99
FILM
SCENES
FOR ACTORS

I00955148

99 FILM SCENES FOR ACTORS

ANGELA NICHOLAS

AVON BOOKS
An Imprint of HarperCollinsPublishers

Permissions, constituting a continuation of the copyright page, are listed on pages v through ix.

AVON BOOKS
An Imprint of HarperCollins*Publishers*
10 East 53rd Street
New York, New York 10022-5299

Copyright © 1999 by Angela Nicholas
Library of Congress Catalog Card Number: 98-92771
ISBN: 0-380-79804-2
www.avonbooks.com

First Avon printing: April 1999

Avon Trademark Reg. U.S. Pat. Off. and in Other Countries, Marca Registrada, Hecho en U.S.A.
HarperCollins® is a trademark of HarperCollins Publishers Inc.

Printed in the U.S.A.

10

Permissions

Acknowledgments

There are so many people to thank when a collection like this is put together. I relied greatly on the brilliance of dozens of gifted and generous writers and filmmakers, the faith of friends, agents and publishers, and the graciousness of studio legal departments from every corner of the world. I started this project knowing that I would need the cooperation of hundreds of people, and I was astounded by the response.

The first people to find out about the book were my fellow actors in class. I was insecure about telling anyone about it; I was scared of ridicule and public failure. I was also afraid of being written off as delusional; so many actors have a ''project'' that never happens. My project was ambitious and daunting, and it was riding on faith. My friends and fellow actors redoubled that faith with their encouragement and support. They constantly reminded me of their need for a book like this, and its value to the acting community. They believed it would fly even when I didn't. They read my manuscripts and tested out the scenes in class. They inspired me with their work. This book is my gift back to them and to all the actors who will come along behind them.

Among those actors whom I count as my friends and supporters was my partner, Richard. He was there through every victory and disappointment along the way. He would listen patiently to the progress reports and sit tirelessly through the endless video viewings. He would read and reread cover letters. He would give me his genuine happiness when I sold the book and his authentic commiseration when I encountered obstacles. He would let me rant and rejoice. He would offer advice and alternatives without controlling and he never, ever let me feel sorry for myself when I was overwhelmed. He didn't doubt for a second that I could succeed. I thank him for his support.

Thanks to my teacher, Mark Monroe, who helped me discover that my process is self-initiated and then helped me rise to that responsibility. And to my teacher before him, Gene Frankel, who gave me the keys to the door between my self and my craft. These wise and giving men continue to inspire me wherever I work. Thanks to The Actors Studio for your standards and ideals, and for giving me something greater to reach for.

Thanks to my supportive family and especially my sister Christina, the real writer in the family, who passed me on to her literary agent, Henry Dunow. Henry took me on, and brought his insight and voice to the process. Thanks to Chris Condry, my editor at Avon Books who saw potential in the book and patiently waited past deadlines for revisions and permissions. And thanks to the other publishers who offered me their interest and took the time to call me and offer their valuable opinions and advice: Eric Kraus at Smith and Kraus and Len Fleischer at Applause Books. Thanks to Joshua Karton, the editor of ''Film Scenes for Actors'' Volumes I and II, the only other collections of this kind ever published, who warmly shared with me his experiences and offered me the unique understanding and compassion of one who has gone before.

Without the incredible Margaret Herrick Library at the Academy for Motion Picture Arts and Sciences, I could never have researched this volume. It is a rich and extensive collection for film studies of all kinds, and stands as a beacon of quality and dedication to the preservation of the art of film. It is run by one of the most knowledgeable and helpful staffs

I have ever seen. They took an interest in my work and gave me the gift of their training and assistance. Thanks to them.

And finally, thanks to all the screenwriters, filmmakers, and studios who gave me their permissions and approvals, and who made this book possible. Jonathan Deckter at Avenue Entertainment, the first person to graciously sign permission for *Drugstore Cowboy* and Dan Yost, the screenwriter. The first permission is the magic link between dream and reality and I thank you for the hope you gave me. All the fabulously talented and fabulously busy giants who took the time to answer my requests and never, ever made money an issue: Quentin Tarantino for *Pulp Fiction*, Spike Lee for *Do the Right Thing*, Oliver Stone for *Born on the Fourth of July*, John Sayles for *Lone Star, Lianna*, and the *Return of the Secaucus 7*, Nora Ephron for *When Harry Met Sally*, Mike Leigh for *Life Is Sweet*, Neil Jordan for *The Crying Game*, Jocelyn Moorhouse for *Proof*, Kurt Luedtke for *Out of Africa*, Tom DiCillo for *Johnny Suede*, Eric Bergren and Christopher DeVore for *Frances*, David Koepp for *Carlito's Way*, Alan Jacobs for *Nina Takes A Lover*, Ted Tally and Alvin Sargent for *White Palace*, Kevin Smith for *Clerks* and *Chasing Amy*, Michael Tolkin for *The Player*, Brad Fraser and Denys Arcand for *Love and Human Remains*, James L. Brooks for *Broadcast News*, Barbara Turner for *Georgia*, John Guare and the Estate of Scott McPherson for *Marvin's Room*, Hossein Amini for *The Wings of the Dove*, Baz Luhrmann, Craig Pearce and Tristam Miall for *Strictly Ballroom*, Shirley Barrett for *Love Serenade*, Adrian Hodges and Michael Hastings for *Tom and Viv*, Michael Thomas for *Scandal*, Woody Allen for *Annie Hall, Manhattan*, and *Bullets Over Broadway*, Stanley Donen and Frederic Raphael for *Two for the Road*, and all the writers whose work is represented here by permission of the studios and publishers. Thank you for your talent, your contribution to the craft of acting, your universal words and timeless stories. I thank each one of you that I didn't get to speak to in the course of putting this collection together. I am so honored to have your work gracing this volume.

The people at the studios who helped me enormously and without whose contribution this book would have been impossible are deserving of personal mention for all the research and time they put into my requests. I want to thank Michael Rothstein at Miramax Films, Cindy Chang and Christiane Townsend at Universal Studios, Debra Waldron and Todd Whitford at MGM, Robin Zlatin at Fine Line, Sharon Lignier at Castle Rock, Judy Noack at Warner Brothers, Diane Charlesbois at Max Films International, Wendy Jaffe at Trimark, and Rebecca Herrera and Jesse Rodriguez at Twentieth Century Fox. I also want to thank all the hard working people in all the legal departments who tried and couldn't get my permission requests approved; thank you for your work and thank you for creating a challenge for me, a challenge to find more wonderful scenes and a challenge to keep believing that I could overcome obstacles and get this book to the actors. I wanted to create something for my fellow actors that was substantial, worthwhile, useful and inspiring. Thanks to all the people who made that dream possible.

For your love, support, and friendship: Anna, Angel, Jonna and Nils, Garrison and Laura, and a very special Baby—thank you.

Contents

Contents

Introduction:
A Message to Actors

I'm an actor, and I know why you bought this book. You're looking for great scenes to work on in your scene study class, or perhaps to prepare for auditions for schools and agents. You may be just starting a college or conservatory drama program, or you may have years of study under your belt. You may even be an acting teacher. Whatever level you're at, you're looking for something juicy, something fresh, something you haven't seen in every scenebook, something "castable," something well written, something exciting. I hope you've found it. I know you thumbed through this book before you plunked down your hard (I know how hard) earned money, looking for a number of scenes you could relate to, get enthused about working on. I know that you're looking for a large selection of roles in your age range, which is probably twenty-fortyish. You want mostly contemporary, naturalistic scenes that speak to who you are as a human being living in this place, time and culture, and who you are as an actor selling yourself in this marketplace. You're looking for scenes about a wide range of experience and perspectives. You're looking for gender-blind and color-blind scenes. And last but not least, you're looking for scenes with a vibrant emotional life. I know what you're looking for because I am you, I want those same things. I chose these scenes for us. I chose these scenes from the hundreds of scripts I've read that

I was excited about and interested in. Scenes that are an appropriate length for classes and auditions. Scenes that live on their own, out of context. Scenes that serve an actor in his/her work on the craft. I'll admit, in all immodesty, that I've put up enough scenes in enough classes to know a really good one when I see it. You'll find a lot of them in here. I only regret stopping at ninety-nine. There are so many great ones out there.

Please read all the material in this book before you eliminate possibilities. I haven't arranged the book by category—drama/comic/seriocomic (whatever *that* means). I believe drama can be very funny, and comedy heartbreaking. I haven't arranged the book by gender—scenes for two women, scenes for two men, etc. Quite a few of these roles can be gender-switched, switched from straight to gay, or gay to straight. I have consciously avoided discussing a character's age; the freedom is yours to make the character any age you choose. I've simply arranged the scenes in alphabetical order, with the characters' and original actors' names. (You'll find indexes at the end that cross reference category, gender, and original actor.) I've also written brief notes about the circumstances of the story and the situations of the characters. As tempting as it was for me to postulate about each character's needs and conflicts and emotional life, I have tried to stick to the facts, just what you need to make your own choices. And those choices are boundless. You may choose to change the setting of the scene, the occupations of the characters, their race, gender, age or orientation. Perhaps the character is an alcoholic, an addict, or a paranoid schizophrenic; it doesn't have to be written in. I've given you the facts of the screenplay as written, but the *scene you do* is up to you. *You* must choose, indeed only you can choose, the character's needs, intentions, conflicts, dilemmas. The craft of acting is about creating emotional truth on stage or film, and your choices will lead you to that truth. Each role becomes unique again as a new actor brings his or her own humanity to it.

The versions of the scenes you find in this book may or

may not differ slightly from the final version on film. This is because scripts undergo so many revisions throughout the course of pre-production and production, and, unless a script is published, it will almost always differ from the final product. The fabulous Academy Library in Los Angeles usually has a copy of the most recent revision, and this is what you'll find here, often corrected to reflect the scene in the film, sometimes not, if I prefer the version in the script. Sometimes I find great scenes that never made it into the film. Sometimes I can't find the script, and have to transcribe the scene from the video. This will always be notated; usually, the screenwriter's work is transcribed verbatim from the script. I've included all the original stage directions; of course, you don't have to use them. I've left them in because they evoke the writer's vision and often can be very revealing—how a character crosses a room or lights a cigarette can tell much about his or her emotional life. Your responsibility, however, is not to the writer's vision; it is to your own process. I hope the scenes collected here can help you through that process with their endless potential to inspire your individuality.

I hope you are glad you bought this book. I hope you find material that inspires you here. I'd be thrilled to get any actor's, teacher's, director's or filmmaker's feedback, comments, or suggestions. If I've left out your favorite scene, let me know. If you loved the book, let me know. And if you want to give me a job, here's my pager number: (just kidding). Write me c/o Avon Books, or e-mail me at *angela531@aol.com*

Enjoy!

Angela Nicholas
Los Angeles, 1997

Interview with
Mark Monroe

I'm pleased to be able to include this interview with Mark Monroe. I was studying with him at the time I compiled this book, and though I'd spent many years in New York studying under many fine teachers, I really came to a full understanding of my craft under Mark's guidance. He is one of the most articulate voices I know when it comes to demystifying method acting. His technique involves a marriage of emotional self-exploration with solid and reliable techniques that allow an actor to reach spontaneous, deep emotional truth—and that's what it's all about.

Mark Monroe started teaching acting in New York and then opened his San Francisco studio in 1987, which has trained thousands of students over the course of eleven years. He founded the Mark Monroe Studio in Los Angeles in 1992, and teaches beginning technique, intermediate and advanced scene study, and singing performance for actors.

Editor: Actors pick up these books. I see them flip through them on the shelves, I see them looking for something. What should an actor be looking for when he or she is choosing a scene? Let's start with an actor looking for a scene to work on in class; are there questions he should ask himself?

Mark: Yes. Am I choosing this material for instrument growth? Or for being able to execute and fulfill the dynam-

ics of the author's intent? Many times both happen simultaneously. Can I find the basic human issue in the scene?
Often this takes time exploring the material. Do I feel compassion or empathy for the dynamic in the scene? Does the
structure of the scene offer opportunities for the actor to
explore and exercise emotions that may feel risky, actions
that have previously been inhibited due to social taboos,
even family history? And, in any good classroom, let's all
hope that it's based on risk, so that actors can expand into
their potential, which is the ultimate goal, to live in that
potential. So, obviously, one is searching for material during the process of expanding their instrument or getting rid
of inhibitions. And so I think one, first, must look at things
with a very sensitive eye, so that they can truly see the
undercurrent of what's going on in the scene. Obviously,
one has to be willing to see what personal connections there
are in the material. Sometimes your passion for the material
is clear; often resistance is an excellent clue that the material in some way should be explored further. Never underestimate resistance: it leads to something richer in
yourself to bring to the material. Repeated acknowledging
and expressing of the resistance is the first and foremost
step in becoming free as an actor.

*So you think resistance to material can be a signal to an
actor, that this is something you should be working on?*

Is a signal to investigate further. In fact, I've seen many, many
actors choose material unconsciously that is the very thing
that, if it were conscious, they wouldn't have picked up.
It's dealing with the unconscious resistance. Another thing
that the actor should look for is exposure, because acting is
exposing something. Within a character, there may be a
hidden agenda, or something hidden within the dynamic of
the script, but for the actor, it's always exposure, and I think
in choosing material an actor needs to be very aware of
what part of themselves they are exposing.

Or want to expose?

Or want to work on exposing. In the classroom. I would say
that choosing material is one of the most important components in the acting process. And I don't think that actors—or often, let me say—actors don't realize how
important it is, or how strong a facilitator the choice of
material should be.

Can be in their process?

Yes. For instance, in the classroom, you don't want to just
look for simple things that you've done over and over, or
for things that are just comfortable; if it's something that
you know is readily accessible to you, other than just keeping up the instrument through practice of it, there's no reason to go back to it.

*Before I get off the subject of choosing material, are there
things that you would say make for a "strong scene"? or
are they different for every actor?*

I feel that many schools would answer it straightforward with
yes, a strong dynamic where the conflict between the two
characters or more characters is very clear, you know. The
environment is very influential and strong, the issues the
play is about can be seen in a humanistic form . . . all of
these kinds of things, I believe that they're all truths. But I
believe that some form of instrument work has to be ac-
knowledged and done before someone can really choose the
best material for them. It's a process of research, it's a process of interest in oneself. Okay? So, if one is making a
committment to the truth in one's life, or discovering the
truth about himself or herself, it will reflect obviously in
the search for scenes. Does that make sense? I have seen
courage be built and enhanced to something truly magnificent through committment. To initiate anything, there's
gotta be that committment, and acting, or finding the ma-

terial that will facilitate the acting process, is the thing. Committment. Discover the truth. Be in the process of un- covering the truth, in yourself. This committment will deepen your vision and understanding of human behavior, feelings, actions, making it easier to discover these com- ponents in a scene or a monologue. Your committment to the process of self-discovery will open your intuitive nature to choose material for your full potential.

I want to talk about the craft that you teach here in the Studio, how you guide actors to finding a need, creating an inten- tion from the need, um, and discovering personalizations, substitutions . . . But actors at all levels may be picking up this book, coming from different techniques with different terminologies. So as the actor begins rehearsals and ap- proaches the character, as he makes the character himself, or himself the character, what are the things about the character that he needs to discover, when he's going into rehearsal, to make the scene live truthfully? To create the truth that he wants—every actor wants to create truth—

Mmm-hm. And bring their truth into . . . the written text and dynamic. So, the uniqueness of the actor's performance and the statement of material . . . marry. Ask the question again.

So, as the actor approaches the text for rehearsal, what are the things he needs to discover about the character in order to achieve what he wants to achieve, which is emotional truth?

Mmm-hm. The bottom line: what the character needs. And the need is just a term for the deepest motivation that may not even be clear to the character, but it must be clear to the actor. Because in that motivation, and making a substi- tution for that motivation, called the need, then spontaneous life through repeated rehearsals starts to grow, and starts to turn behavior into something exciting and unpredictable.

*And how does he turn the need into the finished product?
Does he just stay aware of it through the whole scene? How
does he work with the need? How does he bring the need
into the scene?*

First of all, work—work with the need, work with the need
at the forefront of his consciousness. He must do a rehearsal
that way. So that the minor things within the material, at
first glance or, who knows? third or fourth reading sometimes, become illuminated to him, become personal, *there*
is where the character starts. And there is where all the
controversy is—is there a character, or is there only me? I
believe there is a marriage. And that marriage takes place
within that part, of rehearsing it with the need, keeping the
consciousness of the need in the forefront.

*How does the actor know what the character's deepest need
is?*

First, the actor must have done exploration work on basic
human needs. What are the basic human needs? We all
carry them. That is the one thing that we all do have in
common. All material is written out of basic human needs.
I mean, how can it not be? Needs are simple and universal.
People are not. Like people, characters often seem very
complex. My character may be a drug addict, homeless, and
volatile, who desperately needs rescuing. I may not have
had that personal experience, but I have most definitely felt
the need to be rescued in a different personal circumstance.
So, find a main ingredient in the need that you have felt in
some way before. You find the wound. And from that place
you recognize the need. But you need . . . to be able to identify the hole. It's hard, in this society, to be able to identify
our needs. And unfortunately, we're constantly, socially, as
social beings, choosing the wrong action for the need. And
so, it's natural that this question would come up, around
work specifically identifying the real need. Often we want

to run from the real need because we have expectations of it not getting met or it opening a horrible wound. It's your emotional history. Go and look at the events in your life that stand out. And they will have a through line. This through line in your emotional history will bring up your needs. But be careful to not be seduced by things that you ''want'' as opposed to the things that you need. The ''want'' can lead you to a superficiality for the deeper motivation. Be courageous enough to choose the deeper motivation, which is the need.

What are some other choices that an actor will want to make around the need, as he's preparing the scene?

The next thing I would say is personalizations. Because it's still the being part of the work. It's the being part that we must do so much work on establishing, because that's the part that we generally want to run from. We run because the being part is where we're truly living, it's inside the depths of where we truly live. The personalization is still another being part, which goes along with the need. A personalization is just someone from your life, or your history, that you can pull up, and go into that history with. Bring up feelings; look at them specifically, you know. Put them in an event that will even support the feeling, where the need happened.

An event from your history?

Yes. And then what you may end up wanting to do is, with your scene partner, transpose your personalization onto them, okay? So, therefore, it supports the need, it supports spontaneous behavior, it supports an emotional charge and a directed motivation. The personalization helps you make the need tangible. It grounds the need, um, brings the need tangibly into the scene.

You've talked about these choices—the need, the personalizations—coming from the being and feeling part of your nature . . .

Well, we start there in the process, because the motivation takes us to the action, which I call intentions. The intentions are the actions that are appropriate to getting the need met. There is no separation between the emotional life and the actions that are needed to be taken. The intention being connected this way allows for more spontaneity, gives you so much creative room to take the actions. If you stay motivated from your need, you will experience emotional spontaneity, live in the moment, and embrace your originality, all within the dynamic of the scene. In all of our choices as actors, what we're searching for and working towards is freedom. Not just freedom of action, but freedom of thought, emotion, imagination, desire and passion. Intention work is very important. It's very important to be agile with the intentions in the scene, to free them up instrumentally so that the body is uninhibited enough to, for example, seduce and then turn around and confront. Does that make sense? Because that's where the material can get predictable—we *know* what kind of actions one needs to take if, if we follow the dynamic of the play, you know? That's why they've got to be lived, they've got to be stretched in the classroom, they've got to be taken full on physically and explored. And that's where the individuality of the work lies as well, which is the main point of all these choices. They're based on the individual bringing himself to the technique.

So what you're saying is that when the actor makes the commitment to come into class and stretch the parameters of these choices as fully and courageously as he can, that is what will bring truth, and life, and spontaneity to his work.

Absolutely. Of course there are many other tools that I use within the classes or coachings: sense memory, substitutions, moment to moment work . . . there's so much more to the work, so many more choices to explore and grow from.

Aside from using a scene to expand his process in the classroom, sometimes an actor will pick up a scene to use for an audition; how is that different from all this work he's done in class, and how should he approach it—

For an audition? Very different.

Ok. How about different in the choice of material?

Well, first of all, class is for risk, expanding, exploring, learning . . . that's what class is for. And then solidifying. A personal laboratory. Okay? Auditions—presenting the work for a different kind of agenda, a job, or a play, you know, is very different. Let's assume that the actor has done some work and knows a little bit about what they're good at, what their positive points are, and more importantly, what components make up who they are, the individuality, the uniqueness, that stands out, way beyond the development of the craft. That's a major consideration to look for in a piece of material. So that it shows you're specialness. *And* it also shows the simplicity, at this point, with which you execute your craft. Very important for auditions. Or for work. Obviously, we don't want to see the actor's process at that point. You know? And it's very important that actors have pieces that they've discovered that fit them like a glove or a fine tailored suit that was made exactly for them, from them, you know.

And you get those pieces by—?

You get those pieces by doing work in a classroom, discovering what those components are, because sometimes they lay dormant within, you know. Not always, but often. You get it through self-knowledge, which is going through everything that we've discussed, and breaking down all the terms. It's self knowledge. Self-knowledge and then embodying the experience. It's the self-knowledge that will help you choose the right material for an audition. Help you understand the difference between the acting piece, and the person who is executing the acting, and the person who needs to be there solidly, uniquely, for the interview.

So it's not just a choice about, how am I perceived in the marketplace, but it's a choice about what makes me unique?

Absolutely. Self-generated. Because then self-confidence starts to come into play, and freedom, and back to the blossoming of the individual.

This is not the rote, practical answers that actors see. They see: "Pick something that hasn't been done very often. Pick something that is not too far out of your age range. Pick something comedic." Instead of actors being told: "Pick something that you make work with your specialness. The self knowledge will make you special."

And also, you do know when to be appropriate. You build trust by then. You know if they're looking for a particular type, and if it's the medium of television, you're probably going to have to, more than likely, look like that type, you know? But, to build a craft specifically around that, just hoping that the time will hit, just right, you know . . . It's a long shot, a really long shot. Not to mention, all along the way then you've played a concept of yourself.

Aagh. It's a fearful moment for actors when they wonder if that's what they've been working on for many years. So, in the executing of a scene for an audition as opposed to a class, is the process the same? Is the process of preparing the scene the same as it is for class?

The process of the preparation, yes. Which is a wonderful thing, that that can be consistent, you know. Because you have enough variables to deal with in an auditioning process. But the process of coming up with the scene, the dynamics of the scene, the life that you want to create, are the same, in and outside the class.

Do you think working on film scenes is valuable for an actor?

Oh, absolutely. Just, absolutely I do.

What do you think is good about working on film scenes, for actors?

Oh, some simple things, like the time. They're shorter. And they have to get to the point faster, which I think is very good. Also, working on film scenes, you're left with a lot of interpretation for yourself, although we think it's the other way around, because it's accessible to see someone else do it.

The fact that the scene has been already done on film by a famous actor—do you think that's limiting for an actor?

Do I think that's limiting? No. The truths of the process still remain. What matters is that, if you've seen it, is that you start with the truths for you and that you rehearse the scene with your needs coming first. And that will guide you to many, many differences. Individuality and truth go hand in hand. Make the committment to show up in the moment with your truth and your individuality. My personal experience of seeing so many people audition, is that, it is okay if you do something that's been done before, if you know in your heart that it's something that is special to you and comes from you. So yes, I think that that can be overlooked, that it's been done before. And of course, this process that we're talking about goes across the tables, it's the same thing for music, the same thing for any work of art.

January 1997

Annie Hall
(United Artists, 1977)

Screenplay by Woody Allen
Directed by Woody Allen
Characters: ANNIE (Diane Keaton)
ALVY (Woody Allen)

NOTES: ALVY and ANNIE live in New York City. They used to live together as a couple; they don't anymore, but they have a strong emotional connection. ALVY has a date in his bedroom when ANNIE calls him about an "emergency." ALVY drops everything and rushes over.

INTERIOR ANNIE'S APARTMENT—NIGHT
CUT TO ALVY entering ANNIE's apartment, huffing and puffing.

ALVY: (*off*) What's . . . it's me, open up. Are you okay? What's the matter?

ANNIE: (opens door) Oh.

ALVY: Are you all right? What . . .

ANNIE: (*sighing*)

ALVY: What?

ANNIE: There's a spider in the bathroom.

ALVY: What?

ANNIE: There's big, black spider in the bathroom.

ALVY: That's what you got me here for at three o'clock in the morning? Cause there's a spider in the bathroom?

ANNIE: My God, you know how I am about insects—

ALVY: (*sighing*) Oooh.

ANNIE: . . . I can't sleep with a live thing crawling around in the bathroom.

ALVY: Kill it! For God's—what's wrong with you? Don't you have a can of Raid in the house?

ANNIE: No.

ALVY: (*sighing*) I told you a thousand times, you should always keep, uh, a lotta insect spray. You never know who's gonna crawl over.

They move through the hallway.

ANNIE: I know, I know, and a first-aid kit, and a fire extinguisher . . .

They stop in the living room.

ALVY: Jesus. All right, gimme a magazine, I—cause I'm a little tired. (*ANNIE moves past him and off.*) You know, you joke about me, you make fun of me, but I'm prepared for anything. An emergency, a tidal wave, an earthquake . . . (*he looks over on bookcase and picks up a pamphlet*) Hey, what is this? What? Did you go to a rock concert?

ANNIE: (*off*) Yeah.

ALVY: Oh, yeah, really? Really? How, how'd you like it? Was it, was it—I mean did it . . . was it heavy? Did it achieve total heavy-ocity? Or was it, uh, . . .

ANNIE moves through the room and off again.

ANNIE: It was just great!

ALVY: Oh, humdinger. When . . . Well, I got a wonderful idea. Why don'tcha get the guy who took you to the rock concert, we'll call him and he can come over and kill the spider. You know, it's a . . .

ANNIE: (*off*) I called you. You want to help me—(*she comes back in the room and to ALVY*) . . . or not, huh? (*hands him the magazine*) Here.

ALVY: What is this? What are you . . . Since when do you read "The National Review"? What are you turning into?

ANNIE: Well, I like to try to get all points of view.

ALVY: (*off*) It's wonderful. Then why don'tcha get William F. Buckley to kill the spider?

ANNIE: Alvy, you're a little hostile, you know that? Not only that, you look thin and tired.

ALVY: Well, I was in be . . . It's three o'clock in the morning. You, uh, you got me outta bed, I ran over here, I couldn't get a taxicab. You said it was an emergency, and I didn't ge . . . I ran up the stairs. Believe me, I was a lot more attractive when the evening began. Look, uh, tell, . . . whatta you . . . are you going with a right-wing rock and roll star? Is that possible?

ANNIE: Would you like a glass of chocolate milk?

ALVY: Hey, what am I, your son? Whatta you mean . . . ? I, I came over t' . . .

ANNIE: I got the good chocolate, Alvy.

ALVY: Yeah, where is the spider?

ANNIE: It really is lovely. It's in the bathroom.

ALVY: Is he in the bathroom?

ANNIE: Hey, don't squish it. And after it's dead, flush it down the toilet, OK?—and flush it a couple of times.

ALVY: Darling, darling, I been killing spiders since I was thirty, OK?

He goes down the hall and comes back.

ANNIE: Oh. What?

ALVY: Very big spider.

ANNIE: Yeah?

ALVY: Too . . . Yeah. Lotta, lotta trouble—there's two of 'em.

ANNIE: Two?

ALVY: Yep. I didn't think it was that big, but, it's a major spider. You got a broom, or something with a—

ANNIE: Oh, I, I left it at your house.

ALVY: . . . snow shovel or anything or something.

ANNIE: I think I left it there, I'm sorry.

ALVY: Okay, let me have this. (*He takes her tennis racket.*)

ANNIE: Well, what are you doing, what are you doing with . . .

ALVY: Honey, there's a spider in your bathroom the size of a Buick. (*He goes back into the bathroom.*)

ANNIE: Well, okay. Oooh.

ALVY: Hey, what is this? You got black soap?

ANNIE: It's for my complexion.

ALVY: What—whatta yuh, joining a minstrel show? Geez. (*He goes after spider, banging racket.*)

ANNIE: What are you doing?

ALVY: Don't worry! (*He bangs around some more, then exits*) I did it! I killed them both. What, what's the matter? (*ANNIE is sobbing*) Whatta you . . . whatta you sad about? You . . . What'd you want me to do, capture 'em and rehabilitate 'em?

ANNIE: (*sobbing*) Oh, don't go, okay? Please.

ALVY: Whatta you mean, don't go? Whatta, whatta, what's the matter? Whatta you, expecting termites? What's the matter?

ANNIE: (*sobbing*) Oh, uh, I don't know. I miss you. Tsch.

ALVY: Oh, Jesus, really?

ANNIE: Oh, yeah . . . oh . . . (*she leans on his shoulder and they kiss*) Alvy?

ALVY: What?

ANNIE: Was there somebody in your room when I called you?

ALVY: W-W-Whatta you mean?

ANNIE: I mean, was there another—I thought I heard a voice.

ALVY: Oh, I had the radio on.

ANNIE: Yeah?

ALVY: I'm sorry. I had the television set—I had the television—

ANNIE: Yeah. (*she kisses him*)

Bodies, Rest & Motion
(Fine Line Features, 1993)

Screenplay by Roger Hedden
Directed by Michael Steinberg
Characters: BETH (Bridget Fonda)
*   SID (Eric Stoltz)*

NOTES: BETH and her boyfriend Nick had planned to move away from Enfield, Arizona, the small town they had lived in for the past three years. The decision was mostly Nick's—he was restless, something was missing from his life, and he wanted a change. The day before the move, however, Nick leaves. BETH decides to move anyway, but she doesn't know where to. The house is being painted for the next tenant, who is moving in tomorrow. BETH has made love with the painter, SID, a man who has figured out his own happiness and priorities. She won't stay, however; she sells all her stuff at a garage sale to one widow, including the sofa bed she had promised SID. The next morning, as she's leaving, SID tries to convince her to stay and face herself.

INTERIOR. BEDROOM—CONTINUOUS
SID's finished painting. The room gleams. He pulls a drop cloth off the bureau, then another one off of BETH's two packed suitcases.
BETH: *(O.S.)* *(softly)* Sid?

6

SID turns and looks, smiling. BETH is standing in the door-way, a weariness having settled over her. She steps into the room.

SID: Hi.

BETH: I'm sorry about the sofa bed.

SID: I didn't really need one. When my friends get drunk, they throw up and sleep on the floor.

BETH: But I gave it to you.

He puts his arms around her.

SID: You gave me a lot more.

BETH: No. (*holding him tightly*) It was all even in this department.

SID: (*softly*) . . . Feel me?

BETH: (*whispering*) I know . . . You're hard again.

Holding her tightly, SID runs his fingers down her spine.

SID: I want you all the time.

BETH: (*torn*) Shit.

She kisses him. They kiss, long and hard. Abruptly, she breaks the embrace and moves away from him.

BETH: (*cont.*) (*ironically self-aware*) I just fleeced a widow.

SID: (*protesting*) No . . .

BETH: It was all junk.

She shivers.

BETH: (*cont*) Shit. I've got to get some aspirin . . . (*shaking her head*) I didn't drink enough to be hung over.

She walks away from SID, out of the bedroom.

INTERIOR BETH'S BATHROOM. MOMENTS LATER

BETH gulps down aspirin. She stares at herself in the mirror, wearily searching.

IN THE MIRROR

SID appears in the doorway, his reflection small next to the reflection of her face.

SID: You just feel bad for her like I feel bad for her . . . cause her husband died.

BETH: (*doubting this*) Yeah?

SID: That's about the saddest thing there is . . . losing someone you love.

BETH is struck by a certainty that she's never lost anyone she's loved because she's never really loved anyone.

BETH: It's never happened to me.

SID hesitates, then speaks his heart.

SID: If *you* died, I couldn't stand life.

BETH: I . . .

She steps forward and kisses him. She steps back.

BETH: (*cont*) (*businesslike*) I've got to go now.

She walks out of the bathroom. SID and THE CAMERA FOLLOW as she hurries through the living room toward the bedroom.

IN THE LIVING ROOM

BETH: (*cont*) The new people'll be here.

SID: (*following*) Go to my house.

BETH: (*O.S.*) No.

IN THE BEDROOM

BETH picks up her suitcases. SID steps into the doorway.

SID: While you find a place.

BETH: No. I gotta get out.

She heads to the bedroom door.

SID: I can talk to the realtors, I know they've got a place in Agawam.

BETH stops.

BETH: (*shaking her head*) No . . . Agawam? . . . *no.* I don't know where I'm going. Somewhere else.

She walks past him into the hallway. SID and THE CAMERA FOLLOW.

SID: You can call me when you get there. I'll give you my number.

IN THE LIVING ROOM

BETH: (*gently*) Sid. I'm going away. You're making me way too important. You met me yesterday.

He goes to her.

SID: And today I love you.

She steps back, shaking her head.

BETH: Jesus . . . one day . . .

SID: That doesn't matter. You know that. It can take a second.

BETH loses control, upset with herself for having mixed emotions, upset with her life, and upset he's making this more difficult.

BETH: *No!* That's . . . that's a fuckin' *animal* thing, I've *done* that.

SID: Not with me.

BETH: I mean men, go home with them and *just stay.* No decision involved—it's just what I do. And then I don't have to live my life, I just lead theirs. I can't keep doing that.

SID: (*adamant*) We're not that way!

BETH: What way are we?

SID: We're *passionate.* We're *comfortable.*

BETH: It's *been* passionate, it's *been* comfortable. But it hasn't been . . . *important.* (*after a beat*) Like *you're* making it!

SID: It *is* important! You know that.

BETH: No! It was a *night!* It wasn't real. It was *fun*, it was some great *fucking!* But it's *just something that happened! It's not real!*

SID: It didn't "just happen"! You know *we're it! I'm* the *one* for you!

BETH: The *"one"*? I've had lots of *"ones"*! I look like a baby but I'm twenty-fuckin'-eight years old! You're just the latest!

SID: No. I'm the *last*. You've found me. And it can go on forever.

BETH: No! (*her heart breaking for him*) Oh, Sid . . . forever? (*shaking her head*) You have to understand—*it's just talk.*

SID: It's not.

BETH: (*defiantly disbelieving*) *It is.* C'mon, these things you say . . . c'mon! What?! If I *died* you couldn't *stand* life? That's . . . that's . . .

SID: That's *true*.

BETH: *No.*

BETH can't bear the risk of opening her soul to believe him—and she can't bear to hear the outpouring of his soul without believing him. So she ends it.

BETH: (*cont*) (*after a beat, harshly*) You won't *know* when I die. *You won't be there.*

She picks up her suitcase and heads for the door.

SID: (*following her, certain*) You'd want me there. If I wasn't there, it wouldn't matter who was. You'd be alone.

BETH: *No.*

He grabs her arms and spins her to face him.

SID: (*imploring*) Beth . . . Beth . . . you love me . . .

BETH: (*defiantly*) No!

SID: How do you feel? Think! *You love me.*

She stares at him, breathing deeply, gathering herself. He lets go of her arms and steps back.

BETH: (*her words carefully chosen*) I care about you.

SID: You *have* to be with me.

BETH: No. (*pause*) I *care* about you. But I'm an adult. I can say *no*.

They stare at each other.

SID: (*with controlled anger*) That's what makes you an adult?

BETH: (*unwavering*) Yes. (*pause*) I can say no. (*pause*) No, I won't do that. No, I won't *have* that. No, *I can't*.

SID: (*needing to hear her say it*) You can say *no* to *me*?

BETH: *Yes.*

He looks away from her. She stares at his back.

BETH: I'm going.

She steps toward the door.

SID: Beth!

She stops.

SID: (*cont.*) (*after a beat*) Have someplace to go.

BETH: (*simply*) I don't.

She opens the door.

SID: Why don't . . .

BETH: (*interrupting*) *Don't* tell me what to do.

She goes out the door. SID goes to the door.

EXT THE FRONT LAWN—CONTINUOUS

BETH makes her way to the car. SID stands in the doorway, watching.

SID: What *are* you gonna do?

She turns and faces him.

BETH: I don't know.

BETH tosses her suitcase in the backseat. She gets into the car and starts the engine. SID stands, willing her to stop the car. BETH pulls out to the end of the driveway.

Body Heat
(Warner Bros., 1981)

Screenplay by Lawrence Kasdan
Directed by Lawrence Kasdan
Characters: MATTY (Kathleen Turner)
RACINE (William Hurt)

NOTES: MATTY WALKER is married to a very wealthy man. They have a house in Pinehaven, an upper crust Coconut Grove-like seaside community. MATTY has targeted NED RACINE as a pawn in her plot to kill her husband. She wants her husband out of the way so she can enjoy his wealth alone. NED notices MATTY standing alone on the boardwalk in Miranda Beach, the middle class beach town nearby. NED is a small time ambulance chasing lawyer.

EXTERIOR. THE BEACHFRONT WALKWAY—NIGHT

The woman, MATTY, has walked to the rail. She stands there now lighting a cigarette. She presents her face to the ocean, hoping for a breeze. We move in on her, with RA-CINE. RACINE lights a new cigarette and smiles at her. She looks at him, and for an instant, her eyes race over his body, then she looks back at the ocean.

RACINE: You can stand here with me if you want, but you'll have to agree not to talk about the heat.

She looks at him, and there is something startling about the directness of her gaze. When she speaks, she is cool without being hostile.

MATTY: I'm a married woman.

RACINE: Meaning what?

MATTY: Meaning I'm not looking for company.

She turns back toward the ocean.

RACINE: Then you should have said—"I'm a *happily* married woman."

MATTY: That's my business.

RACINE: What?

MATTY: How happy I am.

RACINE: And how happy is that?

She looks at him curiously. She begins walking slowly along the rail. He walks too.

MATTY: You're not too smart, are you?

RACINE shakes his head "no."

MATTY: I like that in a man.

RACINE: What else you like—ugly? lazy? horny? I got 'em all.

MATTY: You don't look lazy.

RACINE smiles.

MATTY: Tell me, does chat like that work with most women?

RACINE: Some. If they haven't been around much.

MATTY: I wondered. Thought maybe I was out of touch.

She stops again at the rail as a small breeze blows in from the ocean. She turns her back to it and, with her cigarette dangling from her lips, she uses both hands to lift her hair up off her nape. She closes her eyes as the air hits her. RACINE watches very closely.

RACINE: How 'bout I buy you a drink?

MATTY: I told you. I've got a husband.

RACINE: I'll buy him one too.

MATTY: He's out of town.

RACINE: My favorite kind. We'll drink to him.

MATTY: He only comes up on the weekends.

MATTY lets her hair fall and again begins moving down the walkway. She drops her cigarette and steps on it.

RACINE: I'm liking him better all the time. You better take me up on this quick. In another forty-five minutes I'm going to give up and walk away.

MATTY: You want to buy me something? I'll take one of those.

They have come upon a vendor selling snow cones.

RACINE: What kind?

MATTY: Cherry.

RACINE: (*to vendor*) Make it two.

The vendor scoops and pours as RACINE lays some change on the cart.

RACINE: (*to MATTY*) You're not staying in Miranda Beach. (*She shakes her head "no."*) I would have noticed you.

MATTY: Is this town that small?

RACINE hands her a snow cone. They walk over to the rail. RACINE watches her eat the snow cone with enormous interest.

RACINE: Pinehaven. You're staying up in Pinehaven, on the waterway. (*she gives him a look, surprised*) You have a house.

MATTY: How'd you know?

RACINE: You look like Pinehaven.

MATTY: How does Pinehaven look?

RACINE: Well tended.

She looks out at the ocean.

MATTY: Yes, I'm well tended, all right. Well tended. What about you?

RACINE: Me? I need tending. I need someone to take care of me. Rub my tired muscles. Smooth out my sheets.

MATTY: Get married.

RACINE: I just need it for tonight.

For the first time, MATTY laughs. A moment later, she spills the snow cone over the front of her dress. It makes a bright red stain against the white. The thin material clings to the line of her breast.

MATTY: Good. Nice move, Matty.

RACINE: Matty. I like it. Right over your heart.

MATTY: At least it's cool. I'm burning up.

RACINE: I asked you not to talk about the heat.

MATTY: Would you get me a paper towel or something? Dip it in some cold water.

RACINE starts toward the restroom nearby.

RACINE: Right away. I'll even wipe it off for you.

MATTY: You don't want to lick it?

This causes a momentary hitch in RACINE's retreat, but then he hurries off.

Body Heat (2)
(Warner Bros., 1981)

Screenplay by Lawrence Kasdan
Directed by Lawrence Kasdan
Characters: MATTY (Kathleen Turner)
          RACINE (William Hurt)

NOTES: This scene immediately follows the previous one (see notes for previous scene). NED has pulled up to the Pinehaven Lounge, looking for MATTY.

INTERIOR. COCKTAIL LOUNGE—PINEHAVEN—NIGHT

Dark. Almost classy. The place is half full. MATTY is drinking at the end of the bar, her cigarettes next to her glass. The bar chairs near her are empty. RACINE comes in, looks around, walks over and sits in the seat next to her. She looks up, surprised.

MATTY: Look who's here. Isn't this a coincidence?

RACINE looks at her, almost as though he can't place her. But he doesn't push that effect hard. He lights a cigarette.

RACINE: I know you.

MATTY: You're the one that doesn't want to talk about the heat. Too bad. I'd tell you about my chimes.

RACINE: What about them?

MATTY: The wind chimes on my porch. They keep ringing and I go out there expecting a cool breeze. That's what

16

they've always meant. But not this summer. This summer
it's just hot air.

RACINE: Do I remind you of hot air?

The bartender has come up.

RACINE: Bourbon, any kind, on the rocks. (*to MATTY*) Another?

*She thinks, then nods her agreement. The bartender moves
away.*

MATTY: What are you doing in Pinehaven?

RACINE: I'm no yokel. Why, I was all the way to Miami
once.

MATTY: There are some men, once they get a whiff of it,
they'll trail you like a hound.

The bartender brings their drinks and leaves.

RACINE: I'm not that eager.

MATTY: What's your name, anyway?

RACINE: (*offers his hand*) Ned Racine.

MATTY: Matty Walker.

*She takes his hand and shakes it. RACINE reacts strangely
to her touch and doesn't let go right away. She gently frees
it, then refers to his look as she picks up her drink—*

RACINE: Are you all right?

MATTY: (*laughs*) Yes. My temperature runs a couple degrees high. Around 100 all the time. I don't mind it. It's
the engine or something.

RACINE: Maybe you need a tune-up.

MATTY: Don't tell me—you have just the right tool.

RACINE: I don't talk that way.

MATTY: How'd you find me, Ned?

RACINE gives her a look.

RACINE: This is the only joint in Pinehaven.

MATTY: How'd you know I drink?

RACINE: You seem like a woman with all the vices.

MATTY: (*smiles*) You shouldn't have come. You're going to be disappointed.

RACINE looks out over his drink. Several of the men in the place are looking at them.

RACINE: (*referring to the men*) What'd *I* do?

MATTY: (*indicating Racine's chair*) A lot of them have tried that seat. You're the first one I've let stay.

RACINE: (*spotting a few more*) You must come here a lot.

MATTY: Most men are little boys.

RACINE: Maybe you should drink at home.

MATTY: Too quiet.

RACINE: Maybe you shouldn't dress like that.

MATTY: This is a blouse and a skirt. I don't know what you're talking about.

RACINE: You shouldn't wear that body.

MATTY leans back in her seat and glances down at herself. She's magnificent. MATTY watches him, then leans over her drink. Her tone is different.

MATTY: Sometimes, I don't know. I get so sick of everything, I'm not sure I care anymore. Do you know what I mean, Ned?

RACINE: (*He's not sure*) I know that sometimes the shit comes down so heavy I feel like I should wear a hat.

MATTY laughs, studies him.

MATTY: Yeah, that's what I mean.

MATTY drains her glass and stubs out her cigarette.

MATTY: I think I'll get out of here now. I'm going home.

RACINE: I'll take you.

MATTY: I have a car.

RACINE: I'll follow you. I want to see the chimes.

MATTY: You want to see the chimes.

RACINE: I want to hear them.

She looks at him a long time.

MATTY: That's all. If I let you, that's all.

RACINE: (*gestures his innocence*) I'm not looking for trouble.

MATTY: (*very serious*) I mean it. I like you. But my life is complicated enough.

RACINE again accepts.

MATTY: This is my community bar. I might have to come here with my husband sometime. Would you leave before me? Wait in your car? I know it seems silly . . .

RACINE: I don't know who we're going to fool. You've been pretty friendly.

She gives him a look and then slaps him hard! Everyone turns toward them.

MATTY: Now leave me alone.

She stands up, takes her purse and her cigarettes, and walks to the other end of the bar, where she sits down. RACINE watches her with amazed eyes. He stands up and throws some money on the bar. He stalks out of the bar.

Born On
The Fourth Of July
(Universal, 1989)

Screenplay by Oliver Stone based on the book by Ron Kovic
Directed by Oliver Stone
Characters: RON (Tom Cruise)
*   TIMMY (Frank Whaley)*

NOTES: RON KOVIC signed up for the Marines right out of high school, and served in Vietnam. He was badly wounded, spent a long, painful recovery in the VA hospital, and then returned to his parents' home on Long Island, paralyzed from the chest down. He talks with his childhood friend, TIMMY, who also served. It's a summer night. (This version, Fifth Draft, November 1978, differs from the scene that ended up on film.)

64. EXTERIOR. KOVIC BACKYARD AND PORCH—NIGHT (1969)

RON and TIMMY, in semi-shadow, on RON's back porch, late ... drinking beer, insect sounds, the moon drifting by ...

RON: You see that hedge? Right over there?

TIMMY: Yeah ... ?

RON: ... that second telephone pole?

TIMMY: Oh yeah ... yeah.

RON: Yeah, I used to hit 60 home runs over that hedge; I think I counted every one of them.

TIMMY: Yeah, you were the *best*, Ronnie, the best I ever saw. You shoulda gone to that tryout for the Yankees ... when that ...

RON: ... tag? ... remember ... in Sally's woods?

TIMMY: ... tag on Hamilton Avenue ...

RON: ... tag on the river ...

TIMMY: ... tag on the roof ...

RON: ... tag in the supermarket ...

TIMMY: That day, I cut my wrist?

RON: You slipped on an acorn or something ...

TIMMY: I slipped on an acorn? Yeah, I cut my artery and I thought I was going to die fosure. (*giggles*)

RON: (*chuckling like a little kid*) You were a mess ... That time you hit that foul ball right into ole Mrs. Brink's window and she came out screaming, remember?

TIMMY: Yeah—but then we painted her fire hydrant pink ...

RON: And she called the cops!

TIMMY: Yeah ... an' my old man really beat the *shit* out of me! (*laughing, then a pause*)

RON: I wonder what happened to her.

TIMMY: Dead I hope.

RON: I wonder what happened to Donna?

TIMMY: Donna Peters, oh yeah ... ooh, nice right? I heard she was at Stonybrook.

RON: Yeah?

TIMMY: ... going to school. Real bright ... gonna be a lawyer or something ...

RON: (*embarrassed*) I used to write to her, y'know ... long letters from Nam. Real crazy stuff, y'know ... how much I loved her, and everything ... God!

TIMMY: She write back?

RON: Kind of. Couple of times. I don't know. I guess I sounded like an asshole. (*shrugs, looks away*) Who used to play?

TIMMY: You know . . .

RON: Come on, tell me. (*He wants to hear the names again.*)

TIMMY: Well, let's see, Bobby Moore at first, Harry Silvanti at short, Grady Rogers third . . .

RON: No! No! Rogers got sick . . . it was Finelli at third.

TIMMY: . . . Yeah, you're right! Tommy Finelli. He hit .512 one year. I remember that year, yeah . . . He got hit in the First . . . an RPG . . . just blew him away . . . they couldn't even find him.

RON: Rick Jones in left . . . Billy Vorsovich in right; he could hit, he had the power!

TIMMY: Yeah, but he was always flunking English. (*starts to giggle*) He had a hard time with English. You know he got killed by one of his own mortars up at the DMZ. (*giggling*) That's really crazy man.

Another angle—RON can't help it, starts to laugh too—the kind of laugh with hysteria in the eye of it.

RON: Shit! . . . and Phil and Larry Powell? I can't believe it . . .

TIMMY: They were great wrestlers, weren't they fucking tough . . . You know when Phil got killed . . . Larry—he wasn't too much in the brains department either—he went and joined up the next day.

RON: (*laughing harder*) Oh God!

TIMMY: . . . And then he got it . . . There was a land mine or something and he got hit in the head with a tree. Isn't that funny? He goes all the way over there and gets killed by a fucking tree . . . You know it's funny. I think the whole fucking town got devastated. I don't think we have a fuckin' friend left. I think it's really funny.

They laugh again. Mom comes to the window, smiling . . . glances at them, then disappears.

RON: Yeah, yeah—when'd you get hit?

TIMMY: Hunh? . . . Oh, September 18—near Dong Ha . . . you?

RON: Me. Oh January 20, someplace I don't even remember . . . near some river . . . I was already shot in the foot, no big deal . . . I was running around like . . . it was the woods again, like I was John Wayne—you know—"otat tat tat tat come on Charlie Motherfucker!" (*unbelieving*) and then there was this crack above my right ear and . . . (*shifts, sighs*)

TIMMY: How was the hospital?

RON: Bad. Really sucked.

TIMMY: Yeah. I know. Sometimes I get these really bad headaches you know and I'm thinking the dummies in the hospital—they put this plate in backwards or something, man—like I'm going crazy you know, they just come over me . . . they just come . . . and I feel like—like somebody else.

RON: How do you handle it? How do you take care of that when it happens?

TIMMY: (*giggles*) Well mostly I do a lot of drugs.

RON: When I was in the hospital—I kept thinking it wasn't so bad y'know, it was okay, it made sense . . .

TIMMY: Whaddaya mean it made sense?

RON: I mean—I wanted to go over there you know and be a big hero and everything and . . . (*takes a deep breath*)

TIMMY: What's the matter? Ronnie—you don't wanna talk about it, it's . . .

RON: And then—and then there's times I wish . . . I just wish I'd . . .

TIMMY: It was insane, Ronnie.

RON: —I just wished I'd lain down that day—the first time when I got hit, when I took the shot in the heel. I could have just stayed there you know, I had the million dollar wound, I mean who gives a fuck if I was a coward or not, I was castrated that day—why? Because I was so *stupid*— and I'd have my dick and my balls now and I think . . . I think I'd give everything I got . . . *everything*—all my values—just to have my body again . . . just to be whole again . . .

A look between them.

RON: . . . but I still can't feel anything from the chest down, and that's the way it is, isn't it?

Born On
The Fourth Of July (2)
(Universal, 1989)

*Screenplay by Oliver Stone, based on the book by Ron
Kovic
Directed by Oliver Stone
Characters: DONNA (Kyra Sedgwick)
         RON (Tom Cruise)*

NOTES: RON served in Vietnam and has returned in a wheel-
chair (see notes for the previous scene). He lives at his parents'
house on Long Island now and it's not going well. DONNA was
his high school sweetheart, back when he was a wrestling cham-
pion. He didn't ask her to the prom because he had already
enlisted in the Marines and was trying to begin to separate from
his former life. She went with someone else. He changed his mind
and ran to the prom in the rain. Now he looks her up and they
go out. RON is proud of serving his country, but the climate
here at home is becoming anti-war and he learns that DONNA
feels that way too.

83. INTERIOR. RESTAURANT—NIGHT (1970)
RON and DONNA having a quiet dinner in a restaurant—

RON: (*grinning*) Yeah ... the night we sneaked away, remember? You kissed me. That was the first time.

DONNA: No—it was the night of the baseball hat—when I
gave it to you, the Fourth of July? It was your birthday.

RON: That was the same night.

DONNA: (*pause*) Yes . . . yes, you're right—you remember? You never used to.

RON: No. Never . . . in the hospital, in the war.

DONNA: The night of the prom?

RON: Boy was I crazy that night! Running through the rain to get there . . . to dance with you.

DONNA nodding, sharing his spirit.

RON: I just had to dance with you 'fore I went in, y'know I just had to dance with you . . . it was like I knew it.

A shift of mood. He pulls back.

RON: Remember those letters? . . .

DONNA remembering.

RON: (*embarrassed*) Crazy stuff, hunh? Long letters. I guess I told you a lot of stuff I couldn't tell you in high school.

DONNA: They were beautiful letters.

RON: Yeah?

DONNA: (*moved*) They were . . .

RON: I don't think the spelling was too good.

DONNA: But there was a lot of feeling in the words . . . (*her expression shifting*) It's funny the way . . .

RON: What?

DONNA: The way feelings changed . . . about the war.

RON: Yeah.

Starting to eat.

84. EXT. UPPER WEST SIDE STREET—NIGHT (1970)

DONNA pushes RON down a city street, the Upper West Side. Past the Chinese restaurants, Puerto Rican food stands, shoemaker window fronts.

RON: I've been thinking of leaving.

DONNA: Massapequa?

RON: Yeah, I feel like getting out. Seeing a bit of the world.

DONNA: Where?

RON: West. South. South America, maybe. Some place far, some place in the sun.

DONNA: For how long?

RON: Maybe a long time. (*looks at her*) And you?

DONNA: What?

RON: What are you gonna do with yourself?

DONNA: Oh, I got two more years of law school; the first year's the worst though, you go blind. I never had to read so much in my life. End of the day I pass out before my head hits the pillow.

RON: Yeah, must be rough . . . You seeing anybody?

DONNA: Yes . . . someone. I've been living with him 'bout a year now.

RON: Oh?

DONNA: He's a student, at Columbia. He's brilliant, he's poor—very interested in politics—in changing things.

RON: Yeah?

DONNA: Yeah. He took me down to Washington last month, the first time I've ever been to a demonstration . . . to stop the war. It really works, you know? It was incredible—the vibes.

RON: Yeah.

DONNA: You should go down to one, Ron. You could help, really.

RON: Me?

DONNA: You.

RON: Was he over there, this . . . friend of yours?

DONNA: No—but he feels very strongly about it . . .

RON nodding his head.

DONNA: . . . so do I.

Broadcast News
(20th Century Fox, 1987)

Screenplay by James L. Brooks
Directed by James L. Brooks
Characters: JANE (Holly Hunter)
TOM (William Hurt)

NOTES: JANE is a television news editor, a compulsive perfec-
tionist, passionate and obsessive about excellence. She loves her
job and gives it two hundred percent. She meets TOM at a convention where she's just given a speech that bombed because it
had integrity. TOM appreciated the speech. They go out that
night and return to her hotel room. She's attracted to TOM, but
now finds out more about him. TOM is trapped halfway between
his feelings of inadequacy and his extreme narcissism.

INTERIOR. JANE'S ROOM—NIGHT
*A small good room—her working paraphernalia very much
in evidence ... the quality briefcase ... the reams of well-
organized notes, the thick contact book. JANE is sitting on
the bed—TOM, not far away in the room's only chair. One
lamp is on and it serves to place JANE in the shadows and
cast TOM in an enormously flattering light. Music comes
from her miniature portable stereo system.*

JANE: Come on ... Even I'm not that hard on myself.

TOM: No, I really got this job on a fluke and wait till you
hear where it ends up.

JANE smiles a calming smile.

TOM: I was doing sports at the station. The newspaper ran this untrue story that I was leaving and they got all these tons of protest mail—So they made me anchor.

JANE: So great—right?

TOM: Except I'm no good at what I'm being a success at.

JANE: How are you at back rubs?

JANE shifts her position so that her back is to TOM . . . He is immobilized by the sudden turn. JANE waits—just a bit longer than it would take Tom to run from the chair to her side—before experiencing the ghost-like clutch of rejection. She moves briskly past the moment—grabbing a "good night" chocolate from the pillow and munching it as she returns to his agenda.

JANE: It's sort of normal—the way you feel. In graduate school everyone thought the only mistake the admissions committee made was letting them in.

He moves to the bed.

TOM: Listen to me. You keep on thinking I'm somebody who lacks . . . confidence. That's not it. I know I can talk well enough and I'm not bad at making contact with people, but I don't like the feeling that I'm pretending to be a reporter. And half the time I don't really get the news I'm talking about. It isn't that I'm down on myself. Trust me, I stink.

JANE: (*levelly*) I trust you.

TOM: I didn't even have the chance to get really good at sports. I wasn't bad. I thought I was starting to do interesting features but hockey is big at the station and . . .

JANE: (*interrupting*) What about the obvious remedy? Reversing things. Maybe getting a job on a newspaper.

TOM: I don't write.

JANE laughs or, more accurately, scoffs as TOM continues.

TOM: But that didn't stop me from sending out audition tapes to bigger stations and the networks.

JANE: Well, come on—it is your life. Nobody is tying you to the fast track. Did you go to college?

TOM: One year . . . almost one year.

JANE: So, you're not well educated and you have almost no experience and you can't write.

He nods agreement.

TOM: And I'm making a fortune.

JANE laughs very briefly—then rubs her face vigorously with her hands . . . He's making her feel a little crazy. She gets off the bed.

JANE: It's hard for me to advise you since you personify something that I truly think is dangerous.

TOM: Uh-huh.

JANE: (*holding it in*) I agree with you—you're not qualified. (*letting it out*) So get qualified. You can insist on being better prepared. You don't have to leave it at . . . (*mimicking him*) "I don't write. I'm not schooled. I don't understand the news I'm reading. But at least I'm upset about it, folks."

A beat, then he mumbles softly to himself:

TOM: Whoa, this was a mistake.

JANE: Just what do you want from me, anyway? Permission to be a fake? Stop whining and do something about it.

He gets up to leave. She follows him.

JANE: Well, you don't have to start right now.

He turns to her.

TOM: I hated the way you talked to me just now . . . and it wasn't just because you were right.

He exits.

Broadcast News (2)
(20th Century Fox, 1987)

Screenplay by James L. Brooks
Directed by James L. Brooks
Characters: JANE (Holly Hunter)
AARON (Albert Brooks)

NOTES: AARON is Jane's best friend at the station, an excellent field journalist. Intelligent, witty, he has earned Jane's respect and affection. They share a certain level of drive, enthusiasm, and professional integrity. In the office, however, AARON has been feeling a discrepancy between his co-workers' respect for him as opposed to the anchors; he has appealed for a tryout as an anchor and he got his chance the night this scene takes place. It went terribly for him. JANE missed the broadcast; she and Tom have been at a party, a company event, after which JANE agreed to meet Tom at his place. They are in the tentative first stages of a romance, despite JANE's original problems with Tom. She realized after committing herself that she'd planned to go to AARON's, so she hurriedly tries to fulfill the commitment with AARON before she goes to Tom's. She shows up in her rush and excitement at AARON's apartment.

INTERIOR. AARON'S APARTMENT—HALLWAY—NIGHT

It is at the top of a flight of steps. JANE knocks on the door. Rings. Knocks. AARON opens it. He is wearing a sweatshirt and cords.

AARON: I was in the shower.

She enters.

INTERIOR. AARON'S APARTMENT—NIGHT

JANE: How'd it go?

AARON: You didn't see it or speak to anybody?

JANE: No.

AARON: Then it went well.

JANE: Did it really go well?

AARON: Define your terms.

JANE: Do you feel good about it?

AARON: No.

JANE: Do others feel you did well?

AARON: No.

JANE: Then what was good about it?

AARON: I lost six pounds . . .

JANE: Aaron. Will you tell me?

AARON: It was great . . . writing my little first-rate copy, sitting on my jacket, punching my one thought. But I had this historic attack of flop sweat, so they'll never let me anchor again. Oh, I lost one of your shoulder pads. I think it drowned. How was your evening anyway?

JANE: What do you mean, flop sweat?—you're making too much out of it . . . I'll bet you were the only one aware of it . . .

AARON: People phoned in.

JANE: Stop kidding, I want to know what happened.

AARON: I'm not kidding.

JANE: There were complaining phone calls because you were sweating?

AARON: No, nice ones worried that I was having a heart attack.

JANE: If all that happened, how come you're so chipper?

AARON: I don't know. At a certain point, it was so off the chart bad—it got funny. My central nervous system was telling me something. Jane—sweat pouring down my face— makeup falling into my eyes—people turning this fusillade of blow dryers on me—all so I could read introductions to other people who were covering stories, which is what I like to do anyway.

JANE: Yes.

AARON: And I'm chipper because you finally showed up.

AARON kisses her bare shoulder.

AARON: (*continuing*) I'm gonna cook for us. Tequila and eggs sound good?

JANE: I have to be somewhere.

He looks at a clock reading 1:15 in the morning.

JANE: I told what's his name—Tom—that I'd meet him.

AARON: Call him—I mean, it can wait, right.

JANE: (*now the plunge*) I don't know. I may be in love with him.

AARON: I knew it. Get out of my house now. I want you out of here. (*shouting*) I'm not kidding!

JANE stands her ground. AARON gets angrier and shouts:

AARON: Get out of here! You go to hell!

She starts to leave.

AARON: (*softly*) Come back here. Come on. Don't go.

JANE: (*shouting*) This is important to me!

AARON: Yeah. Well . . . I think it's important for you too. Come on. Sit down.

She sits. He walks to a desk and looks at her briefly . . . Silence.

JANE: What?

AARON: (*looking at her*) Let me think a second. It's tough.

A remarkably long silence—her mind wanders, she takes stock . . . it is evident that he is trying to get it right, reaching into himself.

AARON: Aaach . . . Jane . . . (*glancing at note*) Okay. Let's take the part that has nothing to do with me. Let's let me just be your most trusted friend, the one who gets to say all the awful things to you. You know?

JANE: (*testy and wary but fair*) Yes, I guess. Yes.

AARON: You can't end up with Tom because it goes totally against everything you're about.

JANE: Yeah—being a basket case.

AARON: I know you care about him. I've never seen you like this about anyone so please don't take it wrong when I tell you that I believe that Tom, while a very nice guy, is the Devil.

JANE: (*quickly*) This isn't friendship. You're crazy. You know that?

AARON: (*pressing on*) What do you think the Devil is going to look like if he's around? No one's going to be taken in by a guy with a long, red, pointy tail. No. I'm semi-serious here. He will look attractive and he will be nice and helpful and he will get a job where he influences a great God-fearing nation and he will never do an evil thing or deliberately hurt a living thing—he will just bit by little bit lower our standards where they're important. Just coax flash over substance. Just a tiny bit. And he will talk about all of us really being salesmen. (*seeing he's not reaching her*) And he'll get all the great women.

She is getting furious.

JANE: I think you're the Devil.

AARON: No. You know that I'm not.

JANE: How?!

AARON: Because I think we have the kind of friendship where if I were the Devil, you'd be the only one I told.

She's briefly impressed. He has a point.

JANE: You were quick enough to get Tom's help when . . .

AARON: Yes, yes. I know. Right. And if things had gone well for me tonight, maybe I'd be keeping quiet about all this . . . I grant you everything but give me this . . . He does personify everything you've been fighting against . . . And I'm in love with you. (*realizing*) How do you like that?—I buried the lead.

He pauses to catch his breath—breathing deeply through his nose.

AARON: (*an aside*) I've got to not say that aloud; it takes too much out of me.

JANE: (*thawing*) Sit down, stop.

AARON slumps down—it's been a long round.

AARON: I've never fought for anyone before. Does anyone win one of these things?

The Brothers McMullen

(Fox Searchlight, 1995)

Screenplay by Edward Burns
Directed by Edward Burns
Characters: ANN (Elizabeth P. McKay)
JACK (Jack Mulcahy)

NOTES: JACK, Barry and Patrick are first generation Irish brothers who grew up on Long Island, the sons of a "wife-beating, child-abusing alcoholic" and a long suffering mother. When their father dies, Mom buries him and quickly returns to Ireland to rejoin a long lost love. She leaves the house to the boys, saying, "Don't make the same mistake I did"—marrying the wrong person. Five years later, JACK is five years married to Molly and living in the family house on Long Island; Barry, a "lapsed Catholic" and problem drinker, has been through a recent break-up and moved back in; and Patrick, the youngest, has just graduated from college and is facing "real life" with all its decisions. He also has just moved back in. After a dinner party to celebrate Molly's birthday, JACK drives one of the guests, ANN, back into Manhattan. She makes a proposition.

INTERIOR. JACK'S CAR—EVENING
JACK and ANN sit in the front seat. Neither one seems to be in any hurry to leave.

ANN: Thanks for driving me all the way into the city, Jack. I mean, you really didn't have to do that.

JACK: Hey, no problem. I mean, Barry and half a bottle of Irish whiskey is not my idea of safe driving.

ANN: So, other than cook cabbage and corned beef on his wife's birthday, what does a high school basketball coach do with his spare time?

JACK: Oh . . . things like . . . play golf, fish, drink a lot of beers. But I'm actually taking a sports management course in NYU at the moment.

ANN: (*sarcastically*) Oh, very exciting . . . And . . . Molly, what does she do?

JACK: She teaches English at the high school.

ANN: She's a teacher too . . . Really exciting. What, did you two meet at a PTA meeting or something?

JACK: No, it was . . . it was actually during cafeteria duty.

ANN: In the hot-lunch line, I hope.

JACK: Yeah, something like that.

ANN: Uh, I'll . . . bet you were a big jock stud in high school, weren't you? Running around in the backseat of your father's Buick, breaking all the little girls' hearts?

JACK: No, I've . . . I've always been pretty much a one-woman kind of guy.

ANN: That's what my ex-husband said when I met him.

JACK: And he wasn't?

ANN: No, he was . . . I just wasn't a one-man kind of girl.

JACK: I don't buy that. Your problem is that you just haven't found the right man yet.

ANN: I've found plenty of them. My problem is that they all want to marry me. You know, if I was smart, I'd find myself a nice married man.

JACK: What good would that do you?

ANN: Because then there would be no question as to what either one of us wanted from the relationship . . . now, would there?

JACK knows where this is headed and doesn't appear all that comfortable. He takes a look at his watch.

ANN: Yeah, it's getting late.

JACK: Yeah.

ANN: Do you feel like coming up for a cup of coffee or something?

JACK: Oh . . . No, thanks, I should be getting back to the Island . . . traffic and stuff . . .

ANN: All right, some other time then.

JACK: Yeah, some other time.

ANN: Okay, some other time.

JACK: Okay.

ANN: Thanks for the ride, Jack.

ANN leans over and gives JACK a quick kiss.

ANN: Have a good night.

JACK: 'Bye.

The Brothers McMullen (2)
(Fox Searchlight, 1995)

Screenplay by Edward Burns
Directed by Edward Burns
Characters: BARRY (Ed Burns)
*   AUDREY (Maxine Bahns)*

NOTES: BARRY has somewhat conquered his fear of intimacy
long enough to move out of the house on Long Island (*see notes
for previous scene*) and start a relationship with AUDREY. But
when his budding career as a screenwriter/director starts to happen, he backs out of it. Marty is his agent. He has just called
AUDREY's place looking for BARRY, to tell him the good news
about his film deal. BARRY shows up a few minutes later.

INTERIOR. AUDREY'S APARTMENT—DAY

*BARRY enters AUDREY's apartment. She is just finishing
packing her bags.*

BARRY: What's going on with all these bags?

AUDREY: All your stuff's in the blue bag.

BARRY: What do you mean? You going someplace?

AUDREY: I'm moving out.

BARRY: What do you mean? Where are you going?

AUDREY: I'm going home to New Jersey to take care of
my dad for a while.

BARRY: How come?

AUDREY: What do you mean, how come? 'Cause you're a coward.

BARRY: Hey, I don't think this is the right time for me to get involved in a serious relationship.

AUDREY: And why is that? Because as a big-time director you can't be tied down? Don't want to miss out on all the action you could be getting?

BARRY: What is that? Is that what you think? Is that why you think I'm breaking this off?

AUDREY: Can you give me another reason?

BARRY: Yeah, because I'm going to be busy. You know? I mean, I'm not going to have time for this. For us.

AUDREY: You know what? You can have this back, I don't want it.

AUDREY pulls the Claddagh ring off and shoves it into his chest.

BARRY: Hey, Audrey, you knew from day one that I wasn't interested in letting this become, you know, too serious.

AUDREY: I don't care what we thought was going to happen. I fell in love with you, and I think you fell in love with me too. Didn't you?

BARRY: Come on. You know, let's not get into this, all right?

AUDREY: Just answer the question, it won't kill you.

BARRY: What do you want me to say? All right . . . okay, yeah, I do love you.

AUDREY: Then why are you doing this?

BARRY: Because, you know what? I don't want to be in love. All right, and I don't want a wife and I don't want a family either.

AUDREY: Whoever said anything about marriage and a family?

BARRY: I'm sorry, Audrey, it just can't be.

Silence. They stand there looking at each other, neither one sure what to do or say next. The phone rings.

AUDREY: Go ahead and answer, it's Marty. You got what you wanted.

BARRY goes for the phone, and AUDREY goes for the door.

BARRY: Hello?

AUDREY picks up her bags and is almost out of the door.

BARRY: Hey, Marty, hold on a second . . . Hey, Audrey, wait a second. I'm sorry it had to be like this.

AUDREY: I love you, Barry. And I'll never love anyone the way I love you. But I'm not going to be like your mama and wait thirty-five years for you.

AUDREY turns and exits.

BARRY: Hey, Audrey, come on, hold up.

BARRY looks down at the ring in his hand.

BARRY: Hey, Marty, sorry about that . . . No, no, it's nothing . . . Yeah, you know what? Listen, I . . . I can't . . . I can't talk about this . . . All right, I got to go. I got to go.

Bullets Over Broadway

(Miramax, 1994)

Screenplay by Woody Allen and Douglas McGrath
Directed by Woody Allen
Characters: DAVE (John Cusack)
*   CHEECH (Chazz Palmenteri)*

NOTES: It's the Prohibition days in New York, and DAVE is a young playwright. His new play is in rehearsal, as all the kinks get worked out. He has a famous Broadway actress, Helen Sinclair, signed on, and he's being celebrated as the new Golden Boy of the theater scene. His primary investor, however, is a gangster; and one of the conditions of getting the play produced is that the gangster's girlfriend, Olive, plays one of the supporting roles. Olive travels with a bodyguard, a hit man named CHEECH. DAVE soon discovers that CHEECH's ideas about the play are worth exploring, and eventually CHEECH is helping DAVE with rewrites. Nobody knows, and DAVE is embarrassed to tell anyone. Meanwhile, DAVE has been neglecting his girlfriend and has begun an affair with his leading lady. Here DAVE and CHEECH work on the script at CHEECH's hangout (This scene has been transcribed from the video.).

INTERIOR. BILLIARD HALL—NIGHT
DAVE and CHEECH are sitting at the bar, working on the script.

CHEECH: I was thinkin' about, when Sylvia's in the crazy house?

DAVE: The sanitorium.

CHEECH: Yeah, yeah. She gets the D.T.'s and she sees things.

DAVE: She, she uh, hallucinates.

CHEECH: No, she sees things. You know—like visions.

DAVE: Like what kind of visions?

CHEECH: Like her dead husband. And *then* they have that talk. Like she couldn't face up to it—

DAVE: (*over*) What, in the third act?

CHEECH: That's right, and she couldn't face up to it—

DAVE: —with Sylvia's doctor?

CHEECH: —when he was alive.

DAVE: That's great. That's great, that's great.

CHEECH: It is great.

DAVE: I like that.

CHEECH: Joe, gimme a beer.

DAVE: (*muttering under his breath*) . . . that's great, that's all great.

CHEECH: What'sa matter?

DAVE: Nothing, I just gotta take a break.

CHEECH: Wanna take a break?

DAVE: Yeah. (*He takes off his glasses and rubs his nose. CHEECH closes his script.*)

CHEECH: All right.

DAVE: Okay. Cramp. (*he sighs*) Man. It's a nice, nice spot.

CHEECH: I come here a long time.

DAVE: Yeah?

CHEECH: Yeah.

DAVE: You from around here? You, you live around here?

CHEECH: New York, born and raised. West 45th Street.

DAVE: Oh. You got a big family, or—

CHEECH: No. I got a sister, lives in Jersey. I had a brother, but he got killed.

DAVE: Sorry.

CHEECH: It's all right. He welched on some shylocks. They took him out to Canarsie and shot him through the head.

DAVE: Your brother? (*CHEECH acknowledges.*) How did you get into your, line of—work?

CHEECH: My line of work? My father. Was he tough.

DAVE: You ever think about doing anything else?

CHEECH: Like what?

DAVE: Like writing.

CHEECH: Writing?

DAVE: Yeah.

CHEECH: Come on. I been collecting for the mob since I was sixteen.

DAVE: You have a huge gift.

CHEECH: Yeah. Nah—

DAVE: I'm serious. It's really—it's uncanny. I mean, your instincts—

CHEECH: Lemme tell you something.

DAVE: —your dramatic instincts, it's—

CHEECH: Listen to me. Your play was very good.

DAVE: —really, really enviable.

CHEECH: Your play was very good. You just didn't use your head. Sometimes people don't think.

DAVE: Sure, for you it's simple, you know? For someone who can draw, it all seems logical. But for someone who can't . . . I studied playwriting with every teacher, I read every book—

CHEECH: Lemme tell you something about teachers. I hate

teachers. Those blue-haired bitches used to whack us with rulers. Forget teachers.

DAVE: When I was a boy, I mean, when I was growing up, and he played accordian . . .

CHEECH: Yeah?

DAVE: Yeah, and—I loved accordian and I practised and I practised, and I got fluent. Yeah, he would squeeze one single note, and the sound of it would make you cry. Make you cry.

CHEECH: I used to wanna dance. You know that? I mean it, I wanted to dance. You ever seen George Raft dance?

DAVE: Oh, yeah. (*Pause.*) So—

CHEECH: Yeah?

DAVE: Mr. Marx says you, uh, actually rubbed a few people out. Is that true?

CHEECH: What is this, the third degree? Huh?

DAVE: Not, not at all.

CHEECH: Then why are you saying that for?

DAVE: I'm just really . . . the truth is, I'm fascinated.

CHEECH: I took care of a few guys.

DAVE: Why?

CHEECH: Why, why—I don't know why. You know, they cheated Mr V., they went back on a debt—I'll tell you one thing, I never rubbed out a guy who didn't deserve it.

DAVE: (*pause*) So, what does it actually feel like when you, actually—

CHEECH: What?

DAVE: —ki-kill a man?

CHEECH: Feels okay.

DAVE: Feels okay?

CHEECH: Yeah.

DAVE: Even the first time?

CHEECH: The first time? The first time was a punk in prison. He squealed on me and I stuck an ice pick in his back.

DAVE: An ice pick?

CHEECH: An ice pick, yeah. I had to do it over and over. Forty times, it was a mess, forget about it.

Carlito's Way
(Universal, 1993)

Screenplay by David Koepp, based on the novels
Carlito's Way *and* After Hours *by Edwin Torres*
Directed by Brian DePalma
Characters: GAIL (Penelope Ann Miller)
            CARLITO (Al Pacino)

NOTES: CARLITO and GAIL dated before CARLITO was sent to jail. He had been a well-known drug trafficker in his New York neighborhood. Now he's out and determined to change his life, to not get dragged into petty street crime and the drug scene. He finds GAIL at her dance school and surprises her as she's coming out of a class, and they end up at a small West Village restaurant. (For you New Yorkers, this is set in the seventies, and the restaurant bears a striking resemblance to the now-defunct Sandolino's). She tries to hide the fact that she is working as a go-go dancer in a club in Times Square.

43. INTERIOR. RESTAURANT—NIGHT

CARLITO and GAIL are at a table in a restaurant, drinks in front of them.

GAIL: I was in the road company of this show called "Songbird" last year, I played the governor's daughter. It wasn't a lead, but it was a great part. And I did this musical book show last year in Vegas. I hated the weather. You ever been there?

CARLITO: Vegas, yeah. So what, are you in somethin' now? I can come downtown and see you.

GAIL: Um, well, I'm just, you know, doing club dates right now. Mostly one-nighters, so . . . But I'm up for this, um, play that goes this fall, so—

CARLITO's just looking at her, smiling.

CARLITO: Ah, that's great. You're doin' it, livin' what you always dreamed about.

GAIL: Well, getting close. I am getting close. Not there yet, but that's okay.

CARLITO doesn't answer, just looks away, over her shoulder.

GAIL: So, um . . . what was it like inside, Charlie?

CARLITO: No big thing. Lotta pushups and a lotta wasted time.

GAIL: Well, you're out now.

CARLITO: Oh yeah. Yeah, I am. (*pause*) Am I outta line, Gail? Just poppin' up like this, after all these years? You still pissed at me?

GAIL: What do you think? (*pause*) You dropped me hard, Charlie. (*pause*) Now you wanna tell me it was for my own good, right?

CHARLIE: No, it was for mine. It was for mine, Gail. It was for my own good, okay? I mean, I was doing thirty years, what was I supposed to do? I knew you were gonna try and wait for me. You were gonna visit me, you were gonna make me think about you all the time, now what was I supposed to do? There I am, sitting in jail, wonderin', all the time, where you are, what you're doin', who you're with, that would've drove me crazy, Gail. 'At've killed me. Believe me. Best to just cut it clean, you know? Do my time with a clear head.

GAIL: So . . . now what?

CARLITO: Now what? I don't know. It's . . . I'm here, I'm out. For whatever that's worth.

GAIL: Well, what about this club of yours?

CARLITO: Oh, it's not my club, you know, it's, uh, I've just got, got a piece of it. Just tryin' to make enough money . . . But who knows? With my luck, somebody gonna get shot, the cops gonna come close it down, you know.

GAIL: That doesn't sound like you.

CARLITO: It doesn't? Really?

GAIL: You never talked like this before.

He looks at her for a second, hesitant, then starts to talk.

CARLITO: I never *felt* like this before. You know, it's a funny thing, this guy, this counselor at Lewisburg, Mr. Seawald, he once said to me, he said, "Charlie, you run outta steam, you can't sprint all the way, you gotta stop sometime. You can't buck it forever. It catches up to you. It gets you. You don't get reformed; you just run outta wind.

GAIL looks at him, a million thoughts in her mind, and she's not sharing them.

GAIL: Charlie. (*coming out of it*) I gotta go.

She starts to get up. CARLITO jumps up with her.

CARLITO: Can I call you sometime?

She looks at him for a long moment, thinking about it.

GAIL: Why don't you let me call you?

CARLITO: Okay.

GAIL: Okay?

CARLITO: You know where to find me, right?

GAIL: Yeah.

She moves in and they embrace, tightly and long. GAIL pulls out and whispers in his ear.

GAIL: You said you wouldn't break my heart, Charlie.

CARLITO: I know. I'm sorry. I'm sorry.

GAIL: (*sighs*) 'Night.

She gives him a quick kiss on the lips, turns, and she's out the door in a second. CARLITO just watches her leave.

Carlito's Way (2)
(Universal, 1993)

Screenplay by David Koepp, based on the novels
Carlito's Way *and* After Hours *by Edwin Torres*
Directed by Brian DePalma
Characters: GAIL (Penelope Ann Miller)
CARLITO (Al Pacino)

NOTES: CARLITO and GAIL have become live-in lovers since his release from jail. He is living well and seems to be making a success out of his nightclub. He doesn't want his business or himself to be corrupted by crime; he wants to go completely straight, but it's a struggle. His lawyer, Dave, is trying to get him involved in a scheme to break a mobster client out of jail. GAIL sees the danger even if she doesn't understand all the details. They are returning from a night in the club.

64. INTERIOR. GAIL'S APARTMENT—NIGHT
GAIL steams in the door to her apartment, furious. She rips her jacket off as she crosses the living room, slams it on the couch, and continues into the bedroom. CARLITO, right behind her, closes the front door and follows her.

65. IN THE BEDROOM
GAIL pulls her dress over her head and puts on a tee-shirt, for sleeping.
GAIL: I don't like him. I didn't like him the minute I met him.

CARLITO: Well, you're not listening to me.

GAIL: All right,—so what is this boat thing? What is that asshole manipulating you into? *Tell me*!

She balls the dress up and throws it onto the bed, but overshoots, hitting a night table, taking out a framed picture that's on it. It hits the wood floor and smashes.

CARLITO: I'm just helping him out with something, that's all. I owe him.

GAIL: You *owe* him? He's a fucking cokehead, Charlie! I can't even believe you hang around with that guy! He's *sick*! He's going to get you killed, or sent back to prison!

CARLITO: He saved my life, Gail!

GAIL: So now you have to pay him with it?! Jesus Christ, Charlie—you give me this whole song and dance about how you're out of that shit, but you're not!

CARLITO: Song and dance—what does, what does that mean? Song and dance?!

GAIL: You're not.

CARLITO: Where did you get that? From what?

GAIL: Why did you drag me into this?

CARLITO: Drag you into what?

GAIL: Why did you make me believe all the crap about Bahamas and paradise? I feel ridiculous! 'Cause you haven't changed! You haven't changed a bit!

She stalks into the bathroom. In the bathroom, GAIL stands in front of the mirror, taking off her makeup angrily. CARLITO follows her, his anger building too, but he's swallowing it, and it's a little frightening, wondering what his explosion will be like when it comes.

CARLITO: What the fuck are you trying to tell me? That my gettin' out is just some bullshit fantasy trip I'm layin' on you, is that what you're saying? How can you say that, Gail? How can you say that? When you know how close I am? How can you say those words to me? I gotta do this, just this one thing, and then, I'm out. I got, I owe Dave, I gotta—

GAIL: You don't owe him *shit*! You just *think* you do, Charlie! That's the problem with you! That's why nobody like you gets out, no matter what they say!

CARLITO: (*quietly*) You're not listening to me, Gail, it's all—

GAIL: Because everything you ever learned in the neighborhood, every instinct you got won't do anything but get you *killed*.

CARLITO: What the fuck are you talking about? Wh—how do you know what I learned in my neighborhood? You're just, this is stupid, what you say—

GAIL: (*over*) I know how this dream ends, Charlie, and it isn't in paradise. It ends with me carrying you into Sutton emergency room at three o'clock in the morning and standing there, crying like an idiot, while your shoes fill with blood and you die.

CARLITO: Gail, you're not listening—

GAIL: 'Cause you're *bullshitting* me! All your talk is bullshit and your dreams are bullshit and your—

CARLITO smashes his hand into the mirror, spiderwebbing it.

CARLITO: *YOU'RE NOT LISTENING TO ME!*

He stands there, heaving, trying to regain control. He looks down at his hand, which is bloody.

GAIL: Charlie—

She goes to him. They don't speak as she takes a towel from a bar, wets it, wipes the blood from his hand, and wraps the towel around it.

CARLITO: Dave is my friend, Gail. I owe him. That's who I am. That's what I am, right or wrong. I can't change that.

GAIL's shaking now. She speaks quietly, almost a whisper.

GAIL: Charlie. Whatever he wants you to do, don't do it. For me, please, Charlie—don't do it. Please.

CARLITO: Gail—(*he starts to leave*)

GAIL: Just don't do it.

He doesn't answer. He walks out the door.

GAIL: That's the last time I wipe up your blood. (*She slams the door.*)

Carlito's Way (3)
(Universal, 1993)

Screenplay by David Koepp, based on the novels
Carlito's Way *and* After Hours *by Edwin Torres*
Directed by Brian DePalma
Characters: CARLITO (Al Pacino)
            KLEINFELD (Sean Penn)

NOTES: CARLITO and KLEINFELD have a relationship of mutual obligation. KLEINFELD is CARLITO's lawyer; he got CARLITO out of jail, and CARLITO returned the favor by helping KLEINFELD with a dangerous and foolish scheme to break a mobster client out of jail on a boat. KLEINFELD was obliged to help the mob boss because he'd stolen money from him. Once KLEINFELD and CARLITO got the boss on the boat, however, KLEINFELD killed him and now CARLITO is in deeper than he ever feared. Now the mob is after KLEINFELD and suspect CARLITO was on the boat. They have shot KLEINFELD but not killed him and he is in the hospital. CARLITO is trying to get out of the country. It's down to the wire, but he must pay this visit. KLEINFELD, in order to save his own skin, has given the D.A. a false tip that CARLITO is dealing again. This scene is longer than the filmed version and the dialogue differs somewhat.

89. INTERIOR. KLEINFELD'S ROOM—DAY
DAVE KLEINFELD is in his hospital bed, propped up

against pillows, reading a stack of legal briefs. He looks fine, if a little pale. CARLITO's voice comes from the doorway.

CARLITO: (*offscreen*) Hello, Dave.

Kleinfeld doesn't even look, just lunges to his side, groping for something under his pillow, but he moves slowly, bandaged and sore.

CARLITO: (*cont'd*) Relax, Dave. If I was here to whack you, you wouldn't even know it.

KLEINFELD stops, sees who it is, and lays back against the pillows in relief.

KLEINFELD: Fuckin' cop. He's not supposed to let anybody in. I mean, it's you, it's okay, but—

CARLITO closes the door behind him and comes into the room.

CARLITO: Cops aren't gonna help you, Dave. Mob's comin' back for you.

He reaches under KLEINFELD's pillow and pulls out a snubnose revolver. His face goes hard suddenly. He presses the barrel against KLEINFELD's temple.

CARLITO: (*cont'd*) I heard the tape.

KLEINFELD's eyes widen and he tries to hide the guilty look that sweeps across his face.

KLEINFELD: Carlito, what are you—what's the matter with you?

CARLITO doesn't answer, just keeps the gun against KLEINFELD's temple and cocks it. KLEINFELD tries desperately to keep cool.

KLEINFELD: (*cont'd*) Fucking Norwalk. They played that tape for me, tried to leverage me. It's a bunch of bullshit, Carlito. I'm surprised at you. They doctor those things, play them out of context. What's the matter with you, falling for that shit? Don't be a schmuck.

CARLITO: You got a shelf life of about ten minutes, Dave.

He uncocks the gun. He walks across the room, keeping the weapon, playing with it idly while they talk.

CARLITO: (*cont'd*) I woulda done anything for you. I woulda done *anything* for you, Dave, and you fucked me over.

KLEINFELD: Fucked you over? Okay. For the sake of argument, let's say I *did* give Norwalk something to get him off my back. Which *I did not*—but let's say I did. So what? It isn't true, is it? They can't send you to jail for it, can they? So what's the problem?

CARLITO: I can't believe what I'm hearing. Your telling me you didn't do it, but if you did, it doesn't matter 'cause it ain't true? I don't know what that means, Dave. You're missing the point.

KLEINFELD: Yeah, and what's the point?

CARLITO: The point is you don't give up your friends. You don't give up your friends.

KLEINFELD: Hey, let me tell you something. I'm the best fucking friend you've ever had. Let's start with the five times I busted my ass to get you off. And I *got* you off.

CARLITO: Got paid for it too, Dave. Got paid real well.

KLEINFELD: I didn't do it for the money, Carlito.

CARLITO: No? You took the money.

KLEINFELD: I got you out of fucking *Lewisburg*! I saved your life, you admitted it yourself!

CARLITO: This ain't about owing. We don't owe each other, Dave. We're even, remember?

KLEINFELD: Yeah, I remember. You also told me I couldn't make it on your side—well, I got news for you, pal, you don't have a prayer on my side. How many holes does a life like yours leave? Did you plug 'em all? Could you possibly? What about the Italians?

CARLITO: Only way the Italians put me on that boat for sure is if you give me up.

KLEINFELD: Well, if you think I gave you up to Norwalk, what makes you think I won't do the same for the Italians?

CARLITO stares at KLEINFELD for a moment, then down at the gun in his hand.

CARLITO: I'm not sure you won't.

KLEINFELD just looks at him, wounded.

KLEINFELD: (*soft*) Carlito. Do you know what you're saying?

CARLITO: I woulda bled for you. I woulda died for you. I never would've turned you.

KLEINFELD looks at him. He's guilty as charged, he knows it, and now he finally loses his cool.

KLEINFELD: Hey, you know what? Fuck you and your self-righteous code of the street crap! There's only one rule, and you know it—save your own ass! Always been that way, always will be. If I'm the only one who's honest enough to admit it, then good for me!

CARLITO just looks at him, sadly. He walks over and gently puts the gun back under KLEINFELD's pillow.

CARLITO: You're not my friend no more. That may not mean much to you now, but one day it will.

He turns and heads for the door.

KLEINFELD: You know the trouble with you?

CARLITO: The trouble with me is I came up in a time that don't exist no more. See you around, Dave. You got a beautiful future.

Chasing Amy
(Miramax, 1997)

Screenplay by Kevin Smith
Directed by Kevin Smith
Characters: HOLDEN (Ben Affleck)
            HOOPER (Dwight Ewell)

NOTES: HOLDEN and Alyssa are both comic-book artists. He
works out of a loft in New Jersey; she's more into the New York
club scene. They first meet at a comic-book convention, and when
Alyssa invites HOLDEN to a party at a club, he thinks she has
eyes for him and starts to develop a crush. He soon finds out
that she's gay. She makes no secret of it; in fact, she talks openly
about sex and her past. They form a friendship, and hang out
together for a year. Then HOLDEN tells Alyssa that he loves
her. She reacts with anger at first, but then realizes that she loves
him, too. They start an exclusive relationship. This doesn't sit
well with HOLDEN's partner, Banky. He's jealous and threatened. Banky digs up high-school dirt on Alyssa, a story about
her having sex with two guys at once. He tells HOLDEN what
he's found out. HOLDEN doesn't know what to think about all
this and talks to his friend HOOPER, a black gay comic-book
artist who pretends to be straight and militant in order to sell
his work.

INTERIOR. TOWER RECORDS—DAY
HOLDEN and HOOPER peruse laser discs.

HOOPER: Where's that bitch partner of yours been?

HOLDEN: Sulking. He's having a real problem with this Alyssa thing.

HOOPER: I think it's more like Banky's having a problem with all things not hetero right about now. And I'm just a paradigm of said aberration.

HOLDEN: Banky does not hate gays, you know that.

HOOPER: But I do think he is a bit homophobic. And this latest episode between you and Ms. Thing has tapped into that. In his warped perception, he lost you to the dark side—which is she.

HOLDEN: You make it sound like me and him were dating.

HOOPER: Don't kid yourself—that boy loves you in a way that he's not ready to deal with.

HOLDEN: (*beat*) He's been digging up dirt on Alyssa.

HOOPER: And just what has Mr. Angela Lansbury uncovered about your lady fair?

HOLDEN: He heard some bullshit story that she took on two guys.

HOOPER: Really? Well then he's barking up the wrong tree if he wants to split you up, isn't he? He's not going to make you see the error of your ways by pointing out how truly gay she's not. (*holds up a disc*) This one?

HOLDEN: Have it. (*beat*) Actually, it's kind of gotten to me.

HOOPER: How so?

HOLDEN: Banky's not known for believing misinformation. He's got a pretty good bullshit detector.

HOOPER: So, what if it *is* true? Would that bother you?

HOLDEN: Sex with multiple partners?

HOOPER lets out a faux-shock shriek.

HOLDEN: At the same time.

Again, even louder, hands slapped against his chest.

HOLDEN: Thanks for being so comforting.

HOOPER: So, what do you care?

HOLDEN: Well. that's the thing, isn't it? I shouldn't . . . but it gets to me.

HOOPER: Kind of gal Alyssa is, you don't think she's been in the middle of an *all-girl* group-grope?

HOLDEN: You see—that doesn't bother me. But the thought of her and guys . . . Uh!

HOOPER: Oh, Holden, I beg you—please don't drop fifty stories in my opinion of you by falling prey to that latest of trendy beasts.

HOLDEN: Which is?

HOOPER: Lesbian chic. It's oh-so-acceptable to be a gay girl nowadays. People think it's cute, because they've got this fool picture in their heads about lipstick lesbians—like they all resemble Alyssa—while most of them look like you.

HOLDEN: Do I detect a little intersubculture cattiness?

HOOPER: Gay or straight—ugly's still ugly. And most of those boys are scary.

HOLDEN: I thought you fags were supposed to be all supersupportive of one another.

HOOPER: Screw that "all for one" shit. I gotta deal with being the minority in the minority of the minority, and nobody's supporting my ass. While the whole of society is fawning over girls-on-girls, here I sit—a reviled gay man. And to top that off, I'm a gay black man—notoriously the most swishy of the bunch.

HOLDEN: Three strikes.

HOOPER: Hey, Hey! There's a line.

A young black kid approaches HOOPER, holding a comic book.

KID: Are you Hooper X?

HOOPER: (in militant mode) A-salaam Alaikum, little brother.

KID: Could you sign my comic?

HOOPER: (*signs comic; nods to HOLDEN*) See that man there? He's the devil, you understand? Never take your eye off the Man. Our people took their eyes off him one time, and he had us in chains in two shakes of his snakes' tail.

The kid offers HOLDEN an angry look. HOOPER gives him back his comic.

HOOPER: Fight the power, little "G".

KID: Word is bond.

The Kid leaves. HOOPER slips back into his real voice.

HOOPER: Look at what I have to resort to for professional respect. What is it about gay men that terrifies the rest of the world? (*shakes his head*) As for this hang-up with Alyssa's past, maybe what's really bothering you is that your fragile fantasy might not be true.

HOLDEN: What do you mean?

HOOPER: Holden—don't even try to come off like you don't know what I'm saying. Men need to believe that they're Marco fucking Polo when it comes to sex—like they're the only ones who've ever explored new territory. And it's hard not to let them believe it. I let my boys run with it for a while—feed them some of that "I've never done *this* before . . ." bullshit, and let 'em labor under the delusion that they're rockin' my world, until I can't stand them anymore. Then I hit 'em with the truth. It's a sick game. The world would be a better place if people would accept that there's nothing new under the sun, and everything you can do with a person has probably been done long before you got there.

HOLDEN: I can accept that.

HOOPER: Honey, that almost sounded convincing. Do yourself a favor—just ask her about her past, point blank. Get it out of the way, before it gets too big for both y'all to move. (*spotting something OC*) Oooh! *Myra Breckenridge!*

HOOPER trots off. HOLDEN glances at the disc in his hands. Pictured on it are two gorgeous chicks, barely clad, making out. The title is Men Suck . . . and So Do Girls—All XXX Action.

Chasing Amy (2)
(Miramax, 1997)

Screenplay by Kevin Smith
Directed by Kevin Smith
Characters: ALYSSA (Joey Lauren Adams)
*   HOLDEN (Ben Affleck)*

NOTES: HOLDEN has been stewing about the story Banky dug up on ALYSSA. He's pretty sure that it's true, but he doesn't know how to feel about it (*see notes for previous scene*). It's starting to affect the way he relates to ALYSSA. He takes her to a hockey game and tries to broach the subject.

INTERIOR. HOCKEY RINK—NIGHT

On the ice, two teams clash, chasing the puck up and back, checking galore. In the bleachers, amid a slew of fans, ALYSSA watches the game with a large degree of enjoyment. Sitting beside her, HOLDEN doesn't seem to share her enthusiasm.

ALYSSA: Since most of these people are rooting for the hometeam, I'm going to cheer for the visitors. I'm a big visitors fan—especially the kind that make coffee for you in the morning before they go. (*smiles at HOLDEN; no response*) That was a joke. A little wacky word play?

HOLDEN: What do you mean, "visitors"?

ALYSSA: Was I being too obscure? The kind that—until recently—had no dicks and would spend the night.

HOLDEN: So that was until recently?

ALYSSA: Uh, yeah. (*shouting; to ice*) Hey—foul! Foul! He was traveling or something!

HOLDEN: So nobody but me has stayed the night at your place since we got together?

ALYSSA: (*beat*) Something on your mind, Holden?

HOLDEN: No, I was just wondering.

ALYSSA: If I've been "faithful" or something?

HOLDEN: Look, I was just asking.

ALYSSA: (*touches his face*) Oh, sweetie. I only have eyes for you. (*to ice*) CALL THAT FUCKING SHIT, REF! THE GUY ON THE SKATES TOTALLY SHOVED ONE OF MY GUYS! (*to HOLDEN*) I told you I was great at sporting events. Imagine what a bitch I could be if I knew what was going on?

On the ice, things heat up between two opposing players. One snatches the puck away from the other and skates off. The other player gives chase. ALYSSA's very into the game. HOLDEN shakes his head.

HOLDEN: That'd make Banky half right.

ALYSSA: About what?

HOLDEN: He said all the girls from North were bitches and sluts.

ALYSSA: Really. I'm sorry—you two left high school how many years ago? (*grabs his face and kisses his cheek*) Can I put some of my books in your locker? (*goes back to the game*)

HOLDEN: (*under his breath*) How about your yearbook.

On the ice, the player giving chase slashes the player with the puck. ALYSSA jumps to her feet.

ALYSSA: (*to ice*) IF YOU DON'T START USING THAT WHISTLE, I'M GONNA JAM IT STRAIGHT UP YOUR ASS! (*to guy right next to her*) Right?

HOLDEN: What's with "Finger Cuffs"?

ALYSSA: (*sitting back down*) "Finger Cuffs"?

HOLDEN: Yeah. In your senior yearbook, your nickname was "Finger Cuffs." What is that?

ALYSSA: It was? Shit, damned if I can remember. I'd look it up, but I threw all that shit out years ago. (*beat*) Where'd you see a North yearbook?

HOLDEN: Do you know a guy named Rick Derris?

On the ice, the players skid into the corner where Player One checks Player Two into the boards, hard. Player Two scrambles to his feet and throws down his gloves. The crowd around ALYSSA and HOLDEN goes wild.

ALYSSA: Rick Derris? Sure. We used to hang out in high school. (*to ice*) PUNCH HIM IN THE NECK, NUMBER TWELVE!

HOLDEN: Did you go out with him or something?

ALYSSA: (*eyes on the ice*) Date Rick Derris? No. We just hung out a lot.

HOLDEN: Just . . . you and Rick?

ALYSSA: No. Me, Rick, and . . . um . . . what was that guy's name . . . ?

HOLDEN: Cohee?

ALYSSA: Yeah! Cohee Lundin. God, I haven't thought about that name in years.

On the ice, the players square off. Player Two pulls Player One's helmet off and punches him in the face. HOLDEN looks as if he'd like to do the same to his companion. ALYSSA's into the game.

ALYSSA: I remember those guys'd come over almost every-day after school. They'd bug my sisters, look for porno tapes in my dad's closet, raid our fridge. They really took advantage of my parents never being home.

On the ice, Player Two yanks at Player One's jersey and gutpunches him. ALYSSA seems oblivious of HOLDEN's anger, so enthralled with the action is she.

ALYSSA: (*starts laughing*) This one day . . . Rick pulled out his dick and chased me around the house with it! Right in front of Cohee! I couldn't believe it! Guys are weird—I thought the whole size hang-up made you all terrified to show your dicks to each other?

On the ice, Player One staggers a bit, then quickly rights his jersey and lunges at Player Two, landing a barrage of his own punches. Blood sprays across the ice. HOLDEN's face is really sour looking. ALYSSA's still in the game.

HOLDEN: Rick pulled his dick out? Really? What'd you do?

ALYSSA: (*looks him dead in the eye*) I blew him while Cohee fucked me.

On the ice, Player One delivers the kill shot, slamming his fist into Player Two's nose. The blood shoots out like a geyser, and Two goes down hard. HOLDEN stares at ALYSSA, flabbergasted. The crowd around them stares not at the fight on the ice, but at the fight in their midst, shocked. ALYSSA fumes.

HOLDEN: Excuse me?

ALYSSA: That's what you wanted to hear, isn't it? Isn't that what this little cross-examination of yours is about? Well, try not to be so obvious about it next time; there are subtler ways of badgering a witness. (*to bystander*) Am I right?

BYSTANDER: (*to HOLDEN*) Jeez, even I knew what you were getting at.

ALYSSA: (*gathering her stuff*) If you wanted some background information on me, all you had to do was ask—I'd have gladly volunteered it. You didn't have to play Hercule fucking Poirot!

She storms away. HOLDEN chases after her. The Bystander watches them go.

BYSTANDER: (*to companion*) I told you these were good seats.

EXT. RINK PARKING LOT—NIGHT

ALYSSA marches quickly, pulling on her coat. HOLDEN catches up to her. We track with them out into the parking lot.

HOLDEN: So it's true?

ALYSSA: Is that what you want to hear? Is it? Yes, Holden, it's true! In fact, everything you heard or dug up on me was probably true! Yeah, I took on two guys at once! You want to hear some gems you have not unearthed—I took a twenty-six-year-old guy to my senior prom, and then left halfway through to have sex with him and Gwen Turner in the back of a limo! And the girl who got caught in the shower with Miss Moffit, the gym teacher? That was me! Or how about in college, when I let Shannon Hamilton videotape us having sex—only to find out the next day that he broadcast it on the campus cable station? They're all true—those and so many more! Didn't you know? I'm the queen of urban legend!

HOLDEN: How the hell could you do those things?!

ALYSSA: Easily! Some of it I did out of stupidity, some of it I did out of what I thought was love, but—good or bad— they were my choices, and I'm not making apologies for them now—not to you or anyone! And how dare you try to lay a guilt trip on me about it—in public, no less! Who the fuck do you think you are, you judgmental prick?

HOLDEN: How am I supposed to feel about all of this?

ALYSSA: How are you supposed to feel about it? Feel whatever the fuck you want about it! The only thing that really matters is how you feel about me.

HOLDEN: I don't know how I feel about you now.

ALYSSA: Why? Because I had some sex?

HOLDEN: *Some* sex?

ALYSSA: Yes, Holden—that's all it was: some sex! Most of it stupid high school sex, for Christ's sake! Like you never had sex in high school!

HOLDEN: There's a world of fucking difference between typical high school sex and getting fucked by two guys at the same time! They fucking used you!

ALYSSA: NO! I used *them*! You don't think I would've let it happen if I hadn't wanted it to, do you?! I was an experimental girl, for Christ's sake! Maybe you knew early on that your track was from point A to B—but unlike you, I wasn't given a fucking map at birth, so I tried it all! That is until *we*—that's you and I—got together, and suddenly, I was sated. Can't you take some fucking comfort in that? You turned out to be all I was ever looking for—the missing piece in the big fucking puzzle! (*tries to calm down*) Look, I'm sorry I let you believe that you were the only guy I'd ever been with. I should've been more honest. But it seemed to make you feel special in a way that me telling you over and over again how incredible you are would never get across.

She touches his face. He pulls back. She stares at him, hurt and pissed.

ALYSSA: Do you mean to tell me that while you have zero problem with me sleeping with half the women in New York City, you have some sort of half-assed, mealy-mouthed objection to pubescent antics that took place almost ten years ago? What the fuck is your problem?

HOLDEN's eyes are downcast. ALYSSA waits for a response.

HOLDEN: I want us to be something that we can't be.

ALYSSA: And what's that?

HOLDEN: (*beat*) A normal couple.

HOLDEN skulks off. ALYSSA stares after him, and then starts kicking and punching a car beside her, finally slumping to the ground. She cries.

Clerks
(Miramax, 1994)

Screenplay by Kevin Smith
Directed by Kevin Smith
Characters: DANTE (Brian O'Halloran)
           RANDAL (Jeff Anderson)

NOTES: DANTE and RANDAL are good friends, around twenty years old; they work for the same boss in dead-end jobs in a New Jersey town. DANTE works at the Quik Stop Deli and takes it far too seriously, and RANDAL runs the video store next door and doesn't take it seriously at all. DANTE has a girlfriend, Veronica, who goes to college and is urging him to do the same. He has an ex-girlfriend, Caitlin, that he obsesses about and has been talking to lately on the phone. She has a boyfriend, but hasn't told DANTE about him yet, and DANTE is fantasizing about a reunion. RANDAL is an easygoing stoner who lives in the moment and has no illusions about where his life is not going. He can be obnoxious and sensitive at the same time. *CLERKS* follows this hapless pair through the course of a very bad day. DANTE has already been called into work on his day off, and had a fight with Veronica over her past sexual partners. RANDAL comes over to the deli to visit.

INTERIOR. CONVENIENCE STORE—DAY
RANDAL pulls a soda from the cooler.
RANDAL: Want something to drink? I'm buying.

(*Offscreen*) **DANTE:** No, thanks.

RANDAL: Who was on the phone this morning at about two thirty? I was trying to call for a half an hour.

(*Offscreen*) **DANTE:** Why?

RANDAL: I wanted to use your car.

He walks by a row of snacks and grabs one without looking at it.

RANDAL: Snack cake?

DANTE sits in his seat behind the register. RANDAL grabs a paper and joins him behind the counter.

DANTE: You don't want to know.

RANDAL: You called Caitlin again?

DANTE: She called me.

RANDAL: Did you tell Veronica?

DANTE: One fight a day with Veronica is about all I can stomach, thanks.

RANDAL: What do you two fight about?

DANTE: I guess it's not really fighting. She justs wants me to leave here, go back to school, get some direction.

RANDAL: (*opening paper*) I'll bet the most frequent topic of arguments is Caitlin Bree.

DANTE: You win.

RANDAL: I'm going to offer you some advice, my friend: let the past be the past. Forget Caitlin Bree. You've been with Veronica for how long now?

DANTE: Seven months.

RANDAL: Chick's nuts about you. How long did you date Caitlin?

DANTE: Five years.

RANDAL: Chick only made you nuts. She cheated on you how many times?

DANTE: Eight and a half.

RANDAL: (*looks up from paper*) Eight and a half?

DANTE: Party at John K's—senior year. I get blitzed and pass out in his bedroom. Caitlin comes in and dives all over me.

RANDAL: That's cheating?

DANTE: In the middle of it, she calls me Brad.

RANDAL: She called you Brad?

DANTE: She called me Brad.

RANDAL: That's not cheating. People say crazy shit during sex. One time, I called this girl "Mom."

DANTE: I hit the lights and she freaks. Turns out she thought I was Brad Michaelson.

RANDAL: What do you mean?

DANTE: She was supposed to meet Brad Michaelson in a bedroom. She picked the wrong one. She had no idea I was even at the party.

RANDAL: Oh, my God.

DANTE: Great story, isn't it?

RANDAL: That girl was vile to you.

DANTE: Interesting postscript to that story: Do you know who wound up going with Brad Michaelson in the other dark bedroom?

RANDAL: Your mother.

DANTE: Allan Harris.

RANDAL: Chess team Allan Harris?

DANTE: The two moved to Idaho together after graduation. They raise sheep.

RANDAL: That's frightening.

DANTE: It takes different strokes to move the world.

RANDAL: In light of this lurid tale, I don't see how you could even romanticize your relationship with Caitlin—she broke your heart and inadvertently drove men to deviant lifestyles.

DANTE: Because there was a lot of good in our relationship.

RANDAL: Oh yeah.

DANTE: I'm serious. Aside from the cheating, we were a great couple. That's what high school is all about—algebra, bad lunch, and infidelity.

RANDAL: You think things would be any different now?

DANTE: They are. When she calls me now, she's a different person—she's frightened and vulnerable. She's about to finish college and enter the real world. That's got to be scary for anyone.

RANDAL: (*suddenly recalling*) Oh, shit, I've got to place an order.

DANTE: I'm talking to myself here.

RANDAL: No, no, I'm listening. She's leaving college, and . . . ?

DANTE: . . . and she's looking to me for support. And I think that this is leading our relationship to a new level.

RANDAL: What about Veronica?

DANTE: I think the arguments Veronica and I are having are some kind of manifestation of a subconscious desire to break away from her so that I can pursue the possibility of a more meaningful relationship with Caitlin.

RANDAL: Caitlin's on the same wavelength?

DANTE: I think it's safe to say yes.

RANDAL: Then I think all four of you had better sit down and talk it over.

DANTE: All four?

RANDAL: You, Veronica, Caitlin . . . (lays paper flat) . . . and Caitlin's fiancé.

The headline of the engagement announcement reads, BREE TO WED ASIAN DESIGN MAJOR.

Clerks (2)
(Miramax, 1994)

Screenplay by Kevin Smith
Directed by Kevin Smith
Characters: DANTE (Brian O'Halloran)
CAITLIN (Lisa Spoonauer)

NOTES: DANTE's day goes from bad to worse when he gets the news of CAITLIN's engagement (*see previous scene*). Then CAITLIN unexpectedly shows up at the deli, where DANTE is having trouble coping; she's taken the train down from school to see him. She doesn't know what she wants any more than DANTE does, but she thinks she's got it all sorted out. In the process, she sends a different mixed message with every line.

INTERIOR. VIDEO STORE—NIGHT

On counter.

CAITLIN: You're just going to lock the store like that?

DANTE: I want to talk to you about something, and I don't want to be disturbed.

CAITLIN: You saw it?

DANTE: Very dramatic, I thought.

CAITLIN: It's not what you think.

DANTE: What, it's worse? You're pregnant with an Asian design major's child?

CAITLIN: I'm not pregnant.

DANTE: Were you going to tell me or just send an invitation?

CAITLIN: I was going to tell you. But then we were getting along so well, I didn't want to mess it up.

DANTE: You could've broken it to me gently, you know; at least started by telling me you had a boyfriend. I told you I had a girlfriend.

CAITLIN: I know, I'm sorry. But when we started talking . . . it's like I forgot I had a boyfriend. And then he proposed last month . . .

DANTE: And you said yes?

CAITLIN: Well . . . kind of, sort of?

DANTE: Is that what they teach you at that school of yours? Kind of, sort of? Everyone knows about this except me! Do you know how humiliating that is?

CAITLIN: I would've told you, and you would have stopped calling, like a baby.

DANTE: How do you know that?

CAITLIN: Because I know you. You prefer drastic measures to rational ones.

DANTE: So you're really getting married?

CAITLIN: No.

DANTE: No, you're not really getting married?

CAITLIN: The story goes like this: He proposed, and I told him I had to think about it, and he insisted I wear the ring anyway. Then my mother told the paper we were engaged.

DANTE: How like her.

CAITLIN: Then my mother called me this morning and told me the announcement was in the paper. That's when I hopped the train to come back here, because I knew you'd be a wreck.

DANTE: Thanks for the vote of confidence.

CAITLIN: Was I right?

DANTE: Wreck is a harsh term. Disturbed is more like it. Mildly disturbed even.

CAITLIN: I love a macho facade. It's such a turn-on. (*sniffing air*) What smells like shoe polish?

DANTE: And you came here to what? To comfort me?

CAITLIN: The last thing I needed was for you to think I was hiding something from you.

DANTE: But you were.

CAITLIN: No, I wasn't. Not really. I told you I'd been seeing other people.

DANTE: Yeah, but not seriously. Christ, you're ready to walk down the aisle—I'd say that constitutes something more than just seeing somebody.

CAITLIN: I'm giving him his ring back.

DANTE: What?

CAITLIN: I don't want to marry him. I don't want to get married now. I'm on the verge of graduation. I want to go to grad school after this. And then I want to start a career. I don't want to be a wife first, and then have to worry about when I'm going to fit in all of the other stuff. I've come way too far and studied too hard to let my education go to waste as a housewife. And I know that's what I'd become. Sang's already signed with a major firm, and he's going to be pulling a huge salary, which would give me no reason to work, and he's so traditional anyway . . .

DANTE: Sang? His name is a past tense?

CAITLIN: Stop it. He's a nice guy.

DANTE: If he's so nice, why aren't you going to marry him?

CAITLIN: I just told you.

DANTE: There's more, isn't there?

CAITLIN: Why, Mr. Hicks—whatever do you mean?

DANTE: Tell me I don't have something to do with it.

CAITLIN: You don't have anything to do with it.

DANTE: You lie.

CAITLIN: Look how full of yourself you are.

DANTE: I just believe in giving credit where credit is due. And I believe that I'm the impetus behind your failure to wed.

CAITLIN: If I'm so nuts about you, then why am I having sex with an Asian design major?

DANTE: Jesus, you're caustic.

CAITLIN: I had to bring you down from that cloud you were floating on. When I say I don't want to get married, I mean just that. I don't want to marry anybody. Not for years.

DANTE: So who's asking? I don't want to marry you.

CAITLIN: Good. Stay in that frame of mind.

DANTE: But can we date?

CAITLIN: I'm sure Sang and—Veronica?—would like that.

DANTE: We could introduce them. They might hit it off.

CAITLIN: You're serious. You want to date again.

DANTE: I would like to be your boyfriend, yes.

CAITLIN: It's just the shock of seeing me after three years. Believe me, you'll get over it.

DANTE: Give me a bit more credit. I think it's time we got back together, you know. I'm more mature, you're more mature, you're finishing college, I'm already in the job market . . .

CAITLIN: You work in a market, all right.

DANTE: Cute. Tell me you wouldn't want to go out again. After all the talking we've been doing.

CAITLIN: The key word here is *talk*, Dante. I think the idea, the conception of us dating, is more idyllic than what actually happens when we date.

DANTE: So . . . what? So should we just make pretend over the phone that we're dating?

CAITLIN: I don't know. Maybe we should just see what happens.

DANTE: Let me take you out tonight.

CAITLIN: You mean, on a date?

DANTE: Yes. A real date. Dinner and a movie.

CAITLIN: The Dante Hicks Dinner and a Movie Date. I think I've been on that one before.

DANTE: You have a better suggestion?

CAITLIN: How about the Caitlin Bree Walk on the Boardwalk, Then Get Naked Somewhere Kind of Private Date?

DANTE: I hear that's a rather popular date.

CAITLIN: (*hits him*) Jerk. Here I am, throwing myself at you, succumbing to your wily charms, and you call me a slut, in so many words.

DANTE: What about Sing?

CAITLIN: Sang.

DANTE: Sang.

CAITLIN: He's not invited.

DANTE: He's your fiancé.

CAITLIN: I offer you my body and you offer me semantics? He's just a boyfriend, Dante, and in case you haven't gotten the drift of why I came all the way here from Ohio, I'm about to become single again. And yes—let me placate your ego—you are the inspiration for this bold and momentous decision, for which I'll probably be ostracized at both school and home. You ask me who I choose, I choose you.

DANTE: So what are you saying?

CAITLIN: You're such an asshole.

DANTE: I'm only kidding.

CAITLIN: I can already tell this isn't going to work.

DANTE: I'll ask Randal to close up for me—when he gets back.

CAITLIN: Where'd he go? I'd have thought he'd be at your side, like an obedient lapdog.

DANTE: He went to rent a movie, but he hasn't gotten back yet. Ah, screw it; I'll just lock up the store and leave him a note.

CAITLIN: You're too responsible. But no. I have to go home first. They don't even know I left school. And I should break the disengagement news to my mother, which is going to cause quite a row, considering she loves Sang.

DANTE: Who doesn't?

CAITLIN: Well, me I guess. (*gathering herself to go*) So, I shall take my leave of you, but I will return in a little while, at which time—yes—I would love to go for dinner and a movie with you.

DANTE: What happened to the walk and the nakedness?

CAITLIN: I'm easy, but I'm not that easy. (*she kisses his cheek*) See you later, handsome.

DANTE watches her leave. He then explodes in jubilance.

DANTE: Yes!

Clerks (3)
(Miramax, 1994)

Screenplay by Kevin Smith
Directed by Kevin Smith
Characters: CAITLIN (Lisa Spoonauer)
RANDAL (Jeff Anderson)

NOTES: The day is finally almost over. Dante and RANDAL have survived the slings and arrows of the deli and video business, fights with girlfriends and each other, a fire, a trip to a wake (the wrong one) during which RANDAL knocked over the coffin, and it's not over yet. CAITLIN, Dante's ex-girlfriend, has come down from school to visit Dante *(see previous scenes)* and RANDAL is suspicious of her intentions. His loyalty to Dante creates conflict when he sees her. His remark about Chinese food is an insulting reference to CAITLIN's current boyfriend, who is Chinese.

INTERIOR. CONVENIENCE STORE—NIGHT

CAITLIN enters, carrying an overnight bag. RANDAL is watching his porno. The porno is loud and lewd. CAITLIN stares.

CAITLIN: Randal Graves—scourge of the video renter.

RANDAL: Ladies and gentlemen, Mrs. Asian Design Major herself: Caitlin Bree!

CAITLIN: You saw that article? God, isn't it awful? My mother sent that in.

RANDAL: I take it she likes that guy.

CAITLIN: You'd think she was marrying him. What are you watching?

RANDAL: Children's programming. What did your mom say when you told her you weren't engaged anymore?

CAITLIN: She said not to come home until graduation.

RANDAL: Wow, you got thrown out? For Dante?

CAITLIN: What can I say? He does weird things to me.

RANDAL: Can I watch?

CAITLIN: You can hold me down.

RANDAL: Can I join in?

CAITLIN: You might be let down. I'm not a hermaphrodite.

RANDAL: Few are. So what makes you think you can maintain a relationship with Dante this time around?

CAITLIN: A woman's intuition. Something in me says it's time to give the old boy a serious try.

RANDAL: Wow. Hey, I was just about to order some dinner. You eat Chinese, right?

CAITLIN: Dick.

RANDAL: Exactly.

CAITLIN: So where is he?

RANDAL: He went home to change for the big date.

CAITLIN: God, isn't he great?

RANDAL: (*indicating TV*) No, *this* is great.

CAITLIN: Can I use the bathroom?

RANDAL: There's no light back there.

CAITLIN: Why aren't there any lights?

RANDAL: Well, there are, but for some reason they stop working at five-fourteen every night.

CAITLIN: You're kidding.

RANDAL: Nobody can figure it out. And the boss doesn't want to pay the electrician to fix it, because the electrician owes money to the video store.

CAITLIN: Such a sordid state of affairs.

RANDAL: And I'm caught in the middle—torn between my loyalty for the boss, and my desire to piss with the lights on.

CAITLIN: I'll try to manage.

She heads toward the back.

RANDAL: Hey Caitlin... (*cautionary*) Break his heart again, and I'll kill you. Nothing personal.

CAITLIN: You're very protective of him, Randal. You always have been.

RANDAL: Territoriality. He was mine first.

CAITLIN: (*rubs his head*) Awww. That was so cute.

She kisses his forehead and walks away.

The Crying Game
(Miramax, 1992)

Screenplay by Neil Jordan
Directed by Neil Jordan
Characters: FERGUS (Stephen Rea)
           JODY (Forest Whitaker)

NOTES: FERGUS is a "volunteer" with the IRA. Outside of
Belfast, a particularly active IRA stronghold, a small band of
IRA terrorists capture a British soldier and hold him captive,
hoping to trade him for an IRA prisoner that the British are
holding. The soldier is JODY, a young black man. JODY was
seduced by a woman with the gang, Jude, and then captured.
Jude and FERGUS are lovers, but JODY doesn't know this.
They take him to their hideout, an abandoned farmhouse in the
woods. FERGUS takes his turn guarding JODY in the dilapi-
dated greenhouse on the property. JODY can see that FERGUS
has a soft heart, and appeals to his humanity.

INTERIOR. GREENHOUSE—DAY
FERGUS walks to JODY and slowly takes the hood off.
JODY looks up at him, his face bathed in sweat. He breathes
in mighty gulps of air. He smiles.
JODY: Thank you, soldier.
FERGUS smiles.
JODY: Never thought fresh air would taste this good.
FERGUS pours out a cup of tea and brings it to his lips.

JODY: Now, if you took the ropes off, I'd be able to feed myself.

FERGUS: No fucking way.

JODY: Only joking.

FERGUS drinks.

JODY: You know, I was wrong about one thing.

FERGUS: What's that?

JODY: Five ten. Brown eyes. But you're no pinup.

FERGUS: No?

JODY: Nope. Not handsome at all.

FERGUS: You trying to hurt my feelings?

JODY: No. It's the truth.

FERGUS: Well, I could say the same about you.

JODY: Could you?

FERGUS: But I won't. We're more polite around these parts.

JODY: So I've noticed.

FERGUS looks at him. JODY isn't smiling anymore. FERGUS goes back to his seat and drinks his tea. He fingers the gun on his lap.

JODY: Hey—

FERGUS: What is it now?

JODY: You're going to have to do it, aren't you?

FERGUS: Do what?

JODY: Kill me.

FERGUS: What makes you think that?

JODY: They're going to let that guy die. And you're going to kill me.

FERGUS: They won't let him die.

JODY: You want to bet?

FERGUS: I'm not a gambling man.

JODY: And even if he doesn't die—you can't just let me loose.

FERGUS: Why can't we?

JODY: Not in your nature.

FERGUS: What do you know about my nature?

JODY: I'm talking about your people, not you.

FERGUS: What the fuck do you know about my people?

JODY: Only that you're all tough undeluded motherfuckers. And that it's not in your nature to let me go.

FERGUS: Shut the fuck up, would you?

JODY: And you know the funny thing?

FERGUS: No, what's the funny thing?

JODY: I didn't even fancy her.

FERGUS: Didn't look like that to me.

JODY: She's not my type.

He looks at FERGUS.

JODY: C'mere.

FERGUS: No.

JODY: Ah, c'mere. I want to show you something.

FERGUS: What?

JODY: My inside pocket.

FERGUS holds the gun to his face. He fishes inside JODY's inside pocket.

JODY: Take out the wallet.

FERGUS's hand emerges with a wallet.

JODY: Open it.

Close on the wallet. Credit cards, army identification photograph.

JODY: Inside. There's a picture.

FERGUS takes out a picture. It's of JODY, in cricket whites, smiling, holding a bat. FERGUS smiles.

JODY: No, not that one. There's another.

FERGUS takes out another picture of JODY and of a beautiful black woman, smiling.

JODY: Now *she's* my type.

FERGUS: She'd be anyone's type.

JODY: Don't you think of it, fucker.

FERGUS: Why not?

JODY: She's mine. Anyway, she wouldn't suit you.

FERGUS: No?

JODY: Absolutely not.

FERGUS: She your wife?

JODY: Suppose you could say that.

JODY chuckles.

FERGUS: You make a nice couple.

JODY: Don't I know it.

FERGUS: So what were you fucking around for, then?

JODY: You fuckers set me up. That bitch—

FERGUS: She's a friend of mine—

JODY: Okay. That nice lady. Meets me in a bar. I'm saying what the fuck am I doing here anyway. She buys me a drink. She holds my hand. I'm looking at her saying I don't like you, bitch. But what the fuck. Maybe I'll get to understand.

FERGUS: What?

JODY: What the fuck am I doing here.

FERGUS: What the fuck were you doing here?

JODY: I got sent.

FERGUS: You could have said no.

JODY: Can't. Once I signed up.

FERGUS: Why did you sign up?

JODY: It was a job. So I get sent to the only place in the world they call you a nigger to your face.

FERGUS: You shouldn't take it personally.

JODY: (*He imitates a Belfast accent*) ''Go back to your banana tree, nigger.'' No use telling them I came from Tottenham.

FERGUS: And you play cricket?

JODY: Best game in the world.

FERGUS: Ever see hurling?

JODY: That game where a bunch of paddies whack sticks at each other?

FERGUS: Best game in the world.

JODY: Never.

FERGUS: The fastest.

JODY: Well, in Antigua cricket's the black man's game. The kids play it from the age of two. My daddy had me throwing googlies from the age of five. Then we moved to Tottenham and it was something different.

FERGUS: How different?

JODY: Toffs' game there. But not at home.

FERGUS looks at him.

JODY: So when you come to shoot me, Paddy, remember, you're getting rid of a shit-hot bowler.

FERGUS: I'll bear that in mind.

He keeps looking at him.

FERGUS: And by the way, it's not Paddy. It's Fergus.

JODY smiles.

JODY: Nice to meet you, Fergus.

FERGUS: My pleasure, Jody.

The Crying Game (2)
(Miramax, 1992)

Screenplay by Neil Jordan
Directed by Neil Jordan
Characters: FERGUS (Stephen Rea)
            JODY (Forest Whitaker)

NOTES: FERGUS has spent time guarding JODY in the IRA hideout (*see notes for previous scene*), and the two men have begun to develop an emotional connection. JODY tells FERGUS about his life, and about his girlfriend back home, Dil. FERGUS takes a bit of harsh treatment from his cohorts for treating JODY as an individual. They insist FERGUS keep JODY's hood on, and FERGUS knows that, if and when the time comes, they will make him kill JODY to prove his loyalty. In this scene, JODY has been held for a few days already, and time is running out. During this scene, Jude enters; the scene could be played with a third actor or edited for two.

INTERIOR. GREENHOUSE—DAY

JODY sitting with the hood on again. FERGUS enters.

JODY: They giving you trouble, Fergus?

FERGUS says nothing. He takes a plate and brings it toward JODY.

JODY: It happens. Y'see, there's two kinds of people. Those who give and those who take.

FERGUS lifts up JODY's hood to expose his mouth and begins to feed him.

JODY: Ah, take the thing off, man.

FERGUS says nothing and keeps feeding him.

JODY: I will take it by your silence that you don't.

He eats. FERGUS feeds himself, then feeds more to JODY.

JODY: Two types, Fergus. The scorpion and the frog. Ever
heard of them?

FERGUS says nothing.

JODY: Scorpion wants to cross a river, but he can't swim.
Goes to the frog, who can, and asks for a ride. Frog says,
"If I give you a ride on my back, you'll go and sting me."
Scorpion replies, "It would not be in my interest to sting
you since as I'll be on your back we both would drown."
Frog thinks about this logic for a while and accepts the
deal. Takes the Scorpion on his back. Braves the waters.
Halfway over feels a burning spear in his side and realizes
the scorpion has stung him after all. And as they both sink
beneath the waves the frog cries out, "Why did you sting
me, Mr. Scorpion, for now we both will drown?" Scorpion
replies, "I can't help it, it's in my nature."

JODY chuckles under his hood.

FERGUS: So what's that supposed to mean?

JODY: Means what it says. The scorpion does what is in his
nature. Take off the hood, man.

FERGUS: Why?

JODY: 'Cause you're kind. It's in your nature.

*FERGUS walks toward him and pulls off the hood. JODY
smiles up at him.*

JODY: See? I was right about you.

FERGUS: Don't be so sure.

JODY: Jody's always right.

INTERIOR. GREENHOUSE—LATE AFTERNOON

Both men dozing in the heat.

JODY: Where would you most like to be now, man?

FERGUS: Doesn't matter where.

JODY: Come on, man. If this shit was all over.

FERGUS: Having a pint in the Rock.

JODY: You lack imagination, Fergus. Think of something more alluring.

FERGUS: Like what?

JODY: Like having a pint in the Metro—

FERGUS laughs.

FERGUS: Having two pints in the Rock.

JODY: Having a pint in the Metro, and Dil's having a margarita.

FERGUS: Who's Dil?

JODY: My special friend.

FERGUS: Oh, yeah.

JODY: We got simple tastes, you and me.

FERGUS: The best.

JODY: But you fellas never get a break, do you?

FERGUS: Do you?

JODY: Oh, yes. We do a tour of duty and we're finished. But you guys are never finished, are you?

FERGUS: We don't look on it like that.

JODY: I've often wondered how you do it.

FERGUS: Depends on what you believe in.

JODY: What do you believe in?

FERGUS: That you guys shouldn't be here.

JODY: It's as simple as that?

FERGUS: Yes.

JUDE enters.

JUDE: Put that thing back on him, Fergus.

FERGUS: He's hot.

JUDE: Doesn't matter if he's hot. Just cover the fucker up.

JODY: Have you no feelings, woman?

JUDE: You shut your face—

She pulls the hood down over him.

JUDE: You're heading for trouble, Fergus—

JODY: He's a good soldier, Jude.

She whacks him with a pistol.

JUDE: I said shut the fuck up—

JODY: He believes in the future—

INTERIOR. GREENHOUSE—NIGHT

JODY, sitting in the hood. FERGUS lifts it up a bit; JODY's mouth, with blood now on his lips.

FERGUS: Is it bad?

JODY: No. Not bad. Women are trouble, you know that, Fergus?

FERGUS: I didn't.

JODY: Some kinds of women are . . .

FERGUS: She can't help it.

JODY: Dil wasn't trouble. No trouble at all.

FERGUS: You liked her?

JODY: Present tense, please. Love her. Whatever she is. I'm thinking of her now, Fergus. Will you think of her too?

FERGUS: Don't know her.

JODY: Want you to do something, Fergus.

FERGUS: What?

JODY: If they kill me—

FERGUS: Don't think that way.

JODY: But they will. As sure as night follows day. They have to. I want you to find her out. Tell her I was thinking of her.

FERGUS is moved. He can't reply.

JODY: See if she's all right.

FERGUS: I don't know her.

JODY: Take her picture. C'mere.

FERGUS walks toward him.

JODY: Take it. In the inside pocket.

Their faces, close to each other as FERGUS searches out her picture.

JODY: Take the whole lot. I won't need it.

FERGUS: I told you not to talk that way—

JODY: Go to Millie's Hair Salon in Spitalfields. Take her to the Metro for a margarita. Don't have to tell her who you are. Just tell Jody was thinking—

FERGUS: Stop it—

The door opens. Maguire is there, with another.

The Crying Game (3)
(Miramax, 1992)

Screenplay by Neil Jordan
Directed by Neil Jordan
Characters: FERGUS (Stephen Rea)
DIL (Jaye Davidson)

NOTES: FERGUS is now an ex-volunteer with the IRA; the hostage scheme went terribly wrong (*see previous scenes*). The British soldier they captured, Jody, and FERGUS became friends while FERGUS was guarding Jody. When FERGUS was instructed to kill Jody, he let him run instead; Jody ran into the road and was killed by the trucks of the storming British soldiers. FERGUS escaped alone in the fray and got on a boat to London, where he effectively disappeared and became a construction worker named Jimmy. Once there, he locates DIL, Jody's girlfriend; he wants to honor Jody's final wish that he find her and check up on her, tell her that Jody was thinking of her. She is a hairdresser; FERGUS gets his hair cut and has drinks with her a few times. He saves her from a drunken, violent suitor (Dave) and escorts her home. FERGUS doesn't know that DIL is a man, living as a woman. This is the first time FERGUS has been to DIL's flat.

INTERIOR. DIL'S FLAT—NIGHT

DIL comes in in the darkness. FERGUS stands like a shadow in the doorway. The light comes on; she takes off her raincoat.

DIL: Won't hurt you to come in.

FERGUS enters slowly. He looks around the room; there is an exaggerated femininity about everything in it.

DIL: Would you like a drink?

FERGUS: Yes, please.

DIL: What'll it be?

FERGUS: Whiskey.

She goes into a small kitchen. FERGUS looks at the mantelpiece and sees a picture of Jody. The camera tracks into the soldier's smiling face. Then into FERGUS's face. His reverie is broken by the sound of a voice outside—Dave's. She comes through with two drinks.

FERGUS: Someone out there.

DIL: Jesus fucking Christ.

She opens the window door, and we see Dave on the street, in a neck brace.

DIL: Hey, Stirling fucking Moss—

[**DAVE:** It's Dave.]

She goes back into the room and begins taking things up.

[**DAVE:** Talk to me, Dil—]

DIL: Sure, Dave—

[**DAVE:** Please, Dil—]

She flings things down: men's clothes, leather trousers, a suitcase, a teddy bear.

DIL: Take your clothes.

[**DAVE:** Don't throw my clothes out the window!]

DIL: Fuck off back to Essex!

[**DAVE:** Fucking mad!]

FERGUS looks to the man down in the street, a parody of rejection with his things in his arms.

[**DAVE:** Don't chuck my clothes out!]

DIL: Take your fucking goldfish, too!

DIL grabs a large goldfish bowl and flings it down. The bowl breaks to bits on the pavement. Goldfish thrash around in the street.

[**DAVE:** You fucking bitch!]

He tries to pick up the flapping fish in his hands.

[**DAVE:** Murderer!]

Upstairs, DIL closes the window shut.

DIL: Sorry. How'd he drive with his neck in a brace?

FERGUS: Must be in love to answer that.

DIL: Doesn't know the meaning of the word.

FERGUS stands as DIL hands him a glass.

FERGUS: He lived here with you?

DIL: Tried to. Sit down, will you?

FERGUS walks past the photograph and sits down. He looks from her to the picture.

FERGUS: What about him?

He nods toward the picture. She looks down into her drink.

DIL: He was different.

FERGUS: How different?

DIL: As different as it's possible to be.

FERGUS: Tell me about him.

DIL: No.

FERGUS: Shouldn't I go?

DIL: Yes.

And they fall into one another's arms. She stretches up with her whole body over him. They grow suddenly and violently passionate. They fall into the cushions of the couch onto the floor. The photograph above them seems to smile. He draws up her dress with his hands. She suddenly pulls away.

DIL: No—

FERGUS: Did you do that to him?

She comes up toward him once more. She puts her mouth close to his ear.

DIL: You want to know how I kissed him?

FERGUS: Yes ...

DIL: Are you jealous of him?

FERGUS: Maybe.

DIL: That's good ...

She opens the buttons on his shirt and her mouth travels down his chest. FERGUS tries to draw her up toward him, but her hand reaches up to his mouth and presses his head back while her other hand undoes his pants. She kisses his stomach; her mouth moves down his body. FERGUS stares at the picture of Jody. Jody's eyes seem to burn through him. DIL raises her head and kisses his mouth. There are tears in his eyes.

FERGUS: What would he think?

DIL: Can't think. He's dead. In Ireland. He was a soldier. Went there like a fool.

She sits in front of the mirror.

FERGUS: Do you miss him?

DIL: What do you think?

FERGUS: I think you do.

DIL: (*dreamily*) You say that like a gentleman.

FERGUS: Do I?

DIL: Like you're concerned.

FERGUS gets up and stands behind her, gently pushes the hair from her face.

DIL: But you can't stay, you know that?

FERGUS: Didn't think I could.

DIL: A real gentleman ...

She embraces him.

FERGUS: Shouldn't you be in mourning?

DIL: I am.

She sits back down in front of the mirror. FERGUS leaves. She reapplies her lipstick.

The Crying Game (4)
(Miramax, 1992)

Screenplay by Neil Jordan
Directed by Neil Jordan
Characters: FERGUS (Stephen Rea)
            DIL (Jaye Davidson)

NOTES: FERGUS finds out the second time he goes home with DIL that she's a man. He reacts violently, but is immediately apologetic. DIL is hurt, and FERGUS tries to make it up to her. They share an attraction and closeness even though they're not sleeping together. Meanwhile, the two surviving members of FERGUS' gang have tracked him down in London. They have a job for him, an assassination, and they force him to cooperate by threatening to harm DIL. FERGUS knows they're serious; he agrees to the plan and, to keep DIL safe, cuts her hair and dresses her as a man, then hides her in a hotel for the night. The next day, the day he's supposed to do the job, he leaves DIL in the hotel with instructions not to leave. He never shows up at the job. He knows the IRA will be after him and he goes back to the hotel to find DIL has gone. He goes to her flat and finds her walking towards her building, drunk.

EXTERIOR. DIL'S FLAT—NIGHT

FERGUS looks up at her building, but the lights are off in her flat. The sound of feet behind him. He turns and sees DIL walking toward him, a bottle in her hand. He runs toward her.

FERGUS: Dil! Dil! What the fuck are you doing here?

DIL: I'm going home!

FERGUS: Told you to stay in the hotel!

DIL: Thought you was fooling me. Thought you was leaving me.

They are tussling in the darkness of the park. She is very drunk.

FERGUS: I had to go to work!

DIL: Stayed all day in that room thinking every noise was you. There's something you're not telling me, Jimmy.

He takes her arm.

FERGUS: Come on . . .

DIL: No! I'm going home . . .

FERGUS and DIL, on the stairs up to DIL's flat.

DIL: So tell me.

FERGUS: I was trying to get out of something.

DIL: No! Tell me everything, Jimmy.

FERGUS looks at her.

FERGUS: You got to forget you ever saw me, Dil.

DIL: You mean that?

FERGUS: Yes.

And she suddenly faints into his arms. As if on cue.

FERGUS: Stop it, would you?

There is no response. He shakes her.

FERGUS: Give it over, Dil, for fuck's sake—

Still no response. He grows alarmed. He slaps her cheek. She opens her eyes slowly.

DIL: Sorry. I get nervous. I got this blood condition. Just help me inside, Jimmy, then I'll be all right.

INTERIOR. DIL'S FLAT—NIGHT

He walks in holding her. Leans her against the wall, then

goes to the window to check the street outside. She takes a large slug from a bottle of whiskey.

FERGUS: You heard what I said, Dil?

DIL: My pills . . .

She points weakly to a cabinet through the open door of the bathroom.

FERGUS: What pills?

DIL: Prescription. For my condition.

FERGUS: What condition?

DIL: My condition. Ennui.

He goes and gets the pills. She takes a handful of pills. She drinks from the whiskey bottle.

FERGUS: Are you supposed to take that many?

DIL: Only in times of extreme stress.

She walks around the room, drinking, then sits down.

DIL: See, they all say good-bye sometime. 'Cept for him.

She looks at the picture of Jody. Then she looks at FER-GUS.

FERGUS: Are you all right, Dil?

DIL: I will be.

She stares straight ahead, the bottle clutched in her hands between her knees.

DIL: Go on, then.

FERGUS walks slowly toward the door.

FERGUS: Good-bye, Dil.

DIL: Jimmy?

FERGUS: What?

DIL: Don't go like that.

She looks at him, standing up. Something incredibly attractive about her.

DIL: Can't help what I am.

He walks slowly toward her. He kisses her, on the lips. We see the photograph with the soldier's smiling face. FERGUS looks from it to her. She seems to be in a sweet narcotic haze. She reaches out her hand and strokes his.

DIL: Knew you had a heart . . .

FERGUS sits down on the bed. DIL is lying back on it.

FERGUS: Dil. Can I tell you something? I knew your man.

DIL: You knew which man?

FERGUS: Your soldier.

DIL: You knew my Jody?

She still strokes his hand. Her voice is dreamily slurred, her eyes far away.

FERGUS: Lifted him from a carnival in Belfast. Held him hostage for three days.

DIL: You knew my Jody?

FERGUS: Are you listening?

DIL smiles woozily.

DIL: Yes.

FERGUS: I got the order to shoot him. Before I could do it he ran. Ran into a tank and died.

DIL: Died . . .

FERGUS: Did you hear me?

DIL: You killed my Jody?

FERGUS: In a manner of speaking.

DIL: It was you . . .

She is not rational. She is smiling, far away somewhere.

FERGUS: You should scream. You should beat my head off.

She woozily tries to hit him round the face.

DIL: You killed my Jody.

FERGUS: No.

DIL: You didn't.

FERGUS: I suppose I tried.

DIL: You tried.

FERGUS: Don't you want to kill me?

DIL raises an unsteady hand and points it at him.

DIL: Bang . . .

He strokes her cheek. She says very slowly and sleepily:

DIL: Don't leave me tonight. Might kill me, too.

FERGUS: Okay.

Her eyes close. She falls into a deep sleep. FERGUS looks down at her, almost fondly.

Do The Right Thing
(Universal, 1989)

Screenplay by Spike Lee
Directed by Spike Lee
Characters: TINA (Rosie Perez)
MOOKIE (Spike Lee)

NOTES: MOOKIE and TINA have a relationship that is un-defined; they have a son together, but they don't live together. TINA lives with her mother and MOOKIE lives with his sister, but they both live in the same area of Brooklyn. TINA has a hard time getting MOOKIE to spend time with her, so she orders a pizza from Sal's, where MOOKIE works, knowing that he will deliver it. They are in the grip of a heat wave, the hottest time of the summer.

83. INTERIOR. HALLWAY—NIGHT

MOOKIE rings the bell and a fine Puerto Rican sister answers the door.

MOOKIE: Delivery from Sal's Famous Pizzeria.

TINA: What took you so long? Is it hot?

MOOKIE: Lady, I've never delivered a cold pizza in my life.

TINA lets him in.

84. INTERIOR. TINA'S APARTMENT—NIGHT

TINA watches MOOKIE watch her. When she's through

watching, she takes the pizza from his hands and puts it on the floor. MOOKIE grabs her and starts to kiss. TINA is MOOKIE's woman, the one he's been on the phone with earlier. We've heard the voice and now see the person.

MOOKIE: You know you think you're slick, Tina.

TINA: I know. How else was I going to get you up here? I haven't seen you for a week.

MOOKIE: I'm working. I'm making money, getting paid.

TINA: Where's the ice cream? The Haagen-Dazs butter pecan?

MOOKIE: Aw, shit. I forgot.

TINA: Yeah. You know, your memory is really getting ridiculous.

MOOKIE: I just forgot.

TINA: And I really wanted some ice cream too.

MOOKIE: I can run out and get it.

TINA: No! No! You won't come back either.

MOOKIE: I can't be staying long anyway.

TINA: How long then?

MOOKIE: Long enough for us to do the nasty.

TINA: That's out. No! It's too hot! You think I'm gonna let you get some, put on your clothes, then run outta here and never see you again in who knows when?

MOOKIE: A quickie is good every once in a blue moon.

TINA: You a blue-moon fool.

MOOKIE: Then we'll do something else.

TINA: What else?

MOOKIE: Trust me.

TINA: Trust you? Because of trusting you we have a son. Remember your son?

MOOKIE: Trust me.

MOOKIE pushes TINA back into her bedroom.

85. INTERIOR. TINA'S BEDROOM—NIGHT

MOOKIE sits TINA down on her futon bed, turns off the lights, and turns on WE LOVE RADIO as Mister Senor Love Daddy serenades them with slow jams.

MOOKIE: I'm gonna take off ya clothes.

TINA: Mookie, I told you already it's too fucking hot to make love.

MOOKIE: Why you gotta curse?

TINA: I'm sorry, but no rawness is jumping off tonight.

MOOKIE: No rawness.

He laughs his sinister laugh. Mookie unsnaps her bra, then pulls her panties off. TINA is naked as a jaybird.

MOOKIE: Tina, you're sweating.

TINA: Of course I'm sweating. I'm burning up. It's hot, moron, only a hundred degrees in here.

MOOKIE: Lie down, please. (*he gets up*)

86. INTERIOR. TINA'S KITCHEN

MOOKIE walks into the kitchen and sees Carmen, TINA's mother, fixing some food on the stove.

MOOKIE: Hello, Mrs. Rampolla.

Carmen stares at him. It's a look that would definitely stop traffic. She mutters some Spanish and goes into her bedroom, slamming the door behind her. MOOKIE opens the refrigerator and takes out all the trays of ice.

87. INTERIOR. TINA'S BEDROOM—NIGHT

MOOKIE sits down on the bed with a bowl filled with ice cubes. MOOKIE rubs an ice cube on her forehead.

TINA: It's cold.

MOOKIE: It's 'pose to be cold.

TINA: Later for you.

MOOKIE: *Meda. Meda.*

TINA: What?

MOOKIE: Tina, you don't have a forehead, you got a eight-head.

MOOKIE rubs an ice cube on her neck. MOOKIE rubs an ice cube on her full, moist lips, then puts it in her mouth. He rubs an ice cube up and down her thighs.

MOOKIE: Thank God for thighs.

He rubs an ice cube on her round, firm buttocks.

MOOKIE: Thank God for buttocks.

He runs an ice cube on her breast.

MOOKIE: Thank God for the right nipple . . . Thank God for the left nipple . . .

Both TINA and MOOKIE are dying. MOOKIE now has an ice cube on the left and right nipples and we see before our very own eyes both get swollen, red, and erect.

TINA: Feels good.

MOOKIE: Yes, yes, Lord. Isn't this better than Häagen-Dazs butter pecan ice cream? (*he kisses her*) I'll be back tonight.

Do The Right Thing (2)
(Universal, 1989)

Screenplay by Spike Lee
Directed by Spike Lee
Characters: SAL (Danny Aiello)
MOOKIE (Spike Lee)

NOTES: This scene takes place at the end of the film. SAL's Pizzeria in Brooklyn has been smashed and burned in the riot of the night before, a riot exacerbated by racial tensions, misunderstandings, and the relentless heat of the New York summer. MOOKIE, SAL's longtime employee, did not start the riot, but did "throw the first stone" by picking up a garbage can and putting it through SAL's window; then the crowd descended. Despite his part in the destruction of the store, MOOKIE shows up the following morning for his weekly pay.

110. EXTERIOR. SAL'S FAMOUS PIZZERIA—DAY
MOOKIE walks up to Sal's Famous Pizzeria as it still smoulders in the morning light. SAL emerges from the wreckage; he looks like he might have slept there.

SAL: Whatdafuck do you want?

MOOKIE: I wants my money. I wants to get paid.

SAL looks at MOOKIE in disbelief.

SAL: Mookie, I always liked you. Not the smartest kid, but you're honest. Don't make me dislike you.

MOOKIE: Sal, I want my money.

SAL: Don't even ask about your money. Your money wouldn't even pay for that window you smashed.

MOOKIE: Motherfuck a window, Radio Raheem is dead.

SAL: You're right, a kid is dead, but Mook, this isn't the time.

MOOKIE: Fuck dat. The time is fuckin' now. Y'know I'm sorry 'bout Sal's Famous Pizzeria, but I gotta live, too. I gotta get paid.

SAL: We both do.

MOOKIE: We all know you're gonna get over with the insurance money *anyway!* Ya know the deal.

SAL: Do we now?

MOOKIE: Quit bullshitting.

SAL: You don't know shit about shit.

MOOKIE: I know I wants to get my money.

SAL has had it.

SAL: How much? How much do I owe you?

MOOKIE: My salary. Two-fifty.

SAL pulls out a wad and quickly peels off hundred dollar bills.

SAL: One, two, three, four, five.

SAL throws the "C" notes at MOOKIE; they hit him in the chest and fall to the sidewalk.

SAL: Are you happy now? That's five fucking hundred dollars. You just got paid. Mookie, you are a rich man, now ya life is set, you'll never have another worry, a care in the world. Mookie, ya wealthy, a fuckin' Rockefeller.

MOOKIE is stunned by SAL's outburst. He picks up the bills.

SAL: Ya just got paid, so leave me the fuck alone.

MOOKIE: You only pay me two-fifty a week. (he throws two "C" notes back at him) I owe you fifty bucks.

SAL: Keep it.

MOOKIE: You keep it.

SAL: Christmas came early.

Both look at the two hundred-dollar bills on the sidewalk and refuse to pick them up. It's a stalemate.

MOOKIE: This is the hottest Christmas I've known.

MOOKIE counts his money.

SAL: It's supposed to be even hotter today.

MOOKIE: You gonna open up another Sal's Famous Pizzeria?

SAL: No. What are you gonna do?

MOOKIE: Make dat money. Get paid.

SAL: Yeah! . . . I'm goin' to the beach for the first day in fifteen years. Gonna take the day off and go to the beach.

MOOKIE: I can dig it. It's gonna be HOT as a motherfucker.

SAL: Mookie?

MOOKIE: Gotta go.

SAL: C'mere, Doctor.

MOOKIE turns around and goes back.

SAL: Doctor, this is Sal talkin'.

MOOKIE: OK. OK.

SAL: Doctor, always try to do the right thing.

MOOKIE: That's it?

SAL: That's it.

MOOKIE thinks about it, looks at the two "C" notes still smiling up at him. He quickly scoops them up.

MOOKIE: I got it.

Drugstore Cowboy
(Avenue Pictures, 1989)

*Screenplay by Gus Van Sant and Dan Yost, story by
James Fogle
Directed by Gus Van Sant
Characters: DIANNE (Kelly Lynch)
　　　　　　BOB (Matt Dillon)*

NOTES: The year is 1971, and BOB, DIANNE, and their
friends, Rick and Nadine, wander around Washington and
Oregon, staying in any motel or pad, stealing prescription drugs
from drugstores, and using or selling them. Things are status
quo in their non-lives until Nadine overdoses in a motel room
and they are almost caught by the police. BOB decides to return
to Seattle and get on rehab; he is successfully doing this when
DIANNE pays an unexpected visit.

199. INTERIOR. BOB'S ROOM—NIGHT

*A knock comes on the door. BOB is lying in bed playing
solitaire. He gets up and answers the knock. A sad old country & western tune is playing on the little radio by BOB's
bed.*

BOB: Who's there?

DIANNE'S VOICE:　It's me, Dianne.

*BOB throws open the door and smiles. DIANNE steps in
hesitantly and looks around at the room's dismal appear-
ance. She looks shocked.*

DIANNE: Jesus, what kind of dump is this? And where's the female? You might as well trot her out.

BOB: You don't ever change, do you, Dianne?

DIANNE: You're goddam right I don't. Why should I?

BOB: I was just remarking on how good you look. I didn't mean nothing by it.

DIANNE: I'll bet. You're slipperier than an eel, Bob, no one ever catches you off balance because you stay off balance constantly, just to stay on your feet.

BOB: Is that all you got to say? Is that why you come up here, or did you just want to see me down and out?

DIANNE: I just wanted to see you period. How's that methadone thing?

BOB: Oh, so-so. I got a job, bet you never expected to see that.

DIANNE: No shit, where're you working?

BOB: Oh, down at some machine shop on Western.

DIANNE: What do you do there?

BOB: Drill holes.

DIANNE: Drill holes?

BOB: Yeah, you know, like the holes that bolts fit into and such.

DIANNE: Oh yeah? How do you like it?

BOB: Well, to tell you the truth, it's kind of a drag.

DIANNE: Then you're really serious. You're going to go on with this thing.

BOB: Yeah, I am, Dianne. Sit down here, why don't you take off your coat and stay awhile.

DIANNE: Oh, I can't Bob, I got people waiting for me down in the car. I just came up to see how you was doing. Here . . .

DIANNE struggles with something in her purse, and comes up with a small package.

DIANNE: This is from Rick and the rest of us. We kind of thought you might need a taste once in awhile.

BOB smiles and takes the package.

BOB: Thanks, Dianne. I sure do appreciate you all thinking of me.

DIANNE: Bob?

BOB: Yeah?

DIANNE: What happened? What made you turn around that day? Was it me, did I do something wrong? Or was it just that thing with Nadine?

BOB: No, baby, it wasn't you. It was Nadine's death and the hex that she threw on us with the hat. And then I panicked when I looked out into that parking lot and seen all those cop cars. I just knew I was dead. Everything up to then had gone wrong and so I started coping deuces. I prayed like never before. I said, "God, Devil, Sun, whoever you are up there that controls this whirly-girly mad tumbling world, please have pity on me. Please let me get this poor girl's body out of this motel room and into the ground so I don't have to spend the rest of my life in prison. And God, Sun, Satan, if you'll do that for me, I'll show my appreciation by going back to the coast, and getting on a methadone program, getting a job and living the good life." Well, I got out, and I promised, so here I am.

DIANNE: Are you going to stick to it forever?

BOB: Yeah. And, you know, for all the boredom the good life brings, it's not so bad. Even this crummy little room isn't so bad. I'm a regular guy. I got my regular job. And my regular room. Now I got my woman . . .

DIANNE sits down on the bed and sighs.

DIANNE: You're crazy, Bob, you really are crazy. But I see what you mean. Jesus, Bob, if I had known what it was all about, I'd have come along with you. I thought you were mad at me for something.

BOB: Why don't you tell your friends you're going to stay the night, and then come back up here and bed down with me for a while?

DIANNE: I'd like to Bob, (*she lowers her eyes*) but I got another old man now. I work for Rick now, ain't that a gas? There we were teaching the brat to steal, and now I'm on his crew. Things sure can get screwed around, can't they?

BOB nods yes.

DIANNE: I'd like to stay the night with you, really I would. Only I'm Rick's old lady now. And you know me, Bob, I might have been a lot of things, but I never was a tramp.

BOB manages a smile. A long pause.

BOB: I'll see you, Dianne. (*He leads DIANNE out the door*) You stop back by sometime. It sure was good to see you. And you're really looking good. I sure wish I could go with you and win you back.

Dying Young
(20th Century Fox, 1991)

Screenplay by Richard Friedenberg
Directed by Joel Schulmacher
Characters: HILARY (Julia Roberts)
VICTOR (Campbell Scott)

NOTES: HILARY has just been through a "break-up": she has walked in on her boyfriend in bed with another woman. She left, and now she's staying with her mother as she looks for a job. She's not well-educated or particularly skilled in anything. She answers an ad for a live-in nurse. After a long wait in the parlor of an imposing San Francisco mansion, she is turned away from the house, without an interview, by VICTOR's father. VICTOR, however, catches sight of her and has his butler call her back and show her to his private entrance. VICTOR is about the same age as HILARY; he has leukemia and needs constant care. (This version combines the most recent revision with the video transcript. I've kept in as much of the writer's original stage directions and descriptions as possible.)

17. EXTERIOR. THE BASEMENT DOOR

HILARY steps through the slightly open door. A man's voice can be heard, quiet, cultured.

VICTOR: (*voice over*) Yes. Please come in.

She steps into an apartment very different from the main house—high tech, modern, art on the walls. She stands a

114

*beat as her eyes adjust to the dimness and she is striking,
her hair loose now, her color high with exertion and irri-
tation. On the couch VICTOR GEDDES smiles, taken by
her. He is clearly the young man behind the door, and he
is clearly ill, pale and fragile, his head covered by the beret.
He speaks again in the same quiet tone.*

VICTOR: I'm Victor Geddes.

*And he presses a button next to him. Behind her, the door
clicks shut. She jumps slightly. VICTOR grins.*

VICTOR: Trapped.

HILARY: (*had enough*) Hey, what's going on here?

VICTOR: No, no, I'm sorry. A joke. Um—an icebreaker.

HILARY: Oh . . . (*toughening up, wry*) Well, I can see why
the job's still open.

*And VICTOR laughs, surprised by her quickness. He mo-
tions to a wing chair, checking her application form.*

VICTOR: Ms . . . O'Neil.

HILARY: (*shrugs*) Hilary. Yeah.

*She sits instinctively using her best asset, her looks—she
crosses her shapely legs and meets his intense gaze.*

VICTOR: (*pleased*) Hilary. Good. (*pause*) This is going very
well. (*pause*) How old are you?

HILARY: Twenty-three.

VICTOR: I'm twenty-eight. You're not a nurse.

HILARY: No, I am not a nurse . . .

VICTOR: (*reading off form*) But you were a *candystriper.*

HILARY: Well, uh, yeah, in school, but—I dropped out.
(*shrugs*) Well, I was in, uh—Future Nurses of America.
(*embarrassed, proud*) I was the Vice-President.

He's leaning forward, urging her on with his expression.

VICTOR: (*honestly pleased*) Ah—hah . . .

HILARY: Alert the media.

VICTOR: No, that's . . . what did you do?

HILARY: We went to the hospital after school . . .

VICTOR: Mercy?

HILARY: Ah . . . Our Lady.

VICTOR: Oakland.

HILARY: (*bristling*) It's where I'm from.

VICTOR: (*smooth as silk*) I interrupted.

HILARY: (*off balance*) All right . . . I dropped out . . .

VICTOR: You worked there?

HILARY: Right, well, the sisters . . . you didn't go to Catholic school?

VICTOR: (*small laugh*) No.

HILARY: Well, the sisters at the hospital talked to the sisters at school, and if we did something, like, um, wear our skirt too short, or committed some mortal sin, such as . . . (*shrugs*) French kissing . . .

VICTOR: Ah!

HILARY: Then we got all the really terrific duties at the Hospital.

VICTOR: Bedpans.

HILARY: Bedpans, changing sheets, ah, cleaning up . . . all kinds of things . . . um . . . (*memories not pleasant*) . . . But sometimes they'd let us change the babies, and . . . point them out to the parents, you know, through the glass . . . hold them up.

She demonstrates, lapsing into a smile, the toughness leaving her expression, leaving a young, vulnerable girl lit by the filtered sun, her hair a red-gold halo. And VICTOR is smitten.

HILARY: That's about it.

Pause. VICTOR nods absently. There is a lull. HILARY can't help glancing at the antique clock on the wall, ticking intrusively. Then VICTOR sighs, plunging unhappily.

VICTOR: I have . . . Leukemia. (*doesn't miss her look*) I've had it for, ah, ten years. I'm twenty-eight. I said that. So . . . since high school. (*quickly*) Not—the whole time. I've had remissions, I've led . . . a pretty normal life. Been to Europe, and I finished college. Ran the dash, the hundred . . . (*as if forced*) You're not the first woman in my house . . . I, ah . . . Do you know anything about Chemotherapy?

HILARY: (*finding her voice*) Well, I know it's . . . a treatment for . . .

She can't say it.

VICTOR: They give me a course of it every time I fail their blood test. It . . . it's pretty . . .

He stops, gauging her, then shrugs, passing it off.

VICTOR: Well, I need help during it . . . want the job?

HILARY: You make it sound so attractive. Your father said—

VICTOR: (*stiffening*) Forget my father.

HILARY: Well, he said . . . You needed a nurse.

VICTOR: *Forget* what he said.

HILARY: Well, if he's the one hiring . . .

VICTOR: (*suddenly sharp*) He's *not* hiring. He's flying to Japan, in a luxurious airplane. *I* am hiring. Uh . . . if you choose to take this job, you will be working for me. *Not for* my father.

It is precisely the same tone as the argument during her meeting with Richard. HILARY smiles, with an edge.

HILARY: So why would you pick me?

VICTOR: (*caught*) Oh . . .

HILARY: I got it . . . I had the shortest skirt, huh?

VICTOR struggles a moment, but covers himself, smiling slightly, like a little boy, his sophisticated coolness gone, revealing a lonely, hopeful young man.

VICTOR: Uh, actually, no, there was one with a shorter skirt. But he was never a candy striper. (*laughs*) Anyway

... it's room and board, and ... (*sizes her up, then casual*)
Four hundred dollars a week.

He is rewarded by a widening of her eyes, but her voice remains cool.

HILARY: Cash?

VICTOR: Cash. Follow me.

Grinning slowly, swings his feet to the ground, more slowly, as if every move hurts, rises to his feet. She rises with him, alarmed, unsure if she should help. Motioning, he starts down the hallway, and she follows at a cautious distance.

A Fish Called Wanda
(MGM, 1988)

Screenplay by John Cleese and Charles Crichton
Directed by Charles Crichton
Characters: WANDA (Jamie Lee Curtis)
ARCHIE (John Cleese)

NOTES: WANDA and her boyfriend, George, along with her "brother" (lover) Otto, and Ken, have robbed a London bank. The loot was stashed in a safe in a rented garage. WANDA and Otto then promptly turned George in to the police and went to grab the money and jewels, but the loot was gone. Only George knows where the money and jewels are, and in her determination to find out, WANDA poses as an American law student and shows up at the offices of George's attorney, ARCHIE. ARCHIE is typically British: conservative, repressed, with a not very fulfilling marriage. WANDA is a knockout and arrives in a very tight mini dress.

36. INTERIOR. ARCHIE'S CHAMBERS—DAY
ARCHIE sits at his desk, working on a brief. WANDA comes into view outside. He gets up and pulls out a legal tome. As he does so he becomes aware of being watched. He looks out of the window. WANDA waves. ARCHIE stares, then returns the wave. WANDA mouths, "Can I see you." ARCHIE waves her round to the main door. He hurries across the room, opens the door on the corridor and calls to his clerk.

ARCHIE: Davidson. (*Davidson appears from his office*)
There's an American legal student here, wants to see me
for a moment. What time's Sir John due?

DAVIDSON: Half past twelve, sir.

ARCHIE: Right.

*DAVIDSON goes, and ARCHIE hurries back to his room.
He checks himself in the mirror and goes and sits at his
desk. WANDA hands her umbrella to DAVIDSON and
knocks at the door.*

ARCHIE: (*cont'd*) Come in.

She enters.

WANDA: Hi.

ARCHIE: How very nice to see you.

WANDA: Am I interrupting?

ARCHIE: Absolutely not.

WANDA: Really?

ARCHIE: No, no, really. Delighted to see you.

*He offers his hand. WANDA takes it, then steps forward
and kisses him on the cheek, which startles him.*

WANDA: So . . . this is the place, huh? Very nice. I was over
at the courts this morning. Boy, it's fascinating. So much
to know.

ARCHIE: Really, you liked it?

She sees his wig lying beside the bookcase. She puts it on.

WANDA: Everybody wears these. Do you wear one?

ARCHIE: Ridiculous. (*they laugh*) Well . . . um . . . I only
have a few minutes before . . .

WANDA: Oh, I'm sorry.

ARCHIE: But . . . until then, I'm all yours, as they say.

*WANDA puts on her spectacles and sits. ARCHIE goes
round the desk to sit.*

WANDA: I just have a couple of questions. Um . . . I'm having a little problem understanding preliminary criminal procedures.

ARCHIE: Good!

WANDA: What exactly is the committal?

ARCHIE: Ah, interesting. Well, er, basically it's a preliminary investigation where the prosecution presents prima facie evidence that the accused has a case to answer for trial.

As he speaks, WANDA runs an eye over the briefs on his desk for anything on George.

WANDA: Well, that's what it says in the books. Let's just take, for example . . . my friend George Thomason.

ARCHIE: Thomason?

WANDA: Yes.

ARCHIE: George Thomason?

WANDA: Yes . . . do you know him?

ARCHIE: I'm defending him!

ARCHIE is rather pleased.

WANDA: . . . What are you talking about?

ARCHIE: I'm his barrister—his lawyer.

WANDA: That's so great! That's so weird, though. Isn't that weird? Oh, I'm so happy it's you that's defending him.

ARCHIE: (*taking the compliment a little eagerly*) Thank you.

WANDA: He's sure to get off now. Wow! I can watch you work now.

ARCHIE: (*still grinning*) Please . . .

WANDA: Amazing . . . Well, anyway . . . at the committal George will plead . . . ?

ARCHIE: (*obviously*) Not guilty.

WANDA: Really?

ARCHIE: Oh yes, he . . . the evidence against him is largely circumstantial.

WANDA: But there was an identification, wasn't there?

ARCHIE: True, but a very . . . elderly lady. I think they've got the wrong man.

WANDA: . . . You don't think he did it?

ARCHIE: . . . No.

WANDA: Well, let's just say, for argument's sake, that you did think he did it.

ARCHIE is a little confused.

ARCHIE: If further evidence against him came to light, for example . . .

WANDA: Right. You would then advise him to plead guilty and turn turn over the jewels to get his sentence cut. And he would turn them over to who . . . to you?

ARCHIE: . . . Theoretically. Yes, well . . . oh I'm so sorry, I've forgotten your name . . .

WANDA: Wanda.

ARCHIE: Wanda. What a fool, what a fool. Well, Wanda, there are really *three* . . . (*A strange look comes over his face. It begins to dawn on him . . .*) Not Wanda Gershwitz?

WANDA: Yes.

ARCHIE: (*quietly*) Oh my God.

WANDA: What?

ARCHIE: (*almost speechless*) You're his alibi! I can't talk to you. My dear young lady, you are a defense witness. (*he rises*) I'm sorry, I must ask you to leave immediately. I'm so sorry.

WANDA: What did I say?

ARCHIE: Well, it's not ethical for me to talk to a witness.

WANDA: Everybody does it in America.

ARCHIE: Well, not in England. It's strictly forbidden. Please, I must insist, otherwise I may have to give up the case. I'm sorry. Please.

WANDA is looking at ARCHIE oddly. She gets up and goes across to him.

WANDA: Oh, Archie . . . I didn't come here today to talk about boring criminal procedures.

ARCHIE stares.

WANDA: (*cont'd*) Come on, you know . . . you knew the minute I walked in here. I want you.

ARCHIE experiences truly profound puzzlement.

ARCHIE: What?

The intercom buzzes. ARCHIE answers it automatically.

ARCHIE: (*cont'd*) Hallo?

DAVIDSON: (*OOV*) Sir John is here.

ARCHIE: Right. Show him in please.

WANDA: (spelling it out) I want you to make love to me.

DAVIDSON: (*OOV*) Pardon?

ARCHIE: Nothing. Nothing.

WANDA: Will you take me to bed, Archie?

ARCHIE: . . . No. Sorry.

The door opens revealing Davidson and Sir John. WANDA kisses ARCHIE full on the mouth.

WANDA: Bye, Uncle.

She walks out past Sir John. ARCHIE sees Sir John, who looks at him strangely.

ARCHIE: . . . Hi!

Frances
(Universal, 1982)

Screenplay by Eric Bergren, Christopher DeVore,
Nicholas Kazan
Directed by Graeme Clifford
Characters: FRANCES (Jessica Lange)
          CLURMAN (Jordan Charney)

NOTES: FRANCES FARMER is a Hollywood starlet in the early 1940's. When she was a teenager, she won a trip to Moscow to study theatre, and she has an appreciation for the new Stanislavsky approach. But despite her budding success, her life in Hollywood drives her to the brink of insanity. Her selfish, controlling mother, the cruelty of the studio system, and her own alcohol abuse don't help. She leaves the exploitation of Hollywood to join the Group Theatre in New York, and soon becomes the mistress of Clifford Odets, the playwright whose new show, "Golden Boy," she is starring in. The show is about to move to London. She comes home to Clifford's apartment to find the show's producer, Harold Clurman, there.

68A. INTERIOR. ODETS' APARTMENT—DAY
FRANCES comes in the front door with a bag of groceries, removes her key. Walks into the dining room and stops short. CLURMAN is sitting at the table reading a magazine.
FRANCES: Hello, Harold.
CLURMAN: Frances.

FRANCES: (*going to kitchen*) Where's Clifford?

CLURMAN: He's not here.

FRANCES: So, what's up?

She takes off her coat. CLURMAN rises.

CLURMAN: (*raises his glass*) Bourbon?

FRANCES: Okay.

He crosses into the living room and pours her one.

CLURMAN: It's getting cold out.

FRANCES: Yep. (*She unwraps flowers and puts them in a vase*) Pretty, aren't they?

CLURMAN: Lovely. Just lovely.

FRANCES: Thank you.

CLURMAN: Uhm-huhm. (*He hands her her drink and they toast. FRANCES sits down and takes a cigarette from the box on the table.*) I hear you're meeting with the studio lawyers to try and get out of your contract.

FRANCES: (*lights her cigarette*) Well, I just don't want them breathing down my neck while we're in London.

CLURMAN: (*sits down*) Yeah, well, you see, that's the point. You won't be going to London.

FRANCES looks like she's been punched in the stomach.

FRANCES: Don't you think I'm good enough, Harold?

CLURMAN: Well, of course you are. It's not that, it's just— (*sighs*) It's money. We needed backing and, ah ... well, we found it.

FRANCES: Who?

CLURMAN: An actress.

FRANCES: A rich actress?

CLURMAN: (*sighs*) Yes. That's the deal. She plays Lorna Moon.

FRANCES: (*growing angry*) I thought we were supposed to be different, Harold. Clifford says this company is different. A *group* working together!

CLURMAN: I know. I know.

FRANCES: Isn't that what this play is about? What money and greed do to people?

CLURMAN: Right now, we have to be practical.

FRANCES: Well then I'll give you the money, Harold. I'll back the production.

CLURMAN: It's too late, Frances. Well, besides, you don't have that kind of money anymore.

FRANCES: What did Clifford say about this? He doesn't even know, does he? Where is he? I'm going to find him.

CLURMAN: Frances. He knows. He approved it.

CLURMAN takes an envelope out of his jacket pocket and places it on the coffee table. FRANCES looks at it, then at him.

CLURMAN: Now, look. I, I'm sorry. (*he places his hands on FRANCES' shoulders*) Frances, you have done a great service for the group. Your name has helped to draw people. You've helped us grow, you've grown yourself.

FRANCES: Swell. But, Harold, this theatre is everything to me. Don't you understand? What am I going to do now?

CLURMAN: (*sighs*) Well. Hollywood wants you back. Right?

Her eyes fill with rage. She hurls her drink in his face.

FRANCES: You . . . prick!

She turns and leaves the room. He stands and, with as much dignity as he can muster, leaves.

Frances (2)
(Universal, 1982)

Screenplay by Eric Bergren, Christopher DeVore,
Nicholas Kazan
Directed by Graeme Clifford
Characters: FRANCES (Jessica Lange)
SYMINGTON (Lane Smith)

NOTES: FRANCES' rebellious nature, controlling mother, and
the pressures and betrayals of Hollywood have brought her to a
breakdown. Her mother has committed her. She is not insane by
current standards, and her mother's motives are self-serving; she
wants FRANCES to be accepted back in Hollywood. FRANCES
knows she is trapped. Meadow Wood is the psychiatric hospital
her mother has brought her to. DR. SYMINGTON has just
asked FRANCES' mother to leave them alone.

109. INTERIOR. MEADOW WOOD. OFFICE—DAY

Dr. SYMINGTON closes the door. He goes back to his desk,
noticing FRANCES flicking ashes on the rug. As he sits, he
moves an ashtray forward for her to use.

SYMINGTON: I find these initial meetings to be much easier without the concerned relatives in attendance.

FRANCES: What am I supposed to say, "thank you"?

SYMINGTON: Oh, thanks are hardly necessary.

FRANCES: Aw, shucks, ma'am. T'weren't nothin'.

SYMINGTON: I'm glad to see you haven't lost your sense of humor.

FRANCES: It ain't for lack of trying.

SYMINGTON: So it seems. May we be serious for a moment?

FRANCES: Why, Doctor! We've only just met!

SYMINGTON: (*laughs*) Well, I feel like I've known you for a long time. You see, I've followed your career. You, um, you're a fascinating case. I'm looking forward to solving your predicament.

FRANCES' face begins to set in hard planes.

FRANCES: (*chuckles*) Are you really?

SYMINGTON: Among persons such as yourself, creative people under great stress, erratic behavior is not at all uncommon and certainly nothing to be ashamed of. It's just that the anxieties which—

FRANCES rises and leans over his desk.

FRANCES: (*interrupting*) Doctor, do you expect me, for one moment, to believe you have greater insight into my personality than I do?

SYMINGTON: Would you sit back down?

FRANCES: You may discuss my predicament, Doctor. You may discuss it with anyone you like, but not with me. I'm not interested. I can solve my problems without recourse to a veterinarian.

SYMINGTON: I see.

FRANCES: Besides, I don't want to be what you want to make me.

SYMINGTON: And what's that?

FRANCES: Dull. Average. Normal.

SYMINGTON: All right. Will you please take your seat now? (*smiles*) Symington says.

FRANCES: (*chuckles*) Did you actually say that?

SYMINGTON: It's just a little joke, Miss Farmer.

FRANCES: (*slaps her hand on top of the desk, screaming*) This whole fuckin' thing is a joke!

SYMINGTON: Stay calm, please.

FRANCES: No, you stay calm, Doctor. But you're finding that difficult, aren't you? I'm not doing what's expected of me. I'm not sitting here in awe while you carefully dissect my personality. Now you listen to me. All I want is a little rest. A little peace and quiet. And I don't have to talk to you or anybody else about my goddamn "anxieties." You got that?

SYMINGTON: I'll have someone show you to your room.

FRANCES: That's good. That's very good, very professional and controlled. But those tiny little beads of sweat on your upper lip give you away.

SYMINGTON stares at her. He rests his chin on his hand, places his finger on his lip, then looks at the sweat on his fingertip. He looks up at FRANCES.

SYMINGTON: You really should get some rest now. The nurse will meet you outside. Good day.

FRANCES crushes out her cigarette in his ashtray. The butt falls out of the ashtray and sits on top of his desk, burning.

SYMINGTON: (straightening some folders) Is there something else?

FRANCES: Well, you didn't say "Symington says."

SYMINGTON: (*smiles patronizingly*) Symington says.

FRANCES smiles, turns and leaves. SYMINGTON crushes out the cigarette butt into the ashtray.

Georgia
(Miramax, 1995)

Screenplay by Barbara Turner
Directed by Ulu Grosbard
Characters: GEORGIA (Mare Winningham)
SADIE (Jennifer Jason Leigh)

NOTES: GEORGIA and SADIE are sisters. They couldn't be
more different. GEORGIA is older; she is responsible, grounded,
and a talented, successful folk singer. SADIE, on the other hand,
is a loose cannon. She has incredible, undaunted passion and lust
for life, but she is also embroiled in drugs, alcohol, and the party
life. She doesn't take care of herself, and GEORGIA has fre-
quently bailed her out financially. SADIE's behavior is inappro-
priate and often deliberately antisocial. She desperately wants
her own career as a singer but she is not really talented in that
area. SADIE is staying with GEORGIA briefly as she gets her
act together, and the sisters' mutual resentment, jealousy, love
and enmeshment threaten to break through their pretenses. SA-
DIE may or may not have just "shot up" in GEORGIA's bathroom. GEORGIA comes in from the pouring rain.

INTERIOR. FARMHOUSE—DAY
*SADIE comes down the stairs unsteadily, arms loaded with
sheets ... slips a few stairs, catches herself. The camera
stays with her as she starts through the kitchen. GEORGIA's
shedding soaking clothes ... roughing a towel through
drenched hair.*

SADIE: (*on the move*) I stripped the beds.

GEORGIA: You didn't need to do that.

SADIE: Yeah, well. Sure I did.

GEORGIA: It's pouring, Sadie.

SADIE: And you hang them out. How dumb to forget. Well, no harm done. (*about the dress*) I borrowed this, okay.

GEORGIA: Whatever, it's fine. You don't need to clean my house, Sadie.

SADIE: I was cleaning motel rooms. Really. No, really. "Oh God, Sadie reduced to that." Or, is there anything Sadie can't be reduced to.

GEORGIA: You want to give me a break, Sadie.

SADIE: You want to give me one. I can feel what you're feeling.

GEORGIA: (*a long moment, finally*) No. No, you can't, Sadie. No. You can't feel what I'm feeling. You aren't me.

SADIE stands there silent.

GEORGIA: I believe in you. I've always believed in you.

SADIE: I think we should not get into this.

GEORGIA: Fine. Better for me. Oh, shit. (*another moment*) Dad's coming to stay for a week. Friday.

SADIE: I won't be here.

GEORGIA: It gets really tense, Sadie.

SADIE: I won't be here, okay. How's he doing.

GEORGIA: I think fine. I think all right. You need some money?

SADIE: Yeah. Yeah. Something to get started on. I'm good for it.

GEORGIA: I don't want you to be good for it. It pleases me to be able to give it to you. I love being able to give it to you.

SADIE: Okay. Things are going to break for me. There's not a doubt in my mind. This has all got to be about something. This whole adventure. Everything's stored for later use. There must be a pony.

Georgia (2)
(Miramax, 1995)

Screenplay by Barbara Turner
Directed by Ulu Grosbard
Characters: GEORGIA (Mare Winningham)
             SADIE (Jennifer Jason Leigh)

NOTES: SADIE has gotten out on her own, and is living in a
small apartment in town, not too far from GEORGIA. She is
singing with a small time band, playing bars and bar mitzvahs.
She is still drinking and doing drugs. A sweet young man has
moved in with her. Axel is far more naive than SADIE, but he
loves her and wants to take care of her. GEORGIA sees SADIE
using Axel, and she also sees that SADIE is still using drugs, and
knows she may have just shot up in her bathroom. The two
women are in GEORGIA's kitchen area while GEORGIA's
small daughter, MISH, sets the table nearby.

INTERIOR. KITCHEN—LATE AFTERNOON
*Mish sets the table. GEORGIA deals with dinner. Sadie sits
erect on the stool, as though monitoring, not trusting movement . . . hands folded, eyes shining. She'll occasionally
brush something imagined off the tip of her nose, scratch
slowly at her cheek.*

SADIE: I came down to help.

GEORGIA: It's under control. Just sit there.

SADIE: The table looks great, Mish. You know what's so good about us, Georgia? We're so close. Growing up, I can't remember our not doing everything together. Are you okay.

GEORGIA: I'm fine. What are you doing with Axel, Sadie.

SADIE: How do you and Dad find so much to talk about.

GEORGIA: We don't. We don't talk much.

SADIE: I'm going to marry him. (*wiggles her fingers*) His grandmother's ring. And there's only one Jake.

GEORGIA: How old is he, Sadie.

SADIE: He loves me.

GEORGIA: I'm going to stay out of this.

SADIE: So what is it that happens between you when you don't talk.

GEORGIA: Leave Dad alone, Sadie.

SADIE: I do. I do. That's what I do. Will you come to the wedding?

GEORGIA: Sure, okay.

SADIE: I'm going to do it.

GEORGIA: (*won't buy into it*) Fine.

SADIE: You know, I watch you. And I listen to you. This gift from God. And I swell up with admiration and pride and love. And I swear on Mish and Andrew, there's no envy. You know I can't. And here I am, not three feet away, and I talk to you, and I swear, Georgia, it feels like no one's home, you disappear on me.

Mish looks over at her mother.

GEORGIA: You know what I truly want for you, Sadie? I want you to be happy.

SADIE pushes off the counter, works the stool round the room on its wheels.

SADIE: You want to be trouble-free, Georgia.

GEORGIA: Okay. All right. How are you coming with the table, Mish.

MISH: Finished.

GEORGIA: Why don't you see if anyone needs anything.

Mish starts out of the kitchen.

SADIE: Things are going good for me.

GEORGIA: I'm glad. Do you know his last name?

SADIE: Axel? (*a moment*) Yeah, of course.

GEORGIA: Yeah?

SADIE: Yeah, what do you think?

GEORGIA bites the grin.

SADIE: You writing?

GEORGIA: Every day.

SADIE: Working on an album?

GEORGIA: Yes.

SADIE: I should do some backup, if you want.

GEORGIA: Good idea.

SADIE: (*simply, direct*) You haven't come to hear me, why is that.

GEORGIA: I will if you want.

SADIE swallows back the cut.

SADIE: It would be great if you did.

GEORGIA: Well, I will then.

SADIE's left with a hole in her stomach.

SADIE: Okay. Great. I'm interesting, you know.

GEORGIA: You were the one with ambition, Sadie. I never gave a damn.

SADIE: You say.

GEORGIA: You know it's the truth.

SADIE: Funny how things work out.

GEORGIA: Not what I meant. (*a little laugh*) You know, I let you talk to me this way. And I manage to make myself think it's okay. And I'm always glad you've been here. And I can't stand it when you're hurting. And I've made peace with ... that nothing's enough for you. I don't want to know what you do locked away in the bathroom for half an hour. I don't want my kids to know.

SADIE: I wouldn't do that in your house, Georgia.

GEORGIA: (*accepts the lie*) Okay.

Georgia (3)
(Miramax, 1995)

Screenplay by Barbara Turner
Directed by Ulu Grosbard
Characters: GEORGIA (Mare Winningham)
SADIE (Jennifer Jason Leigh)

NOTES: After SADIE's short-lived attempt to get her life together (*see notes for previous scene*), she once again sank deep
into her substance abuse. She lost her singing job with the band,
and Axel, tired of caretaking and getting nothing in return, left
her. Over the last several months, GEORGIA has seen SADIE
through a serious withdrawal and rehab ordeal. Now SADIE is
once again staying with GEORGIA, back at square one, dry for
now. The sisters have been through the mill together, taken and
given all they can take and give. The truth finally comes out.

EXTERIOR. PORCH—NIGHT

*It's late. The house is silent. SADIE comes out the screen
door, glass in hand. GEORGIA's in a robe, leaning against
the porch post.*

SADIE: (*a moment*) What are you doing.

GEORGIA: (*a moment*) Nothing. My favorite thing.

GEORGIA turns, smiles wonder at her.

GEORGIA: Hello Sadie.

SADIE: (*a moment, about the drink*) Water. "First the man
takes a drink. Then the drink takes the drink. Then the drink
takes the man."

136

GEORGIA turns back, looks out into the quiet.

GEORGIA: Sometimes I wish I could vanish—

SADIE: For how long.

There's no response.

GEORGIA: Mish has got the ticket. She can become weight-less. Thin air. It's something I'm apt to encourage. Are you going to need money?

SADIE: Not a lot.

GEORGIA: It's not a bottomless pit, Sadie.

SADIE: Well, Sis. I know that, Sis. I'm keeping accounts. (*to Georgia's grin*) You didn't know that.

GEORGIA: You're so funny, Sadie.

SADIE: You haven't asked my plans.

GEORGIA: No. I haven't . . .

SADIE: Do you care.

GEORGIA laughs.

GEORGIA: I knew you'd tell me.

SADIE: Uncertain. I think L.A. I think in stages.

GEORGIA: Oh. Good.

SADIE: Good what.

GEORGIA: I don't know, Sadie. As long as you're okay.

SADIE sits into the porch chair.

SADIE: (*a long moment*) I was just thinking, you know. You never left home, Georgia.

GEORGIA: I guess so.

SADIE: I must scare the shit out of you. I must be your worst nightmare.

GEORGIA: Sadie's out there gobbling it up. Always. It's always how I see you. Gobbling it up again. I hate the desperation. Everything's so desperate. Everything needs to be so desperate.

SADIE: Yeah. Well you don't do anything desperate. Don't feel anything desperately. It's not in your nature. Feeling isn't your strong suit, Georgia.

GEORGIA: Not that kind of hunger, no.

SADIE: Nothing consuming.

GEORGIA: No. Not like you.

SADIE: Not passion . . .

GEORGIA: Passion? Okay, passion.

SADIE: Or pain.

GEORGIA: No. Or suffering. Well, that's a gift you mistake for voice, Sadie. I don't want your pain. You're wed to it. My God, it's how you define yourself. But it's yours, I'll give you that. For God's sake, nothing else is. Your whole life's borrowed. Borrowed's kind. Except for Sadie's pain. That's Sadie's own. Sadie's cross. And Sadie's pain has to be fed, goddamn it. Kept alive. Nurtured. And we're all here. Ready to serve. You don't sing, Sadie. You can't sing.

SADIE: (*wide smile, choked laugh, small, generous*) You wish.

There's been a lot of venom. GEORGIA's wasted her. GEORGIA smarts, hurts for it. Ther's no way to come back round. SADIE ignores the wound, unable right at the moment to cope with the break. She wraps hands round the edge of the chair, looks out into the night.

Good Will Hunting
(Miramax, 1997)

Screenplay by Matt Damon and Ben Affleck
Directed by Gus Van Sant
Characters: SEAN (Robin Williams)
WILL (Matt Damon)

NOTES: WILL HUNTING is a young man from the "wrong side of the tracks" in South Boston, gifted to the point of genius, but struggling emotionally. He works as a janitor at MIT, a highly respected technical institution in Boston. His parole officer got him the job. He's had a long history of brushes with the law, from assault to grand theft auto. He's also an orphan, but his only "family" now is his loyal band of buddies from "Southie." His foster family was a nightmare; he suffered severe physical and emotional abuse at the hands of his foster father. When WILL sees an advanced mathematical theorem posted on the board at MIT (a competition to see which student, if any, can solve it), he proves the theorem and writes the answer, sending the math professor Lambeau (a genius himself) on a wild goose chase looking for the brilliant mind among his students. When he discovers it's WILL, he tries to get WILL to work with him. When Lambeau bails WILL out of jail for his latest screw up, he has a golden opportunity; the judge releases WILL under Lambeau's supervision, allowing WILL to work with Lambeau, under the provision that WILL have weekly counseling sessions. WILL's difficult nature, however, has already cost him three therapists. Lambeau, in desperation, goes to his old college friend

SEAN, a psychologist. SEAN lost his wife to cancer two years ago, and has his own difficulties adjusting to life, but he is very wise and from a similar background to WILL's. This is their first session.

INTERIOR. SEAN'S OFFICE—DAY

After an awkward moment, Lambeau and Tom go, leaving SEAN and WILL alone. WILL sits. WILL doesn't look at SEAN for more than one second. He seems more interested in the room. There is a long silence as SEAN watches WILL.

SEAN: How are you?

WILL: 'Kay.

SEAN: Where are you from in Southie?

WILL: I like what you've done with the place.

SEAN: Thanks.

WILL: Did you buy all these books retail, or do you send away for, like, a "shrink kit" that comes with all these volumes included?

SEAN: Do you like books?

WILL: Yeah.

SEAN: Did you read any of these books?

WILL: I don't know.

SEAN: How 'bout any of these books?

WILL: Probably not.

SEAN: What about the ones on the top shelf—you read those?

WILL's eyes flicker up to the shelf for an instant.

WILL: Yeah, I read those.

SEAN: Good for you. What did you think about them?

WILL: Hey, I'm not here for a fuckin' book report. They're your books, why don't you read them?

SEAN: I did. I had to.

WILL: That must have taken you a long time.

SEAN: Yeah, it did.

SEAN says this with pride. His determined stare and confident manner catch WILL a bit off guard. WILL rises from his chair and goes to the shelf.

WILL: *(looking at a book)* The United States of America, A Complete History, Volume I. Jesus. If you want to read a real history book, read Howard Zinn's *A People's History of the United States*. That book will fuckin' knock you on your ass.

SEAN: Better than Chompsky's *Manufacture and Consent*? You think that's a good book?

WILL: You people baffle me. You spend all your money on these fuckin' fancy books, you surround yourselves with them—and they're the wrong fuckin' books.

SEAN: What are the right fuckin' books, Will?

WILL: Hey. Whatever blows your hair back.

SEAN: Yeah. I ain't got much hair left. Hey—you know I'd be better off shoving that cigarette up your ass. It'd probably be healthier for you.

WILL: Yeah, I know. It really gets in the way of my yoga.

SEAN does not seem at all affected by WILL's attitude. He remains behind the big desk with almost a half smile on his face. WILL is aware of SEAN's confidence.

SEAN: You work out, huh?

WILL: What—you lift?

SEAN: Yeah.

WILL: Yeah—Nautilus?

SEAN: Nah—free weights.

WILL: Oh really?

SEAN: Yeah.

WILL: Free weights, huh?

SEAN: Yeah, big time.

WILL: Yeah?

SEAN: Just like that.

WILL: What do you bench?

SEAN: Two eighty-five. What do you bench?

WILL gets up again and moves around his chair to SEAN's painting. It is a picture of an old sailboat in a tremendous storm—by no means a masterpiece. WILL studies it.

WILL: You paint this?

SEAN: Yeah. You paint?

WILL: Uh-uh.

SEAN: You sculpt?

WILL: No.

SEAN: You like art? You like music?

WILL: This is a real piece of shit.

SEAN: Oh—tell me what you really think.

WILL: Nah, it's just the—the linear/impressionistic mix makes a very muddled composition. It's also a Winslow Homer ripoff, except you got whitey uh, rowing the boat there.

SEAN: Well, it's—

WILL: (*over*) That's not really what concerns me, though.

SEAN: What concerns you?

WILL: It's the coloring.

SEAN: You know what the real bitch of it is? It's paint by number.

WILL: Is it color by number? Because the colors are fascinating to me.

SEAN: Are they really? What about her? (*referring to figure in painting*)

WILL: (*over, he's not listening*) I think you're about one step away from cutting your fuckin' ear off.

SEAN: Really?

WILL: Oh yeah.

SEAN: You think I should move to the south of France, change my name to Vincent?

WILL: You ever heard the saying "Any port in a storm"?

SEAN: Yeah.

WILL: Well, maybe that means you.

SEAN: In what way?

WILL: Maybe you were in the middle of a storm, a big fuckin' storm.

SEAN: Yeah? Maybe.

WILL: (*over*) The sky is falling on your head, the waves are crashin' over your little boat, the oars are about to snap, you're just pissin' your pants, you're cryin' for the harbor. So maybe you do what you gotta do, to get out. Maybe you became a psychologist.

SEAN: Bingo. That's it. Let me do my job now, you start with me. Come on.

WILL: Maybe you married the wrong woman.

SEAN: Maybe you should watch your mouth. Watch it right there, chief, all right?

WILL: That's it, isn't it? You married the wrong woman. What happened? What—she leave you? Was she—you know, bangin' some other guy?

In a flash, SEAN has WILL by the throat. WILL is helpless.

SEAN: If you ever disrespect my wife again . . . I will end you. I will fuckin' end you. Got that, chief?

WILL: Time's up.

SEAN: Yeah.

Good Will Hunting (2)
(Miramax, 1997)

Screenplay by Matt Damon and Ben Affleck
Directed by Gus Van Sant
Characters: SKYLAR (Minnie Driver)
           WILL (Matt Damon)

NOTES: WILL's therapy sessions with Sean had a rough start (see previous scene), but they finally hit their stride and WILL has already told Sean about a girl he's seeing, SKYLAR. She is the opposite of WILL—has an easy life, attends college—or so WILL thinks. SKYLAR and WILL have become closer and are in a "relationship." She will be graduating and leaving Boston soon, however, to go to med school in California. SKYLAR is an intelligent, strong woman, but has her own history of grief; her father died when she was younger, leaving her enough money for her education. (She is from England and speaks with an accent.) Her invitation to WILL to accompany her to California is rather unexpected, but then, so was their relationship.

INTERIOR. SKYLAR'S ROOM—NIGHT

Close-up on WILL asleep in SKYLAR'S bed.

SKYLAR: Are you awake?

WILL: No.

SKYLAR: Yes you are. Will, come with me to California.

WILL: What?

SKYLAR: I want you to come to California with me.

WILL: Are you sure about that?

SKYLAR: Oh, yeah.

WILL: Yeah, but how do you know?

SKYLAR: I don't know. I just know.

WILL: Yeah, but how do you know?

SKYLAR: I know because—I feel it.

WILL: 'Cause—that's a serious thing to say, honey.

SKYLAR: I—I know.

WILL: We could be in California next week, you know, you might find out somethin' about me you don't like and, you know, maybe you'll wish you hadn't said that. But, you know, it's such a serious thing that you can't take it back, and now I'm stuck in California with someone who doesn't really want to be with me who wishes they had a take-back.

SKYLAR: A what? What's a "take-back"? I don't want a take-back. I just want you to come to California with me.

WILL: Well—I can't go to California.

SKYLAR: Why not?

WILL: One, because I got a job here and two, because I live here—

SKYLAR: Look, um—if you don't love me you should just tell me because it's—

WILL: I'm not sayin' I don't love you.

SKYLAR: Then why? Why won't you come? What are you so scared of?

WILL: What am I so scared of?

SKYLAR: Well, what aren't you scared of? You live in your safe little world where no one challenges you and you're scared shitless to do anything else because that would mean you'd have to change—

WILL: (*over*) Don't, don't, don't tell me about my world. Don't tell me about my world! I mean, you just want to

have your fling with, like, the guy from the other side of
town and then you're gonna go off to Stanford, you're
gonna marry some rich prick who your parents will approve
of, and just sit around with the other trust fund babies and
talk about how you went slummin', too, once.

SKYLAR: Why are you saying this? What is your obsession
with this money? My father died when I was thirteen and
I inherited this money. You don't think every day I wake
up and I wish I could give it back. I would give it back in
a second if I could have one more day with him. But I
can't. And that's life. And I deal with it. So don't put your
shit on me, when you're the one that's afraid.

WILL: I'm afraid? What am I afraid of? What the fuck am
I afraid of?!

SKYLAR: You're afraid of me. You're afraid that I won't
love you back. And you know what? I'm afraid, too. Fuck
it! I want to give it a shot! And at least I'm honest with
you.

WILL: I'm not honest with you?

SKYLAR: What about your twelve brothers?

WILL: Ah—(*He reaches for his jeans.*)

SKYLAR: No. You're not going. You're not leaving.

WILL: What do you want to know? What? That I don't have
twelve brothers? That I'm a fuckin' orphan?

SKYLAR: (*over*) Yes, Will. I didn't even know that. I didn't
know it.

WILL: No, you don't want to hear that. You don't want to
hear that I got fuckin' cigarettes put out on me when I was
a little kid.

SKYLAR: I didn't know that—

WILL: (*over*) That this isn't surgery—that the motherfucker
stabbed me.

WILL reveals a six-inch scar on his torso.

WILL: You don't want to hear that shit, Skylar!

SKYLAR: I do want to hear it!

WILL: Don't tell me you want to hear that shit!!

SKYLAR: I want to hear it because I want to help you! Because I want to be with—

WILL: Help me?! What the fuck? What, do I got a fuckin' sign on my back that says "save me"?! Do I look like I need that?

SKYLAR: No! No, God. (*she reaches for him*) I just want to be with you, because I love you. I love you!

WILL, full of self-loathing, pushes her away and against the wall.

WILL: Don't bullshit me! Don't you fuckin' bullshit me! (*He pounds the wall next to her head.*)

SKYLAR: (*she is weeping*) I love you. I want to hear you say that you don't love me. Because if you say that, then I won't call you, and I won't be in your life. (*she kisses his face*)

A beat. WILL looks SKYLAR dead in the eye.

WILL: I don't love you.

He walks out. He leaves, clothes in hand.

Good Will Hunting (3)
(Miramax, 1997)

Screenplay by Matt Damon and Ben Affleck
Directed by Gus Van Sant
Characters: SEAN (Robin Williams)
*   WILL (Matt Damon)*

NOTES: WILL has been on a job interview at the N.S.A. that Lambeau, the math professor, set up for him (see *previous scenes*). He wasn't impressed. He told the N.S.A. just what ethical problems he had with the job, and here he relates the experience to SEAN. Meanwhile, he's just broken up with Skylar, but doesn't tell that bit of news to SEAN.

INTERIOR. SEAN'S OFFICE—NIGHT
WILL sits across from SEAN.

WILL: Say I'm working at N.S.A. Somebody puts a code on my desk, something nobody else can break. So I take a shot at it and maybe I break it. And I'm real happy with myself, 'cause I did my job well. But maybe that code was the location of some rebel army in North Africa or the Middle East. Once they have that location, they bomb the village where the rebels were hiding and fifteen hundred people I never met, never had no problem with get killed. (*rapid fire*) Now the politicians are sayin', "Send in the Marines to secure the area" 'cause they don't give a shit. It won't be their kid over there, gettin' shot. Just like it wasn't them when their number got called, 'cause they were pullin' a tour in the National Guard. It'll be some guy from Southie takin' shrapnel in the ass. He comes back to find that the plant he used to work at got exported to the country he just got back from. And the guy who put the shrapnel in his ass got his old job, 'cause he'll work for fifteen cents a day and no bathroom breaks. Meanwhile my buddy from Southie realizes the only reason he was over there was so we could install a government that would sell us oil at a good price. And of course the oil companies used the little skirmish over there to scare up domestic oil prices. A cute little ancillary benefit for them but it ain't helping my buddy at two-fifty a gallon. They're takin' their sweet time bringin' the oil back, of course, maybe they even took the liberty of hiring an alcoholic skipper who likes to drink martinis and fuckin' play slalom with the icebergs, and it ain't too long 'til he hits one, spills the oil and kills all the sea life in the North Atlantic. So my buddy's out of work, he can't afford to drive, so he's got to walk to the job interviews, which sucks 'cause the shrapnel in his ass is givin' him chronic hemorrhoids. And meanwhile he's starvin' 'cause every time he tries to get a bite to eat the only blue plate special they're servin' is North Atlantic scrod with Quaker State. (*beat*) So what'd I think? I'm holdin' out for somethin' better. I figure, fuck it. While I'm at it, why not just shoot my buddy, take his job and give it to his sworn enemy, hike up gas prices, bomb a village, club a baby seal, hit the hash pipe and join the National Guard? I could be elected president.

SEAN: You feel like you're alone, Will?

WILL: What?

SEAN: Do you have a soul mate?

WILL: Do I—define that.

SEAN: Somebody who challenges you.

WILL: I have Chuckie.

SEAN: No, Chuckie's family. He'd lie down in fuckin' traffic for you. No. I'm talkin' about someone who opens things up for you, touches your soul.

WILL: Ah—I got, I got—

SEAN: Who?

SEAN waits.

WILL: I got plenty.

SEAN: Well, name them.

WILL: Shakespeare, Nietzsche, Frost, O'Connor, Kant, Pope, Locke—

SEAN: That's great. They're all dead.

WILL: Not to me, they're not.

SEAN: Well, you don't have a lot of dialogue with them. You can't give back to them, Will.

WILL: Not without a heater and some serious smelling salts, no . . .

SEAN: That's what I'm saying. You'll never have that kind of relationship in a world where you're always afraid to take the first step because all you see is every negative thing ten miles down the road.

WILL: You're goin' to take the professor's side on this?

SEAN: Don't give me a line of shit. No.

WILL: Look, I didn't want the job.

SEAN: It's not about the job. I don't care if you work for the government. But you could do anything you want. You are bound by nothing. What are you passionate about? What do you want? I mean, there are guys who work their entire lives layin' brick so their kids have a chance at the opportunities you have here.

WILL: I didn't ask for this.

SEAN: No. You were born with it. So don't cop out behind "I didn't ask for this."

WILL: What do you mean, cop out? I mean, what's wrong with layin' brick?

SEAN: Nothing.

WILL: There's nothing wrong with layin' brick. That's somebody's home I'm buildin'.

SEAN: Right. My dad laid brick. Okay? Busted his ass so that I could have an education.

WILL: Exactly. That's an honorable profession. What's wrong with—with fixin' somebody's car—someone'll get to work the next day 'cause of me. There's honor in that.

SEAN: Yeah, there is, Will. There's honor in that. And there's honor in, you know, taking that forty-minute train ride so those college kids can come in in the morning and their floors are clean and their wastebaskets are empty— that's real work.

WILL: That's right.

SEAN: Right. And that's honorable. I'm sure that's why you took that job, I mean, for the honor of it. I just have a little question here. You could be a janitor anywhere. Why did you work at the most prestigious technical college in the whole fuckin' world? And why did you sneak around at night and finish other people's formulas that only one or two people in the world could do and then lie about it? 'Cause I don't see a lot of honor in that, Will. So what do you really want to do?

A beat. WILL says nothing.

WILL: I wanna be a shepherd.

SEAN: Really?

WILL: I wanna move up to Nashua, get a nice little spread, get some sheep, and tend to them.

SEAN: Maybe you should go do that.

He goes to the door and opens it.

WILL: What?

SEAN: You know, if you're gonna jerk off, why don't you just do it at home with a moist towel?

WILL: You're chuckin' me?

SEAN: Yeah. Get the fuck out.

WILL: Hey, no, no, no. Time's not up yet.

SEAN: Yeah, it is.

WILL: I'm not leavin'. No.

SEAN: Listen, you're not gonna answer my questions, you're wastin' my fuckin' time.

WILL: What? I thought we were friends. What do you mean, you're—

SEAN: Play time is over, okay?

WILL: Well, why are you kickin' me out, Sean? I mean, what—I mean, you're lecturing me on life? Look at you, you fuckin' burnout! What winds your clock?

SEAN: Working with you?

WILL: Where's your "soul mate"?! You wanna talk about soul mates? Where is she?

SEAN: Dead.

WILL: That's right! She's fuckin' dead! She fuckin' dies— and you just cash in your chips and you walk away?

SEAN: Hey. At least I played a hand.

WILL: Oh, you played a hand and you lost. You lost a big fuckin' hand! And some people would lose a big fuckin' hand like that have the sack to ante up again!

SEAN: Look at me. What do you want me to do?

A beat. WILL looks up.

SEAN: You and your bullshit. You got a bullshit answer for everybody. But I asked you a very simple question and you can't give me a straight answer. Because you don't know. (*He opens the door.*) See ya, Bo Peep.

WILL walks out.

WILL: Fuck you.

SEAN: (*closing the door behind him*) You're the shepherd.

SEAN goes to his chair and sits down. He takes his glasses off and wipes them.

SEAN: Shepherd. Right, little prick.

Good Will Hunting (4)
(Miramax, 1997)

Screenplay by Matt Damon and Ben Affleck
Directed by Gus Van Sant
Characters: LAMBEAU (Stellan Skarsgard)
*   SEAN (Robin Williams)*

NOTES: WILL is becoming increasingly disaffected and/or terrified with the prospect of following the plan LAMBEAU has for
him (*see previous scenes*). He even goes so far as to send his
friend Chuckie in his place to one of his job interviews. LAM-
BEAU is threatened and fears SEAN's influence on WILL. He
confronts WILL in his office. Their conflict is about much more
than WILL. They have a long history of mutual resentment, even
though they can recognize each other's gifts.

INTERIOR. SEAN'S OFFICE—DAY

LAMBEAU stands across from SEAN, seething.

LAMBEAU: This is a disaster, Sean! I brought you in here
    because I wanted you to help me with the boy, not to run
    him out—

SEAN: I know what I'm doing with the boy.

LAMBEAU: I don't care if you have a rapport with the boy!
    I don't care if you have a few laughs, even at my expense,
    but don't you dare undermine what I'm trying to do here.

SEAN: Undermine?

LAMBEAU: This boy is at a fragile point right now.

SEAN: I do understand. He is at fragile point right, okay? He's got problems.

LAMBEAU: Well, what problems does he have, Sean? That he's better off as a janitor? That he's better off in jail? Better off hanging out with a bunch of retarded gorillas?

SEAN: Oh, why do you think he does that, Gerry? Do you have any fucking clue why? Hmm?

LAMBEAU: He can handle the problems. He can handle the work. And he obviously handled you.

SEAN: Why is he hiding? Why doesn't he trust anybody? Because the first thing that happened to him was that he was abandoned by the people who were supposed to love him the most!

LAMBEAU: Oh, come on, Sean, don't give me that Freudian crap—

SEAN: No, no, listen Gerry. And why does he hang out with those "retarded gorillas," as you call them? Because any one of them, if he asked them to, would take a fuckin' bat to your head, okay? That's called loyalty!

LAMBEAU: Yeah, that's very touching.

SEAN: And who's he handling? He pushes people away before they have a chance to leave him. It's a defense mechanism! And for twenty years he's been alone because of that. And if you push him right now, it's going to be the same thing all over again. And I'm not going to let that happen to him!

LAMBEAU: Now don't do that.

SEAN: What?

LAMBEAU: Don't you do that! Don't infect him with the idea that it's okay to quit. That's it's okay to be a failure, because it's not okay, Sean! If you're angry at me for being successful, for being what you could have been—

SEAN: I'm not angry at you, Gerry—

LAMBEAU: Oh yes, you're angry at me, Sean. You resent me. But I'm not going to apologize for any, any success that I've had. You're angry at me for doing what you could have done. But ask yourself, Sean, ask yourself if you want Will to feel that way, if you want him to feel like a failure.

SEAN: It's always this arrogant shit! That's why I don't come to the goddamn reunions! Because I can't stand that look in your eye, you know? That condescending, embarrassed look. You think I'm a failure! I know who I am. And I'm proud of what I do. It was a conscious choice. I didn't fuck up! And you and your cronies think I'm some sort of pity case! You and your kiss-ass chorus, following you around, going ''the Fields medal, the Fields medal!'' Why are you still so fuckin' afraid of failure?

LAMBEAU: It's about my medal, is it? Oh God, I could go home and get it for you. You can have it.

SEAN: Oh, please don't. You know what, Gerry? Shove the medal up your fuckin' ass, alright? 'Cause I don't give a shit about your medal. 'Cause I knew you before you were Mathematical God, when you were pimple-faced and homesick and didn't know what side of the bed to piss on!

LAMBEAU: Yeah, you were smarter than me then and you're smarter than me now! So don't blame me for how your life turned out. It's not my fault.

SEAN: I don't blame you! It's not about *you*, you mathematical dick! It's about the boy! He's a good kid! And I won't see you fuck him up like you're trying to fuck me up right now! I won't see you make him feel like a failure too!

LAMBEAU: He won't be a failure, Sean!

SEAN: But, but if you push him, Gerry, if you ride him—

LAMBEAU: Sean! I am what I am today because I was pushed. And because I learned to push myself!

SEAN: He's not you! You get that??

A beat. LAMBEAU turns, something catches his eye. SEAN turns to look. It's WILL. He's standing in the doorway.

Good Will Hunting (5)
(Miramax, 1997)

Screenplay by Matt Damon and Ben Affleck
Directed by Gus Van Sant
Characters: WILL (Matt Damon)
*   SEAN (Robin Williams)*

NOTES: This is a continuation of the previous scene. SEAN and Lambeau don't know that WILL has heard about half of their conversation. WILL has opened the door, stopping their fight. He offers to come back, but Lambeau says no and leaves. WILL is really at a crucial point in his process with SEAN; he's depressed and confused. SEAN is a bit shaken from his confrontation with Lambeau, but sensitive to WILL's needs right now.

INTERIOR. SEAN'S OFFICE—DAY

There is an awkward moment as LAMBEAU leaves. WILL shuts the door.

SEAN: Look, a lot of that stuff goes back a long way, between me and him, you know. It's not about you.

A beat. WILL sees a file on SEAN's desk.

WILL: What is that?

SEAN: That's your file. I have to send it back to the judge for evaluation.

WILL: Hey, you're not gonna fail me are you?

SEAN smiles.

WILL: What's it say?

SEAN: You want to read it?

SEAN offers the file.

WILL: Why?

WILL doesn't take the file. SEAN opens the file and looks at polaroids of WILL's scars.

WILL: Have you had any uh, experience with that?

SEAN: Twenty years of counseling, yeah, I've seen some pretty awful shit.

WILL: I mean, have you had any—*experience* with that?

SEAN: Personally?

WILL: Yeah.

SEAN: Yeah, I have.

WILL: (*smiles*) It sure ain't good.

SEAN: (*after a pause*) My father was an alcoholic. Mean fuckin' drunk. He'd come home hammered, looking to wail on somebody, so I'd provoke him, so he wouldn't go after my mother and little brother. The interesting nights were when he wore his rings.

WILL: He used to just put a wrench, a stick and a belt on the table and just say, "Choose."

SEAN: Well, I gotta go with the belt, there . . .

WILL: I used to go with the wrench.

SEAN: Why the wrench?

WILL: 'Cause fuck him, that's why.

SEAN: Your foster father?

WILL: Yeah. So, you know, what is it, like, "Will has an attachment disorder," is it all that stuff?

SEAN nods.

WILL: Fear of abandonment? Is that why I—is that why I broke up with Skylar?

SEAN: I didn't know you had.

WILL: Yeah, I did.

SEAN: Do you want to talk about that?

WILL: Nah.

SEAN: (*beat*) Hey, Will? I don't know a lot. But see this? (He holds up WILL's file.) All this shit . . . It's not your fault.

WILL: Yeah, I know that.

SEAN: Look at me, son.

WILL, who had been looking away, looks at SEAN.

SEAN: It's not your fault.

WILL: (*nonchalant*) Oh, I know.

SEAN: It's not your fault.

WILL: (*smiles*) I know.

SEAN: No, no, you don't. It's not your fault.

WILL: I know.

SEAN: It's not your fault.

WILL: (*laughs nervously*) All right.

SEAN: It's not your fault.

WILL is silent, looking at the floor.

SEAN: It's not your fault.

WILL: Don't fuck with me.

SEAN: It's not your fault.

WILL: (*shoves SEAN in the chest*) Don't fuck with me, all right? Don't fuck with me, Sean, not you!

SEAN: It's not your fault.

WILL starts to to cry.

SEAN: It's not your fault.

SEAN takes WILL in his arms and holds him like a child. WILL sobs like a baby.

WILL: Oh God, oh God, I'm so sorry . . .

He wraps his arms around SEAN and holds him even tighter. We pull back from this image. Two lonely souls being father and son together.

SEAN: Fuck them, all right?

Grand Canyon
(20th Century Fox, 1991)

Screenplay by Lawrence Kasdan and Meg Kasdan
Directed by Lawrence Kasdan
Characters: CLAIRE (Mary McDonnell)
MACK (Kevin Kline)

NOTES: CLAIRE and MACK live in LA; they have a comfortable life and a teenage son who is just at the age when a boy starts to separate from his mom. Their son is at summer camp, and MACK is at work when CLAIRE, out jogging one morning, hears a baby crying. She follows the sound into a small wooded area where she finds the child, abandoned. She brings it home, bathes it, feeds it, cares for it all day, and doesn't report it to the police. Now MACK returns home from work.

51. INTERIOR. FRONT HALL—NIGHT

MACK comes in, puts his things on the hall table, and begins glancing through the mail.

MACK: Claire! I'm here.

CLAIRE comes to the top of the stairs.

CLAIRE: Hi, Mack.

MACK: You never brought in the mail. There's something here from Carol.

CLAIRE: Mack, come on up here. I want to show you something.

MACK finally looks up from his mail. He leaves everything and heads up the stairs. CLAIRE waits for him at the top and when he reaches her, she puts her arms around him and kisses him, a real one.

MACK: Is something wrong?

She shakes her head, kisses him once more and leads him by the hand into the master bedroom.

52. INTERIOR. MASTER BEDROOM—NIGHT

CLAIRE leads MACK over to the bed. He is about to sit down on it, imagining the most romantic explanation, when she stops him. She puts her fingers to her lips for "quiet" and points to a jumble of blanket in the center of the big bed. It takes MACK a second to sort out what he's looking at. When he spots the baby sleeping in the center, he smiles reflexively. The conversation starts in whispers.

MACK: Whose is it?

CLAIRE: She's beautiful, isn't she?

MACK: (*agreeing*) Is that the Wilson kid? (*CLAIRE shakes her head*) Who?

CLAIRE: I don't know.

MACK digests this. It takes a few beats. He looks again at the infant, then back to CLAIRE. He's not sure he's got it yet, but he thinks he's going to hate it when he does.

MACK: What do you mean?

CLAIRE: I don't know who the parents are.

MACK: (*voice a little louder*) Come on, Claire, don't make me guess. Where'd it come from?

Again, CLAIRE puts a finger to her lips. This upsets MACK more. With a last glance at the baby, he leads CLAIRE from the room.

INTERIOR. MASTER BATHROOM—NIGHT

MACK deposits CLAIRE on the closed toilet seat. He takes off his jacket and starts pulling off his tie.

MACK: What's the story?

CLAIRE: I found her. I was jogging and I heard this crying and I looked—

MACK: (*sits on the tub*) Where is this?

CLAIRE: On Carmelina, just around the corner. (MACK nods, "go on") So I looked under the bushes and there she was. There were bugs crawling on her. And in this dirty blanket that was wrapped around her.

MACK: Where's the blanket?

CLAIRE: I threw it out.

MACK: (*makes a face*) I'll get it out of the garbage.

CLAIRE: What for?

MACK: When was this?

CLAIRE: This morning.

MACK: This morning? What time?

CLAIRE: Around 9:30, I guess.

MACK: What did the police say?

CLAIRE: Hmm?

Now MACK knows for sure. He knew it right away, but he was hoping he was wrong. He's pretty calm.

MACK: My guess is that the police did not say "Hmm?" So I guess my next guess is that . . . *you haven't called the police?* (*CLAIRE admits it*) You know, it's possible this baby was kidnapped and someone has been frantically looking for it all day.

CLAIRE: I don't think so. (*MACK gives her a look*) I could tell. But I listened to the news three times and there wasn't a thing about it.

MACK: Claire, that doesn't mean anything. They may not have announced it yet or they may be waiting to hear from—

CLAIRE: This baby wasn't kidnapped. I can tell you that, Mack. This baby was deserted by its mother and it's going to need a new one.

There's something strange enough in her tone to worry MACK.

MACK: Claire, are you okay?

CLAIRE: *(irritated)* I'm fine!

MACK: Claire, you know we have to call the police right now?

CLAIRE: Of course. Mack, I haven't taken leave of my senses.

MACK accepts that, but continues to look at her.

CLAIRE: I just wanted you to see her. So I waited 'til you got home. That's all. She's so beautiful, I wanted you to see her.

Grand Canyon (2)
(20th Century Fox, 1991)

Screenplay by Lawrence Kasdan and Meg Kasdan
Directed by Lawrence Kasdan
Characters: DEE (Mary Stuart Masterson)
MACK (Kevin Kline)

NOTES: DEE works for MACK as his secretary/assistant. They
have had a one-night stand, but it didn't blossom into an affair.
MACK is married, relatively happily, but something is missing
from his life. He's recently met a man, a tow-truck driver who
helped him out of a dangerous situation when MACK broke
down in a crime-ridden neighborhood. MACK has introduced
the man to DEE's single friend and confidante, Jane. DEE,
meanwhile, has stayed in love with MACK, and kept hoping for
something more.

118. INTERIOR. MACK'S OFFICE—DAY

*MACK is working at his desk. DEE comes in and closes the
door. MACK looks up, distracted.*

MACK: What's next?

DEE: Nothing.

*Her tone stops him. He puts down his pen. She sits in the
chair in front of his desk. He waits.*

DEE: I'm quitting.

He's not shocked, but he's not happy.

MACK: Tell me.

DEE: (*sharp*) You make me miserable.

MACK: I'm sorry. I don't want to.

DEE: Stop it.

MACK: What happened?

DEE: This is intolerable. I can't do this anymore. It's sick. I need to go on.

MACK looks at her, understanding.

DEE: Don't act like you're not relieved. I know you are.

MACK: I don't want you to go.

DEE: Do you know what your trouble is? You just never want to be the bad guy. You want everything you do to be okay. But it isn't.

They look at each other. She can't hold the look, so she stands up and goes to the window.

DEE: If you really didn't want this to happen, then you shouldn't have fucked me.

MACK: I'm sorry. I think I've said that before.

DEE: You've denied me in every way you can. Everything I've wanted, you've denied me.

MACK: I've been honest with you all along. Even that night.

DEE: Who gives a shit. Don't you see what you do? Even now, you want to deny me what's rightfully mine.

MACK: Which is?

DEE: To resent the hell out of you. (*turns on him*) To feel totally rejected and hate it. To hate you for doing it to me.

MACK: I fucked up. But I didn't think I was fucking up when I did it. And I didn't think that the next morning, either.

DEE: You see! You're doing it again. Shut up. (*looks away*) There are a lot of good men out there who are going to treat me like I'm the very thing they want.

They're silent for a while.

DEE: And then—then you do that thing with Jane.

MACK: (*confused*) What?

DEE: You know, with the guy, the tow-truck guy.

MACK: What about it? What's that got to do with anything?

DEE: You don't know, do you? You don't know why that hurts me so much.

MACK looks at her, puzzled.

DEE: Jane's in love. She thinks this could be the one.

MACK: Is that bad? I thought she was your friend.

DEE: She is my friend. I'm happy for her. But it makes me feel like shit that you're out there finding her the love of her life. And I'm here, what, I'm here like shit. How do you think that's going to make me feel?

MACK: Look, Dee, I understand you're angry with me, but why would—

DEE: Forget it. It doesn't have to make sense.

She crosses to the door.

DEE: I'll stay for two weeks, but you better find someone else.

The Grifters
(Miramax, 1990)

*Screenplay by Donald E. Westlake, based on the novel
by Jim Thompson
Directed by Stephen Frears
Characters: LILLY (Anjelica Huston)
            BOBO (Pat Hingle)*

NOTES: LILLY is a very handsome and sexy woman, hovering
around forty. She is tough when she needs to be but quietly
desperate. She can "take care of herself" and is more sophisticated than most other women of her class and education level.
She has never worked a "legit" job in her life; she's always been
a grifter. She runs playback money for the mob; they pay her
to go to the track and bet money on the long shot to lower the
odds and protect them from big payouts. She always skims a bit
off the top for herself and stashes it in a suitcase in the trunk of
her car. She has a good chunk of cash by now, but she skims
carefully and her boss, BOBO, expects that sort of thing. BOBO
has sent LILLY out of her regular territory in Baltimore to La
Jolla, California; she decides to stop in L.A. and drop in on her
son Roy. It's been eight years since they've seen each other. She
finds him sick and checks him into the hospital; he's been hit in
the stomach. She stays until she's sure he's okay, then heads up
to La Jolla late. She misses the race she's supposed to fix and is
in big trouble with BOBO. He shows up at the track soon after.

EXTERIOR. DELMAR—DAY

An angle on the exit doors toward the parking lot. LILLY comes out, self-absorbed, then sees something ahead of her, falters briefly, keeps walking, tries a very shaky smile. BOBO JUSTUS, 50, a blunt hoodlum in a good suit and a civilized veneer, stands leaning against the car, arms folded, squinting behind sunglasses.

LILLY: Hi, Bobo.

BOBO: Did I buy you that dress, you piece of shit?

LILLY's scared, startled, but trying to figure out how to play this.

LILLY: Well, I guess so. You're the guy I work for.

BOBO: You work for me, huh? Then I just may flush you down the toilet. Drive me to the Durando.

BOBO gets in the passenger seat, while LILLY nods convulsive agreement and hurries around to get behind the wheel. The car jolts forward, then smooths, and heads for the gate.

INTERIOR. CHRYSLER—DAY

Driving along the highway. LILLY concentrates on traffic. BOBO heavily watches her profile, finally speaks.

BOBO: Bluebell.

LILLY's eyes briefly close, her shoulders sag. Then she goes back to the silent, alert person she'd been. BOBO nods.

BOBO: How'd you figure you were gonna get away with that?

LILLY: I'm not getting away with anything, Bobo.

BOBO: You're fuckin' right you're not. How much did your pals cut you in for on that nag, huh? Or did they give you the same kind of screwing you gave me?

LILLY: I was down on that horse, Bobo. Not as much as I should have been, but there was a lot of action on those—

BOBO taps a finger against the side of her head to shut her up. She shuts up.

BOBO: One question. Do you want to stick to that story, or do you want to keep your teeth?

LILLY: I want to keep my teeth.

BOBO: Now I'll ask you another. You think I got no contacts out here? That nag paid off at just the opening price. There wasn't hardly a flutter on the tote board from the time the odds were posted. There ain't enough action to tickle the tote, but you claim a ten grand win! You send me *ten thousand dollars*, like I'm some mark you can blow off!

LILLY: (*terrified, broken*) Bobo, no, I—

BOBO: You wanna talk to me straight up?

LILLY: My son—

BOBO: Your *what*?

LILLY: My son was in the hospital—

BOBO: What the fuck are you doin' with a son?

LILLY: He left home a long time ago. He was in the hospital, up in Los Angleez, real sick.

BOBO: (*utter scorn*) Motherhood.

LILLY: I never fucked up before, Bobo.

BOBO: You expect me to buy this?

It's time for LILLY to show tough, and she knows it.

LILLY: You do buy it, Bobo. I cost you, and I'm sorry.

BOBO thinks this over.

BOBO: I got a lot of people work for me, Lilly. I can't have shit like this.

LILLY: (*begging*) It'll never happen again. I swear.

BOBO: It happened once. With me, that's making a habit of it.

LILLY drops back to her final position; fatalism.

LILLY: You're calling the shots.

BOBO: You got any kind of long coat in the car? Anything you can wear home over your clothes?

LILLY: (*deadened with fear*) No.

BOBO: (*doesn't matter*) I'll loan you a raincoat.

LILLY drives, holding herself together.

INTERIOR. HOTEL SUITE—DAY

Living room of a high-floor suite. Camera faces across the room to the balcony and the view of the ocean. Entrance door to one side. A supermarket shopping bag is on the coffee table. Two thugs sit on the sofa, watching TV. The door opens and LILLY enters, followed by BOBO. The thugs immediately rise and switch off the TV.

BOBO: (*to the thugs*) Take a walk.

The thugs leave the room as LILLY crosses to stand between us and the view, followed by BOBO, neither looking out. LILLY turns to BOBO, who abruptly punches her hard in the stomach. She falls to the floor. Another angle as BOBO steps across her and goes over to close the drapes over the view. LILLY sits up, watching him, waiting obediently. BOBO looks at her.

BOBO: Get me a bath towel.

She gets up, hurting, and hurries to the bathroom. BOBO sits on the sofa, crossing his ankles on the coffee table next to the supermarket bag. He takes out and lights a cigar. LILLY comes back with a large white bath towel.

BOBO: You ever hear about the oranges?

LILLY: You mean, the insurance frammis?

BOBO: Tell me about the oranges, Lilly.

He kicks over the supermarket bag. Oranges roll on the floor.

BOBO: While you put those in the towel.

LILLY's very scared. She drops to her knees, spreads the towel, crawls around gathering oranges while she talks.

LILLY: You hit a person with the oranges in the towel, they get big, awful-looking bruises, but they don't really get hurt, not if you do it right. It's for working scams against insurance companies.

BOBO: And if you do it wrong?

LILLY: It can louse up your insides. You can get puh, puh, puh . . .

BOBO: (*impatient*) What's that, Lilly?

LILLY pauses, bent over, tightly holding an orange.

LILLY: Permanent damage.

BOBO: You'll never shit right again.

He gets to his feet, leaving his cigar in an ashtray.

BOBO: (*hard, impatient*) Bring me the towel.

Fumbling slightly, she folds the towel edges together to make a bag, then stands, brings the towel to BOBO. He makes a production out of getting his grip on the edges just right. She stands as limp as she can, just wanting to get through this. He looks at her without expression, rears back with the towel, swings it forward, lets it drop open. Oranges roll on the floor. LILLY stares, wide-eyed, recognizing reprieve. BOBO tosses the towel behind him onto the sofa, then gestures contemptuously for her to pick up the oranges again. Two shot, closer, as LILLY turns, bending toward the oranges, and BOBO picks up his cigar, then lifts a foot and kicks her, flat-footed, hard, in the back. She sprawls on the floor. He follows and drops to his knees on her back. An angle close on LILLY on the floor, BOBO's knees grinding back and forth into her back. An angle on BOBO, grimacing as he bears down, pressing his weight onto her back. He leans forward, left hand bracing himself on the floor beside her head as he reaches down with the cigar held in his right hand and presses the ember against the back of her splayed-out right hand. Extreme close-up, LILLY, clenching her teeth, tears squeezing from her eyes, simply bearing it. An angle on BOBO, catching a bad smell, looking back down behind himself at LILLY's body. This is the result he wanted, but it disgusts him. He straightens up, still kneeling on her, puts the cigar in his mouth, doesn't like the taste, removes it, his left hand against her back while he lifts off her, getting back up onto his feet. Wide shot, BOBO stepping over her, expression repulsed.

BOBO: Go clean yourself up.

He puts the cigar back in the ashtray as she rises, cradling her burnt hand. Not looking toward BOBO, hobbling with knees together, she starts from the room.

BOBO: The raincoat's on the bed.

She leaves. He opens the drapes, then picks up an orange from the floor and steps out onto the balcony. BOBO stands looking out at the ocean. He enjoys breathing the sea air. He slowly peels the orange, dropping pieces of peel over the side. LILLY appears in the doorway, wearing a too-large man's raincoat. BOBO doesn't seem to notice her at first, then nods to her.

BOBO: Almost forgot. That ten grand of yours. It's in the envelope by the door.

LILLY: (*tries for animation*) Oh, thanks, Bobo.

BOBO: You want a drink?

LILLY: Gee, I better not, if it's okay. I still gotta drive back up to Los Ang-gleez.

BOBO: See your son, huh? Well, that's nice. A side of you I didn't know, Lilly.

LILLY chances taking a step out onto the balcony. It's vital that she encourage this forgive-and-forget dialogue.

LILLY: He's a good kid. A salesman.

BOBO: On the square, huh? And how are *you* making out these days? Stealing much?

BOBO'S being jolly now. LILLY's scared, but has to be jolly, too.

LILLY: From you? My folks didn't raise any stupid kids.

BOBO's joshing now. He raises a humorous eyebrow.

BOBO: Not skimming a thing, Lilly?

LILLY: Oh, well, you know. I just clip a buck here and a buck there. Not enough to notice.

BOBO: (*honest approval*) That's right. Take a little, leave a little.

LILLY: A person that doesn't look out for himself is too dumb to look out for anybody else. He's a liability, right, Bobo?

BOBO: (*this is his creed*) You're a thousand percent right!

LILLY: Or else he's working an angle. If he doesn't steal a little, he's stealing big.

BOBO: You know it, Lilly.

LILLY: You know, I like that suit, Bobo. I don't know what there is about it, but it somehow makes you look taller.

BOBO: (*delighted*) Yeah? You really think so? A lot of people been telling me the same thing.

LILLY: Well, you can tell them I said they're right. (*looks at sky*) I better get going. Roy'll wonder where I am.

BOBO: Worries about his mother, eh? Give him a hug for me.

LILLY: I will. So long, Bobo.

LILLY leaves the balcony. BOBO eats more orange, looking out at the ocean. His expression is stern but calm.

The Grifters (2)
(Miramax, 1990)

*Screenplay by Donald E. Westlake, based on the novel
by Jim Thompson
Directed by Stephen Frears
Characters: MYRA (Annette Bening)
               ROY (John Cusack)*

NOTES: ROY is Lilly's son (*see notes for the previous scene*), a
small-time grifter, about twenty-five. He lives alone in a cheap
hotel in L.A., working the short con—cheating people at cards,
switching bills on bartenders, any small hustle. He learned his
trade from an older hustler who also taught him a "code": never
work with partners, etc. He tells Lilly he's getting off the grift
and going straight, but he keeps a very large stash of money
hidden in his cheap hotel room, in the hollowed-out backs of two
clown paintings. He's pretty much a loner who plays it close to
the vest, trusting no one. When Lilly finds him, they have a
strained, antagonistic reunion before she takes him to the hospital. (He's been punched in the stomach by a bartender he was
trying to cheat.) His girlfriend, MYRA, is a hustler herself—she
often pays the rent with sexual favors—but she's worked the
"long con" before—for ten years, with a partner who went insane. It is her game of choice, but she hasn't found a suitable
partner since. She has been sleeping with ROY a few months
before she realizes that he's a talented grifter like herself. She
pitches a partnership, but ROY is holding out.

INTERIOR. LIVING ROOM—DAY

ROY's room. He has one of the clown pictures face down on the coffee table. He takes money from his jacket pockets, crams it into the space, which is now just about full. As he's tightening the wing nuts closing the back, the doorbell rings. He hurries, finishing the job, hanging the picture on the wall, then crossing to open the door. MYRA enters, ebullient.

MYRA: Darling, guess what? I had to tell you right away.

She gives him an enthusiastic kiss, then marches into the living room.

ROY: (*grinning*) And hello to you, too.

MYRA: I called a fellow I know in Tulsa, the one who plays my chauffeur. There's a sucker there he says is *made* for us. And a broker that just shut down, we can use their office, not change a thing! Now, I can scrape up ten grand without much trouble. That leaves fifteen or twenty for your end. We could start this weekend, get the sucker into position—

ROY: Wait a minute! When did this happen, that we're partners?

MYRA: (*bewildered*) What?

ROY: The last I looked, we were just talking things over.

MYRA: You're too good for the small time, Roy.

ROY: Maybe I like it where I am.

MYRA's need breaks through her good sense.

MYRA: Well, maybe I don't! I had ten good years with Cole, and I want them back! I *gotta* have a partner! I looked and I looked and believe me, brother, I kissed a lot of fucking frogs, and *you're* my prince!

ROY tries to treat this lightly.

ROY: Don't I get any say in this?

MYRA: No! Because I—

ROY: (*pointing at her*) That's what I say.

MYRA: (*thrown off course*) What?

ROY: What I say is, no. We don't do partners.

She stares at him, trying to find a chink in the armor, trying to find a reason, trying to find something.

MYRA: What is it? What's going on?

ROY: I'm happy the way I am.

MYRA: By God, it's your mother. It's Lilly.

ROY: (*doesn't get it*) What?

MYRA: Sure it is. That's why you act so funny around each other.

He frowns at her, not believing he understands her right.

ROY: What's that?

MYRA: Don't act so goddamned innocent! You and your own mother, *gah*! You like to go back where you been, huh?

He takes a step toward her, rising toward fury.

ROY: You watch that mouth.

MYRA: I'm wise to you. I should have seen it before, you rotten son of a bitch. How is it, huh? How do you like—

He slaps her openhanded but hard, and she staggers back. He pursues her.

ROY: How do you like this?

He slaps her as hard with the other hand. Astonished, frightened, befuddled, she backpedals, bringing her forearms up to protect her face. He grabs her two wrists in one hand, holds them out of the way, slaps her a third time.

MYRA: *STOP*!!

He suddenly gets control of himself, releases her, steps back into the middle of the room. He's angry, but also remorseful, sorry he lost control but still enraged at the enormity of her suggestion.

ROY: That's not like me. I don't do violence.

She cowers against the wall, peering in terror at him through her raised arms. He settles down, becomes heavily calm.

ROY: That's why we wouldn't work together. You're disgusting. You're mind's so filthy, it's hard to even look at you.

He crosses to the apartment door, pulls it open. Sunlight pours in.

ROY: Goodbye, Myra.

She lowers her arms slowly, as though her whole body aches. She's still scared, but angry now, too. She'd like to tell him off, but discretion tells her not to. She moves across the room toward the open door, but stops, not wanting to be that close to him. Understanding, he backs away from the doorway, gestures with cold irony for her to proceed. She moves to the threshold, looks back at him.

MYRA: And you don't even know it.

Angry again, ROY steps forward. She hastily steps outside, and he slams the door.

The Grifters (3)
(Miramax, 1990)

Screenplay by Donald E. Westlake, based on the novel by Jim Thompson
Directed by Stephen Frears
Characters: LILLY (Anjelica Huston)
ROY (John Cusack)

NOTES: After Myra is rejected by ROY (*see notes for previous scenes*), she decides that LILLY is in her way. She spies on LILLY at the track, and finds out about her stash. She tips off the mob, sending LILLY on the run. Then she follows LILLY, stopping at the same motel, and tries to kill her. LILLY, defending herself, shoots Myra in the face. The police think LILLY has committed suicide, as the corpse is unrecognizable. LILLY now has a little time to get away, before Bobo finds out the truth. She goes directly to ROY's apartment; he isn't there. She takes down the clown paintings and opens up the back, stuffing ROY's cash into a rickety attache case. She plans on taking all ROY's money and hitting the road. ROY returns from "identifying" LILLY's body. At the end of the scene, LILLY inadvertently kills ROY; the glass he's holding smashes and cuts into his throat. He bleeds to death in front of her as she collects the money and runs.

INTERIOR. LIVING ROOM—NIGHT
LILLY enters, puts the case on the coffee table beside the

*picture, scoops the money out of the picture and puts it in
the case. Then she unceremoniously dumps the picture on
the floor. LILLY takes the second picture from the wall, puts
it face down on the coffee table, opens the back, transfers
the money to the case. She closes the case, attaches the one
clasp that works, picks up the case.*

ROY: (*OC*) Hello, Lilly.

*Two shot, as Lilly whirls around, terrified and then relieved.
ROY stands in the open apartment doorway, blackness behind him.*

LILLY: Oh! Roy! You scared me.

ROY enters the room and shuts the door.

ROY: Going somewhere?

LILLY: Somewhere *else*, that's for sure.

ROY: I just came back from Phoenix.

LILLY: (*anxious*) Oh, yeah? Is the frame holding?

ROY: Looks very solid, Lilly. Sit down. Take a minute, tell
me about it.

LILLY: I've really got to—

ROY: You're dead, Lilly. It worked.

LILLY: Not for long. Not when they do a fingerprint check.

ROY: Why should they? The cops are satisfied.

LILLY: *Bobo* won't be. He'll spend the money to make sure.

ROY: Even so. You still got time. Relax a minute, tell me
what happened. Sit down.

*He gestures at the sofa. LILLY's holding the attache case.
The gutted pictures are lying around, one on the coffee table
and one on the floor. She looks around at everything, awkward and embarrassed. But ROY hasn't said anything. And
he's between her and the door.*

LILLY: Just for a minute.

*She backs up, sits on the sofa, puts the case on her lap.
ROY pulls a chair over so it's directly between LILLY and
the door. He sits, looking at her with polite interest.*

ROY: Myra followed you, huh?

LILLY: She must have been the one to blow me off with Bobo. I guess to get me running. Did you tell her about my stash?

ROY: (*isn't worth discussing*) No.

LILLY: No, you wouldn't. That's what she was after, though. But why hit on *me*?

ROY: I wouldn't go in with her on a deal. She blamed you for it.

LILLY: (*a shaky laugh*) As though you do what I say.

ROY: (*cold grin*) That's pretty funny, all right. What happened in Phoenix?

Remembered emotion makes LILLY talk in little fast clusters of words.

LILLY: Roy, it was terrible. You read about people killing people and all that, but when it *happens*, my God.

LILLY stares across the room, breathing hard, reliving the experience.

LILLY: I sat in there with her, I thought, what do I do now? Run and I've Bobo *and* the law after me. Stay, and how do I explain?

ROY: This way's perfect.

LILLY sits back, showing that relief again.

LILLY: It is, isn't it? And maybe it's a break for me after all. I've been wanting out of the racket for years, and now I'm out. I can make a clean start, and—

ROY: You've already made a start. Doesn't look that clean, though.

Here's the awkwardness. LILLY looks guilty and embarrassed.

LILLY: I'm sorry. I hated to take your money, but—

ROY: Don't be sorry. You're not taking it.

LILLY reacts as though he's slapped her. But then she gets her determination back. She splays out both hands, palms down, on the attache case on her lap.

LILLY: I *need* this, Roy. I can't run without money, and if I can't run I'm dead.

ROY: You must have *some* money.

LILLY: Just a few bucks.

ROY: And Myra's stuff?

LILLY: (*scornful*) Her credit cards. How far am I gonna get with that?

ROY: Far enough. Maybe up to San Francisco. Or St. Louis, someplace new. Start over.

LILLY: At *what*?

ROY: You're smart, Lilly, and you're good-looking. You won't have any trouble finding a job.

LILLY: (*appalled*) A job? I've never had a legit job in my life!

ROY: Well, you're gonna start, if you hope to live through this. A square job and a quiet life. You start showing up at the track or the hot spots and Bobo's boys will be all over you.

LILLY: (*exasperated*) Roy, I know what to do with myself! It's a big world out there.

ROY: Not any more. Lilly, listen, I'm giving you good advice. I'm following it myself.

LILLY: (*doesn't get it*) What?

ROY: I thought it over, and you were right. You wanted me out of the rackets, and now—

LILLY: (*bedeviled, aggravated*) Roy, that's fine, but I don't have time for this. Bobo—

ROY: I thought you'd be happy for me. After all, you—

LILLY: Bobo isn't after *you*! Bobo's after me, and he's goddam good! But so am I. I'm a survivor, Roy. I *survive*.

ROY: I know you do, so that's why—

LILLY: And to survive, *my* way, I need money. Bobo knows about the stash in the car, so I didn't dare touch it, not if Lilly Dillon's dead. So that leaves *this*.

ROY: (*isn't worth discussing*) No.

LILLY sits back again, brooding at ROY, trying to think how to get to him, how to get through him or around him. She sighs, licks her lips.

LILLY: You want a drink?

ROY: I don't think so. You probably shouldn't either.

LILLY: No, but I'm godamned thirsty. Ice water?

ROY: Yeah, sure, that sounds nice.

LILLY: I'll get it.

She stands, putting the attache case on the sofa next to where she was sitting. ROY, with a faint smile, watches her leave the room. LILLY switches on the kitchen light as she enters, then leans against the counter, fists clenched and trembling on the counter in front of her. She grits her teeth, hyperventilates, stares around the room in search of escape, an answer, something. CU on LILLY's face, desperate, grim, but not giving up.

INTERIOR. LIVING ROOM—NIGHT

LILLY enters with the tray, crosses to ROY, presents the glasses, speaks as he reaches for one.

LILLY: Take whichever one you want.

ROY hesitates. It hadn't occurred to him that LILLY might try to poison him or knock him out. He grins at her and takes a glass.

ROY: You wouldn't do that.

LILLY takes the other glass, puts the cookie sheet on a table, looks down at ROY.

LILLY: You don't know what I'd do, Roy. You have no idea. To *live*.

ROY: (*easy*) Oh, you'll live, Lilly.

LILLY crosses back to the sofa, sits beside the attache case, pats it absently as though it's a pet and she's glad it didn't move, waited for her. She sips water, puts the glass on the end table.

LILLY: I know what's bugging you, of course.

ROY: Oh? I didn't know anything was.

LILLY: *(twisted grin)* Oh, really? You've got a legitimate complaint, Roy, I don't deny that. I wasn't a very good mother when you were a kid.

ROY: *(full laugh)* Not very *good*!

She nods, accepting the correction.

LILLY: A bad mother. By any standards. I've thought about it, you know, from your side, since then. I know just how bad I was.

ROY: *(closed against her)* Uh-huh.

LILLY: I wonder did you ever think about it from my side.

ROY: *(not worth discussing)* Never.

LILLY: No. I guess not. It was pretty lousy of me, I guess, to be a child at the same time you were. Not to stop being a child just because I had a child. I guess I was a real stinker not to be a grown-up when you needed a grown-up.

ROY didn't expect to be made uncomfortable and defensive, and he resents it.

ROY: What do you want me to do? Pin a halo on you? You're doing a pretty good job of that yourself.

LILLY: And making you feel bad at the same time, huh? But that's the way I am, you know, the way I've always been. Always picking on poor little Roy.

ROY: For God's sake, Lilly!

LILLY: *(intense)* I gave you your life twice. I'm asking you to give me mine once. I *need* the money.

ROY: *(not worth discussing)* No.

LILLY subsides back onto the sofa. One hand rests on the attache case. With the other, she sips water, puts the glass back down. ROY watches her, unmoving, expressionless. LILLY frowns, not quite looking at him.

LILLY: You're getting off the grift?

ROY: That's right.

LILLY: That's good. You don't really belong on this side of the fence, you know.

ROY: *(amused)* I don't?

LILLY: If you stayed a crook, do you think you'd live to be *my* ripe age?

ROY: I don't see why not.

LILLY: Well, I guess I got it wrong, then. Seems to me I heard about a guy just about your age that got hit so hard in the guts it almost killed him.

ROY's again unexpectedly uncomfortable. He shifts uneasily in his chair, trying to think of a response.

ROY: Well, uh . . .

LILLY: Sure, sure, that doesn't count. That's different.

ROY: Well, it doesn't matter, does it? I'm getting out.

LILLY: *(intense)* And that's why you've got to get rid of this money. If you keep it around, it'll just make you think how clever you are. It'll be a temptation to get back into the game.

ROY: *(full laugh)* Oh, *that's* it! You're stealing my money for my own good! How very motherly of you, Lilly.

Once again, LILLY drops back against the sofa back. Another round in the fight is over. ROY watches her, patient, waiting for her to give up, seeing no other outcome. An angle on LILLY, frustrated, feeling the need to move, the pressure of pursuit. Her head turns back and forth, her body starts false gestures. Finally, abruptly, she gets to her feet, looks at ROY, looks away, picks up the attache case. CU, ROY, alert. He won't let her reach the door. An angle pan-

ning with LILLY as she prowls the room, pacing back and forth, the attache case swinging at her side. Finally, she stops, standing the attache case on the coffee table, her hand still on its handle.

ROY: Lilly.

She looks at him, attentive without hope.

ROY: If *I* should get out of the racket, that goes double for you. That's why you've got to change your life completely, go to some town, get a square job, live like a john yourself. If you try to do it your way, what future is in it?

LILLY: *A* future. The only future I've got.

ROY: That money wouldn't last forever. And then what? You'd be back in some other part of the rackets. Another Bobo Justus to slap you around and burn holes in your hand. This way, you've *got* to go the square route. You could send me a card when you're settled, I could maybe help out sometimes . . .

LILLY: (*bitter laugh*) That's what it is, isn't it? Keep me down. Your turn to be in charge, have the power.

ROY: (*stonewalling*) Just trying to help, Lilly.

She sits on the sofa again, this time leaving the attache case to stand on the coffee table. She studies ROY, calculating.

LILLY: Roy . . . What if I told you I wasn't really your mother? That we weren't related?

ROY: (*bewildered*) What?

LILLY leans back again, but this time her manner is different; languorous, sexy. She crosses her legs, the upper leg swinging gently, encouragingly, at ROY.

LILLY: You'd like that, wouldn't you? Sure you would. You don't need to tell me. Now, why would you like it, Roy?

An angle on ROY, understanding and not wanting to understand.

ROY: (*hoarse*) What's that all about? Of course you're my
mother. Of course you are.

Two shot. LILLY leans forward toward ROY, inviting him.

LILLY: (*very soft*) Roy . . . Roy . . .

ROY will not let anything complicated come to the surface.

ROY: There's nothing more to talk about.

LILLY: (*very soft*) I have to have that money, Roy. What
do I have to do to get it?

*An angle on ROY, his face bruised-looking, eyes scared. He
will not know what's going on. He shakes his head, not
trusting himself to speak. An angle on LILLY, leaning forward, tension showing through the seductive manner.*

LILLY: No? Won't you give me the money, Roy? Can't I
change your mind? What can I do to change your mind?

*Two shot, as LILLY gets to her feet and takes a step toward
him. ROY's pressed back into his chair, trying to maintain
a cold facade.*

ROY: Lilly, Jesus, what are you doing?

LILLY: Is there *nothing* I can do, Roy, nothing at—

ROY: NO!

*They both turn away at the same instant. ROY turns to the
side to pick up the glass of water, to break the spell and the
tension. LILLY turns back toward the coffee table and picks
up the attache case. ROY, lifting the glass to drink, turns
forward again as LILLY spins forward, swinging the attache
case at his head with all her might. The case crashes into
the glass and into his face. ROY screams, and topples off
the chair, as the one remaining clasp on the case lets go
and money goes flying, filling the air.*

Johnny Suede
(Miramax, 1992)

Screenplay by Tom DiCillo
Directed by Tom DiCillo
Characters: JOHNNY (Brad Pitt)
DEKE (Calvin Levels)

NOTES: JOHNNY and DEKE are friends. They live the downtown life in New York. Their goals are pretty simple: DEKE wants a motorcycle, JOHNNY wants to be a singer; he frequents the clubs. His blue suede shoes are very important to him. Recently, however, JOHNNY has been seeing Yvonne; she works, and lives uptown. She wants him to move in and he's pretty frightened of giving up his freedom. He appeals to DEKE after they finish a painting job.

2-19. EXTERIOR. JOHNNY'S ROOF—TWILIGHT

JOHNNY and DEKE lean against a low brick wall bordering the edge of the roof. Both are wearing their paint clothes. DEKE counts out some bills while JOHNNY stares broodingly at the city gleaming softly in the fading light.

DEKE: That's 500 Big Ones, man. Minus the forty you owed me. A little better than our first job, huh?

DEKE hands the bills to JOHNNY who takes them, barely looking at them.

DEKE: I'm gonna buy a motorcycle. That's right: I'm gonna take a trip somewhere. Just hop on my bike and take off.

What are you gonna do with your money? (*no response*)
All right, I'm out of here.

JOHNNY: Stick around.

DEKE: Aren't you seeing Yvonne tonight?

JOHNNY: It's my night off.

Both men stare out at the city in silence for a long moment.

JOHNNY: Want to hear something funny?

DEKE: Why not?

JOHNNY: (*pause*) Yvonne wants me to move in with her.

DEKE laughs, then stops, seeing JOHNNY isn't joining him.

DEKE: You goin' to?

JOHNNY: I don't know. Sometimes I think maybe I should, you know? Then other times I think, what am I, crazy?!!

DEKE: You should make a list.

JOHNNY: What kind of list?

DEKE: You put down all the Reasons For moving in and all the Reasons Against; then just add 'em up and the choice is made. Right there on paper—no more thinkin' about it for weeks and weeks.

JOHNNY smashes his beer bottle against the wall and heads for the stairs.

JOHNNY: Deke! That's a great idea!

DEKE: Hold on, I'll give you a hand.

2-20. INTERIOR. JOHNNY'S APARTMENT—NIGHT

Deke finishes lining out a section of blank wall with the headings: Reasons For and Reasons Against.

DEKE: What I would suggest is startin' with the Reasons For 'cause they're the hardest.

JOHNNY: Good idea.

DEKE: OK, let's have a couple.

JOHNNY: (*thinking*) You're right; these are hard.

DEKE: Off the top of your head.

JOHNNY: She's got a color TV.

DEKE: There you go. Color TV. (*writes it on the wall*)

JOHNNY: But would I watch it.

DEKE: I would.

JOHNNY: All right. (*thinks*) She's got an extra room she says I could play my guitar in. Like my own private room. But would I play my guitar if every time I had to get up and go into another room?

DEKE: Good question.

JOHNNY: Put it down.

DEKE: Private room. That's two.

JOHNNY thinks for another long moment.

JOHNNY: She's always got these nuts and crackers around to eat.

DEKE: You could eat them when you watch TV.

JOHNNY: You're right. We'll call that Snacks.

DEKE: Good. Anything else?

JOHNNY: I don't think so.

DEKE: OK, we've got Color TV, Private Room and Snacks. That's three reasons for. Let's proceed to Reasons Against.

JOHNNY: (*quickly*) She lives Uptown.

DEKE: Out of Your Element.

JOHNNY: That's good. I like that.

DEKE: Next.

JOHNNY: I'd be locked up with her 24 hours a day. Go to bed at night, there she is. Wake up in the morning, there she is again. What if I had to cut a fart? Hell, I'd probably have to go into my Private Room just to cut a fart!

DEKE: So you're sayin' you'd feel . . .

JOHNNY: I'd feel like I was in prison.

DEKE: Prison Similarities?

JOHNNY: That's it.

DEKE: OK. Number three?

JOHNNY: She's a little crazy.

DEKE: That's no good.

JOHNNY: Why not?

DEKE: You just can't say she's crazy. You got to be specific.

JOHNNY: She threw a shoe at me once.

DEKE: There, that's specific. Shoe Throwing Tendencies. All right, pal. Three to three.

JOHNNY: Let's be honest for a second, Deke.

DEKE: You got to be honest, man. It's the only way this list is any good.

JOHNNY: She's not my type. She's got a weird job, she dresses funny. Hell, do you know she's never been to a club?

DEKE: Are you serious?

JOHNNY: See what I'm saying? She's like the exact opposite of the type of girl I would be attracted to.

DEKE: Different Types.

JOHNNY: That's us.

DEKE: Alright. There it is, man. Three Reasons For, four Reasons Against.

JOHNNY: (*shakes Deke's hand*) Deke, thanks alot. That was a great idea.

DEKE: Numbers don't lie.

JOHNNY: Maybe I'll get a motorcycle too.

DEKE: Now you're talkin'!

JOHNNY: Sure! I got places I want to go in life; things I want to do!

DEKE: Hey, New Mexico, man!

JOHNNY: Wyoming!

The two men beam grins of comradeship at each other.

JOHNNY: Let's go down to Club G. I'll buy you a beer. Maybe that blonde from Queens will be there.

DEKE: She's still dyin' to meet you.

JOHNNY: I know she is. See, that's my kind of style, Deke. Two or three contrasting types of girls that I could call whenever I felt like it. And if Yvonne could accept that, fine. Just because I don't move in with her doesn't mean I have to stop seeing her, does it?

DEKE: Hell no.

JOHNNY: Cause hey, I do like the girl.

DEKE: Sure you do.

JOHNNY: I'll tell you one thing; she's great in bed.

DEKE: Nothin' wrong with that.

JOHNNY: No sir! No problems there with Yvonne.

JOHNNY and DEKE stop simultaneously just as they are about to go to the door. They stare at each other for a moment.

JOHNNY: Should I put that down?

DEKE: You said you were going to be honest.

They return to the wall and DEKE adds Great Sex to the list of Reasons For.

JOHNNY: Dammit.

DEKE: It's tied up again. Four to four.

JOHNNY: All right, be quiet. Let me think for a moment.

JOHNNY paces in front of the wall. Suddenly he stops and scrutinizes the list intently.

JOHNNY: Hold it. See this? (*points to Color TV*) I wouldn't watch it.

DEKE: You're sure?

JOHNNY: Positive.

DEKE: Well, if you wouldn't watch it then . . .

JOHNNY: Then we just cross it right off.

JOHNNY grabs the marker and crosses off Color TV. He and DEKE stare at each other for a moment.

JOHNNY: All I got to do now is find a way to tell her.

DEKE: Here's an idea. Make a copy and mail it to her.

Johnny Suede (2)
(Miramax, 1992)

Screenplay by Tom DiCillo
Directed by Tom DiCillo
Characters: YVONNE (Catherine Keener)
        JOHNNY (Brad Pitt)

NOTES: JOHNNY has moved in with YVONNE (*see previous scene*); it's now his birthday and she has prepared a celebration at home with cake and presents. JOHNNY, however, doesn't show. He has followed a girl he saw in the grocery store to her apartment and had sex with her. He falls asleep by accident, then wakes up to realize how late he is. The girl he's been with is very odd; he runs out of her apartment and rushes home.

3-16 INTERIOR. YVONNE'S APARTMENT—NIGHT
YVONNE jerks open the door and flies into JOHNNY's arms.

YVONNE: Johnny!!

JOHNNY: Hi, babe.

YVONNE: Where have you been?

JOHNNY: You won't believe it.

YVONNE: Are you all right?

JOHNNY: Me? Yeah, I'm all right.

YVONNE: (*grabs his hand*) You're bleeding!

JOHNNY: No, that's not mine. That's somebody else's. (*the "blood" is actually ink from the red china marker*)

YVONNE: What happened?

JOHNNY: Some guy got shot on the train. This fat guy; sitting right next to me—got it right in the head. I was asleep so I didn't see who did it but of course the cops got to keep me down there for six hours asking every goddam question you can imagine, over and over—

YVONNE: Why didn't you call me?

JOHNNY: They wouldn't even let me use the phone, can you believe it? I ran all the way from the station.

YVONNE: I'm so glad you're OK. I was so worried. You must be starved. Come on, you're dinner's in the fridge.

JOHNNY: I think I'll hop in the shower first.

YVONNE: (*laughs*) You do smell kind of ripe.

JOHNNY: (*jumps*) That train was like a sweatbox.

YVONNE: Well, hurry up and shower and maybe we can salvage what's left of your birthday.

JOHNNY: (*notices the cake*) Hey, you bought a cake.

YVONNE: Bought it hell. I made it.

JOHNNY: (*amazed*) You made me a cake?

YVONNE: I made you a cake; what's the big deal?

On a sudden impulse JOHNNY embraces YVONNE. As she nuzzles his neck a brief look of puzzlement passes across her face before JOHNNY quickly moves away.

INTERIOR. YVONNE'S BEDROOM—NIGHT

JOHNNY enters the room, followed by YVONNE. A small pile of gift-wrapped packages lie on the dresser.

JOHNNY: What the hell is this—Christmas? Look at these presents.

JOHNNY picks up a small package and shakes it.

YVONNE: Open it.

JOHNNY: No, I'll save it till we eat the cake.

JOHNNY kicks off his shoes and takes off his shirt. YVONNE immediately notices the red hand-shaped splotches spreading faintly across his chest.

YVONNE: What's that?

JOHNNY: (*jumps*) What?

YVONNE: (*looking closer*) Those red marks.

JOHNNY: (*turning away*) Some kind of heat rash, I guess.

YVONNE: (*pause*) Are you sure you're alright?

JOHNNY: What do you mean?

YVONNE: You're acting kind of funny.

JOHNNY: How the hell would you act if you just saw some guy get his head blown off!

At that moment JOHNNY furiously yanks down his pants. To his horror Ellen's powder-blue panties suddenly fall out and flutter to the floor at YVONNE's feet. They both stare down at them in silence.

YVONNE: (*quietly*) Look, I don't care who it was. I don't care where it was. Just tell me one thing: why did you do it?

JOHNNY: (*sighs deeply*) I don't know. I've been thinking and thinking about it and all I can say is it seems like this giant hand was behind me all day, shoving me along, and I couldn't stop it, you know?

YVONNE: A giant hand.

JOHNNY: Right. It just kept shoving me and shoving me and I was just rolling along like an old tire.

YVONNE: Rolling along.

JOHNNY: Like an old tire.

YVONNE: Too bad you weren't on the edge of a cliff!

JOHNNY: All right, I'm going to tell you something. I didn't want to move in with you in the first place. It's not my style. I've got things I want to do in my life, places I want to go. Hell, I could meet somebody tomorrow who wants me to be the lead singer in their band or go to France and make a record or anything like that and I've got to be able to go, you know? Just move, like I always have!

YVONNE: Who's stopping you?

Despite his floundering panic, JOHNNY had built a little momentum with his "explanation." YVONNE's question stops him cold.

JOHNNY: (*confused*) Nobody's stopping me.

YVONNE: Then what's the problem?

JOHNNY thinks hard for a long agonized moment.

JOHNNY: The problem is that I'm in this thing with you.

YVONNE: What thing?

JOHNNY: This . . . relationship! And I don't know how it got started and I don't know how it's going to end! That's what it is!

YVONNE: So you want it to end.

JOHNNY: No! I mean, I like you babe, I really do, but . . . (*a long silence*)

YVONNE: (*suddenly*) But what?!

JOHNNY: But . . .

YVONNE: You want to keep seeing her?

JOHNNY: Hell no. She was nothing.

YVONNE: She must have been something.

JOHNNY: She wasn't. (*pause*) She was just sitting there and I was looking at her legs. That's what it was really; she had a great pair of legs. And the next thing I know she was walking down the street and I was following her, and then I was in her place and . . . it happened. And it's not that I really enjoyed it cause I didn't, but for the first time in my life I felt like I was home. You know? Home.

JOHNNY turns to YVONNE in hopeful expectancy. She looks at him for a moment, then suddenly snatches one of the presents on the dresser and hurls it at him. It misses him and goes out the window.

JOHNNY: Hey!!

YVONNE picks up one of JOHNNY's shoes.

JOHNNY: Don't even think about it!

YVONNE hesitates for a brief moment then whips the shoe at him. JOHNNY ducks wildly and the shoe flies out the window too. He stares after it in disbelief.

JOHNNY: Goddammit!!!

Just as YVONNE turns to find something else to throw, JOHNNY grabs her by the back of her hair and slams her onto the bed on her back. Still holding her down by the hair JOHNNY cocks his other fist and tenses his entire body in preparation for punching YVONNE in the face. It is only at the last minute that he stops himself. Trembling in rage he glares down at YVONNE's terrified face.

JOHNNY: What did I tell you about throwing shoes at me!!? Huh!!? What did I tell you!!?

YVONNE merely stares at him, frozen in fear. JOHNNY recoils from the look of panic in her eyes and pulls away, suddenly horrified at what he has almost done.

Lianna
(The Winwood Company, 1982)

Screenplay by John Sayles
Directed by John Sayles
Characters: LIANNA (Linda Griffiths)
**   DICK (Jon DeVries)**

NOTES: LIANNA is the young wife of a film studies professor
at a small college. She used to be his student; they had an affair
and now have been married several years, much of it unhappily.
DICK still sleeps with his students, and takes no pains to hide it
from LIANNA. He can't or won't give it up. They have two
children now, Spencer, an adolescent, and Theda, in grade
school. They live on campus in a house provided by the school.
LIANNA wants to be defined by more than her family; she starts
taking a night school course, with little support from DICK. He
wants her to show up at faculty functions because he's hoping
for a promotion and tenure. He's very afraid he'll be passed
over. LIANNA takes her course anyway, and soon has an affair
with her professor, who happens to be a woman. This hasn't
happened to her before; she once had a teenage crush on her
camp counselor, but she's lived as a straight person her whole
adult life. She doesn't question it, however; she feels she is in
love, and almost immediately tells DICK. They've just come back
from another faculty party. DICK has been out of town at a film
festival. (This scene has been transcribed from the video.)

INTERIOR. DICK AND LIANNA'S BEDROOM—NIGHT

DICK is removing his tie and LIANNA sits on the bed, undressing.

DICK: . . . I mean, it was sort of my responsibility to stay.

LIANNA: I'm sorry, I thought you might wanna come home and talk to me. I thought you'd be tired from your trip.

DICK: I am tired, but it's part of my job. You know that. These parties are where all the "teacher evaluation" goes on. (*he goes to the closet*)

LIANNA: You're exaggerating. (*she removes her dress; she's wearing a slip*)

DICK: I'm not ex—(*he takes off his jacket and hangs it up*) Forget it. So what did you do with yourself while I was off viewing Lithuanian masterpieces?

LIANNA: Nothing. (*pause*) I had an affair.

They are sitting on opposite sides of the bed; he turns to look at her. She is looking right back at him.

DICK: Oh. Congratulations. Anyone I know?

LIANNA: Not really.

DICK: Good. Jerry Carlson was acting kind of strange tonight; I'd hate to think that he had anything on me. An affair, huh? Feel like you've gotten even?

LIANNA: That's not why it happened. (*she gets off the bed and walks to the far side of the room from him*)

DICK: Was it worth it? Was it the man of your dreams?

LIANNA: It wasn't a man.

DICK: Huh?

LIANNA: I said, it wasn't a man.

DICK starts to laugh, puts his head in his hands.

LIANNA: What's so funny?

DICK: You've come a long way from Alberta. (*He continues to undress, takes off his shoes.*) How was it—like a drug store paperback?

LIANNA: None of your business. (*she takes a step toward him*) I don't know what you're feeling so humorous about.

DICK: It's just different than if it had been a man.

LIANNA: Why? She touched me the same way you—

DICK: I don't wanna hear what you did in bed, damnit. Who is it?

LIANNA: Ruth Brennan.

DICK: Ah-ha. The pieces fall into place. I always thought there was something fishy about her.

LIANNA: There's nothing fishy about her.

DICK: She engaged in an unnatural act with my wife, I think that's pretty damn fishy. Professor Brennan, huh?

LIANNA: That's right.

DICK: (*He stands and walks away from the bed, toward the dresser.*) So you're still fucking your teachers.

LIANNA: And you're still fucking your students!

DICK: At least they're the right sex! What'd she do? Come on to you after class, offer you a friendly shoulder to cry on? (*he empties his pockets nonchalantly, puts the contents on the dresser*) Tell me, I'm interested in how they operate.

LIANNA: Who's "they"?

DICK: Campfire girls, what the hell do you think I mean?

LIANNA: Why are you being this way? You're making everything worse.

DICK: What the hell, you said it was no big thing.

LIANNA: I never said that, Dick.

DICK: It is a big thing?

LIANNA: I know it's probably never occurred to you, but it is possible that I might fall in love with somebody.

DICK: With somebody else. (*He fiddles with his change on the dresser.*)

LIANNA: With somebody.

DICK: Well, don't let me stand in your way.

LIANNA: I don't intend to.

DICK: Are you gonna keep seeing her?

LIANNA: If she wants me to.

DICK: (*an angry outburst*) The hell you are! Not while you're living with me.

LIANNA: Okay, if that's what you want. We'll get a separation.

DICK: (*he approaches her*) Where do you think you're gonna live? How do you think you're gonna support yourself?

LIANNA: What do you mean?

DICK: Move in with the professor, if you want, whatever. But I want you out of here tomorrow.

LIANNA: The hell I will!

DICK: Did you ever consider what the kids are gonna think? Or our friends and neighbors here in Faculty Land?

LIANNA: You're not telling the kids.

DICK: No. I'll leave that up to you. You'll have to think of something to explain why you're moving out.

LIANNA: Why are you being this way?

DICK: You're giving me a perfect escape route, honey. I'm taking it, that's all. (*He walks past her and sits on the bed.*)

LIANNA: You fucker. You prick!

DICK: That's it, Lianna, let it all out.

LIANNA: You always have to win, don't you? And if you lose, you make the other person lose more.

DICK: Very good, you're psych classes must be finally paying off. Must be all that private tutoring.

LIANNA: You made up your mind in Toronto, didn't you? You came back to ask for a separation, and then I dumped it right in your lap.

DICK: I did a lot of thinking while I was in Toronto.

LIANNA: You're not taking the kids from me, Dick.

DICK: (*He stands.*) That depends on you, and whether you're a true convert to the fold, or just hot for the first friendly piece of ass you—

LIANNA: God damn you—!

She flies at him. He grabs her arms and they struggle. He falls back onto the bed, still grappling with her. She grabs the telephone and starts to pummel him with it. He quickly gets the better of her and brings her to her knees. He grabs her hair and pulls her head back. He screams in her face.

DICK: I'll hurt you back, Lianna! I will! No matter how much you think you can hurt me. I can hurt you more! Understand?

She just looks at him, afraid and defiant at once. He pushes her away. She falls to the floor, then scrambles out of the room. He puts the phone back on the receiver calmly. Then he explodes. He throws something from the dresser across the room. He picks up her dress and tries to rip it. He picks up the phone and repeatedly bangs it against the dresser. Then he just sits with his head in his hands.

Lianna (2)
(The Winwood Company, 1982)

Screenplay by John Sayles
Directed by John Sayles
Characters: LIANNA (Linda Griffiths)
JERRY (John Sayles)

NOTES: LIANNA has moved out of the house she shared with Dick (*see previous scene*). She has her own apartment; it's very tiny and spare. She's gotten a job checking groceries. She hasn't been able to see her children often; Dick is making it difficult for her. She also hasn't seen a lot of her lover; Ruth has been out of town. LIANNA knows that Ruth is seeing her former lover and trying to decide who she will commit to. She has been alone a lot and it's been hard for her, adjusting all by herself. She's known JERRY for many years; he's a faculty member like her ex-husband, teaching film studies. He's lovable and he cares for her but he's also a bit of a casanova, and she knows that. (This scene has been transcribed from the video.)

INTERIOR. LIANNA'S APARTMENT—NIGHT

LIANNA is sitting in her tiny apartment, alone, reading a book. There is a knock at the door. She goes to answer it. It's JERRY.

JERRY: Hi, gorgeous.

LIANNA: Jerry! Come in!

JERRY: Hi, how're you doing? (*he kisses her*)

LIANNA: Fine.

JERRY: Hey, you've done a real nice job in here.

LIANNA: Thanks. Take a seat.

She indicates the "sitting room"; it's about as big as a foyer, with one armchair in it.

JERRY: Which one?

LIANNA: Would you like a beer or something?

JERRY: Yeah, a beer'd be great. (*She goes to get one from the fridge.*) I'm not interrupting anything, am I?

LIANNA: Nah, I was just reading.

JERRY: Reading . . . oh yeah, those funny little lines on paper, what they had before film? What're you reading?

LIANNA: *The Well of Loneliness.*

JERRY: Sounds like a riot. How much do you pay for this?

LIANNA: Too much. Two seventy five without utilities. I was kinda pressed for time.

She brings his beer and a chair from the kitchen table for herself. She sits across from him.

JERRY: Thank you. (*She hands him the beer.*) So. How's it been?

LIANNA: Not too bad. I've been, uh, a little lonely lately . . .

JERRY: I felt it in my bones. That's why I came over.

LIANNA: You could make a living with bones like that.

JERRY: Get much sun in here?

LIANNA: In the afternoon. It's nice. In the morning it comes in through my bedroom window.

JERRY: Good, I like that.

LIANNA: What?

JERRY: I said, I like that. It's a nice way to wake up.

LIANNA: Oh.

JERRY: Have you been, uh, seeing anybody since—you and Dick had your falling out?

LIANNA: If you're asking, did I leave him for somebody— no. Not really. Should've done it long ago.

JERRY: Good. (*he smiles at her*)

LIANNA: Jerry! Are you intimating what I think you are?

JERRY: I don't intimate, Lianna, you know that. I'd love to sleep with you.

LIANNA: (*she laughs*) You don't waste any time, do you?

JERRY: Well, I figure it's been a while since you and Dick split, and you said there wasn't another guy involved... You're a grown, healthy woman, and I figured I'd come over and—

LIANNA: —help me out? Like the Welcome Wagon?

JERRY: Ah—you know I've been interested in you since I've known you, and I know you've been interested in me—

LIANNA: I'm not interested. Not in sleeping with you.

JERRY: (*a bit taken aback*) Sorry if I came at you a little sudden, but ... my technique must be getting ragged. I really like you, and I wanted to—

LIANNA: I'm not interested in you, Jerry. Not at all. (*gently*) Okay?

JERRY: Sure. The Welcome Wagon knows when it's not welcome.

LIANNA: Of course you're welcome. I'm really glad to see you. I just—don't want to sleep with you. Okay?

JERRY: Okay.

Pause.

LIANNA: So how are your courses going? Have any of your students finished their films?

JERRY: Oh, they're fine. Yeah. As a matter of fact, I—I should probably go help in the cutting room tonight. I've uh, got, uh—

LIANNA: I thought you were all set to spend the night.

JERRY: Well, I've got this kid, she's a bit of a loose wind, she could use a hand, so—

LIANNA: Jerry, you don't have to—

JERRY: I'm sorry, I—I made a mistake.

LIANNA: Good night, Jerry.

He gets up and heads for the door, touching her shoulder as he goes.

JERRY: I'll see you around, okay? Um, Dick gave me your number—I'll give you a call.

She stays in her chair.

LIANNA: Good night.

JERRY: Take care.

He goes. She stays in her chair.

Life Is Sweet
(October Films, 1991)

Screenplay by Mike Leigh
Directed by Mike Leigh
Characters: NICOLA (Jane Horrocks)
          WENDY (Alison Steadman)

NOTES: WENDY is NICOLA's mother. Their small family lives in a lower-middle-class area of London. WENDY got pregnant with twins, NICOLA and her sister, when she was sixteen. She married the father; they have not had an easy life, but they haven't lost hope. NICOLA is a young woman with frustrated passions and no direction; she's deeply depressed, but she doesn't know it. WENDY has tried over and over to reach her and now makes a last-ditch attempt.

INTERIOR. NICOLA'S BEDROOM—DAY
In NICOLA's bedroom, WENDY is gathering up the vacuum cleaner. NICOLA is sitting on her bed, hugging a pillow and smoking a fag.

WENDY: Blimey day, Nicola—look at the state of you. You're sittin' there like there's a grey cloud over you, it's like the sun's gone in. You've got no energy 'cos you don't eat your dinners. And you've got no joy in your soul.

NICOLA: 'Ow do you know?

WENDY: I know, because you've given up. 'Cos you're not 'appy, that's 'ow I know. (*She takes the vacuum cleaner out on to the landing.*)

NICOLA: I am happy.

WENDY: You've lost all your friends. I don't see them knockin' on the door anymore.

NICOLA: I don't want friends. They disappoint you.

WENDY: I mean, you say you wanna change the world— you're supposed to be political, but I don't see you doin' anything about it.

NICOLA: I am political. And shut the door.

She stubs out her fag. WENDY comes to the doorway.

WENDY: How are you political?

NICOLA: I read the paper, I watch the news. I'm more political than you.

WENDY: Oh, blimey, Nicola, we can all watch the telly. You should be out there, 'elping the Old Age Pensioners or goin' on marches or whatever.

NICOLA: Marching's a waste of time. It's boring.

WENDY: If you put your money where your mouth is, you should be joining one of these Socialist . . . whatsit groups, or the Nuclear Disarmament whatever, but you don't. All you do is sit 'ere in this room, starin' at the walls, and tweakin' and twitchin'. (*She makes to go, closing the door almost completely.*)

NICOLA: And you're so perfect!

Pause. WENDY opens the door again and leans on the frame.

WENDY: No . . . I'm not perfect, but I 'aven't given up. I'm still out there, fightin'. And I tell you what, Nicola . . . Every time I look out that window and I see that rusty old caravan sittin' there, do you know what it says to me? It says to me there's a man who 'asn't given up either, who's still out there fightin', lookin' for his dream.

NICOLA: Well, it says to me, there's a man who's gettin' greedy.

WENDY: Greedy? Your dad? 'E's the most unselfish man I've ever met. D'you know, he's up six o'clock every mornin', sloggin' 'is guts out in a job he 'ates—which is more than you do. And 'e still comes home at the end of the week with sod all.

NICOLA: I'm not prepared to be exploited.

WENDY: Exploited? You're not prepared to work, full stop.

NICOLA: You've accepted Nat as a plumber, and you didn't like that at first.

WENDY: No, I didn't; I didn't like it. But I can see now I was wrong, because he's happy.

NICOLA: I don't know what I want to do, yet.

WENDY: Oh, don't you? Well, you 'ad your chance, Nicola, when you were seventeen, when you were at the college doin' your three A-levels. You were goin' great, and then suddenly you stopped. You stopped eatin', you stopped everything—you ended up eight weeks in the 'ospital.

NICOLA: Well, you put me there—I didn't wanna go.

WENDY: Oh, for God's sake, Nicola, you were at death's door.

NICOLA: You were trying to control my life!

WENDY: You were dying!

NICOLA: No, I wasn't.

WENDY: Yes, you were!

NICOLA: I'd know if I were dying!

WENDY: Dr. Harris told us, you had two weeks to live!!

Pause. NICOLA is shaken by this news.

WENDY: (*cont'd*) You didn't know that, did you? The three of us, comin' 'ome every night, cryin' our eyes out. You were lucky. Life's not easy, Nicola. I could've given up, right? Sixteen, I was doin' me A-levels.

NICOLA: What A-levels?

WENDY: English and Business Studies, if you must know. And then I got pregnant with twins.

NICOLA: Well, why didn't you 'ave an abortion?

WENDY: Because I didn't want one, because I 'ad two little lives growin' inside me. I don't believe in it—that's the easy way out. Your dad was only seventeen. 'E was at catering college, and he was workin' in hotels at night, tryin' to get a bit extra. We got a little flat together; begged and borrowed—couple o' cots. And when the two of you were born, we were thrilled to bits. Because we 'ad two lovely little babies. We came through, laughin'.

NICOLA: Well, don't blame me! I didn't ask to be born!

WENDY: I'm not blamin' you, Nicola. I just want you to be happy, that's all, and you're not. I wouldn't care what bloomin' job you did, I wouldn't care 'ow scruffy you looked, as long as you were happy. But you're not. Something inside you's died. You've given up. And if one day I could just walk through that door, and you could look at me and you could say, "Look, Mum, help me, please— I don't know what I'm doin', I don't know where I'm goin' . . . Then I'd say, "Great, because now we can be honest with each other. Now we can start talkin'."

NICOLA: But I'm not in a mess.

WENDY: Aren't you?

NICOLA: You're givin' me a problem when I 'aven't got one.

WENDY: Christ, Nicola . . .

Pause.

NICOLA: If you 'ate me so much, why don't you throw me out?

WENDY: We don't hate you. We love you, right? You stupid girl!

She goes out, closing the door. NICOLA sobs uncontrollably. Whilst downstairs in the living room, WENDY is also having a quiet cry.

Lone Star
(Sony Pictures Classics, 1996)

Screenplay by John Sayles
Directed by John Sayles
Characters: SAM (Chris Cooper)
          PILAR (Elizabeth Pena)

NOTES: SAM DEEDS is sheriff of a small Texas border town. SAM's father, Buddy Deeds, was a deputy in the late fifties under a corrupt sheriff, Charlie Wade, but Buddy stood up to Charlie's bullying and Charlie disappeared soon after, never to be heard from again. Buddy then became sheriff, and was loved and respected by the whole town, even though he didn't always do things by the book, either. SAM has to live in the shadow of his father, who is now dead. He did marry and move away, but he came back when his marriage failed. Human bones have recently been found in the desert, and SAM thinks they belong to Charlie Wade. He begins to question the older people of the town, knowing he might find out that his father was responsible. His teenage love, PILAR, still lives in the town and teaches school. She is a widow, with two teenage children. Her mother runs the town cafe. SAM and PILAR were always kept apart by their parents; they thought for the obvious reasons. They didn't know that Buddy and Mercedes, PILAR's mother, were lovers, and that Buddy is PILAR's father. They are half brother and sister. They have always had a special love and it still lives. They are tentative around each other. They are both at the unveiling of a special statue of Buddy at the courthouse.

EXTERIOR. SAN JACINTO STREET—DAY

The bystanders laugh. SAM steps away, intercepting Mercedes as she steps away—

SAM: Nice to see you, Mrs. Cruz.

Mercedes just looks at him, keeps going. His gaze brings him to PILAR, standing on the sidewalk, watching. SAM steps over from the dispersing crowd—

SAM: Field trip?

PILAR: Lunch hour. My next class isn't until one-thirty.

SAM: Want to take a walk?

EXTERIOR. RIVERSIDE—DAY

SAM and PILAR walk together alongside the Rio—

SAM: Your mother still doesn't like me.

PILAR: I can't name anybody she does like these days.

SAM: I see she built a place up here by the river.

PILAR: A real palace. She rattles around alone in that thing—

SAM: She's done well for herself—on her own and all—

PILAR: So she tells me three times a week.

She looks at him—

PILAR: I thought you got through that pretty well.

SAM: They cooked the whole thing up without asking me.

PILAR: People liked him.

SAM: Most people did, yeah.

PILAR: I remember him watching me once. When I was little—before you and I—

She shrugs.

PILAR: I was on the playground with all the other kids, but I thought he was only looking at me. I was afraid he was going to arrest me—he had those eyes, you know—

SAM: Yeah.

PILAR: Weird what you remember.

They walk in silence a moment—

SAM: Your boy, there—

PILAR: Amado.

SAM: Nice-looking kid.

PILAR: He hates me.

SAM: No—

PILAR: With Paloma, it's more like she tolerates and pities me—totally age-appropriate. But Amado—he's—he's never been book-smart. Had a hard time learning to read. Me being a teacher and caring about those things is like an embarrassment—like a betrayal.

SAM: Fernando did okay, and he dropped out—

PILAR: Fernando wasn't pissed off at everybody. He just wanted to fix their cars.

SAM: It might be just the age. I spent my first fifteen years trying to be just like Buddy and the next fifteen years trying to give him a heart attack.

She looks at him—

PILAR: So why did you come back here, Sam?

SAM: Got divorced. I wasn't gonna work for my father-in-law anymore. The fellas down here said they'd back me—

PILAR: You don't want to be Sheriff.

SAM: I got to admit it's not what I thought it'd be. Back when Buddy had it—hell, I'm just a jailer. Run a sixty-room hotel with bars on the windows.

PILAR: It can happen so sudden, can't it? Being left out on your own.

SAM: You've got you mother, your kids—

PILAR: They've got me. Different thing.

They stop at a spot where you can climb down the bank—

SAM: Remember this?

PILAR looks at the spot. She isn't ready to deal with whatever memory it brings back—

PILAR: I should get back.

SAM: Pilar—

PILAR: Looks real bad if the teacher's late for class. It's really nice to talk with you, Sam.

She waves and walks away, feeling awkward. SAM watches for a minute, then turns and steps down to the bank. He looks at the water—

Lone Star (2)
(Sony Pictures Classics, 1996)

Screenplay by John Sayles
Directed by John Sayles
Characters: SAM (Chris Cooper)
             BUNNY (Frances McDormand)

NOTES: SAM was once married to BUNNY (*see notes for previous scene*) and he worked for her father, but the marriage failed, and they now live in different towns in Texas. BUNNY is, indeed, unbalanced. She is depressed, has obviously had some episodes with fire, and covers her deep anxiety with a football obsession. SAM shows up to pick up some things he stored with her; he has taken over the job of sheriff in his home town like his father before him and he thinks in his father's belongings might be a clue to a murder mystery from the town's past that he is trying to unravel. SAM and BUNNY are in their thirties.

INTERIOR. LIVING ROOM, KINCAID HOUSE—DAY
SAM's ex-wife, BUNNY KINCAID, shuffles across her living room in slippers, crossing to turn off a big-screen TV playing football highlights. BUNNY wears shorts, a Houston Oilers sweatshirt and a Dallas Cowboys cap. The living room is like a sports museum—signed footballs, team posters, a bookcase filled with tapes of Texas pro and college football games—

BUNNY: The Longhorns gonna kick some serious butt this Saturday, just you watch. We got a kid at tailback from down your way—outta El Indio—

SAM: (*OS*) That's in Maverick County.

She brings us to SAM, sitting uncomfortably beneath a full-size blow-up of Tony Dorsett hurdling a tackler—

BUNNY: Oh. Right. And you're in—?

SAM: Rio.

BUNNY: Right. This kid, Hosea Brown? Does the 40 in 3.4, soft hands, lateral movement—the whole package. Only a sophomore—

SAM: You still going to all the home games?

BUNNY: Well, Daddy's got his box at the stadium, of course, and I'll fly to the Cowboy away games when they're in the Conference. Then there's the high school on Friday nights—West Side got a boy 6'6", 310, moves like a cat. High school, we're talkin'. Guess how much he can bench-press?

SAM: Bunny, you—uhm—you on that same medication?

BUNNY: Do I seem jumpy?

SAM: No, no—you look good. I was just wondering.

BUNNY: Last year was awful rough—Mama passing on and the whole business with O.J.—I mean it's not like it was Don Meredith or Roger Staubach or one of our own boys, but it really knocked me for a loop—

SAM: You look good—

BUNNY: —and that squeaker the Aggies dropped to Oklahoma—sonofabitch stepped in some lucky shit before he kicked that goal—

SAM: Yeah, well—

BUNNY: —they hadn't pulled me off that woman I would have jerked a knot in her.

SAM: You were in a fight—

BUNNY: Daddy calls it an "altercation." How you doing, Sam? You look skinny.

SAM: Same weight as I always was.

BUNNY: You look awful good in that uniform, though.

SAM: Best part of the job.

BUNNY: Daddy hired a pin-head to take your job. He says so himself. Says, "Even my son-in-law was better than this pin-head I got now."

SAM: Bunny, is that stuff I left in the garage still there?

BUNNY: Least he never called me that. With me, it was always "high-strung." "My Bunny might have done something with her life, she wasn't so high-strung." Or "tightly wound," that was another one. You seeing anyone?

SAM: No. You?

BUNNY: Yeah. Sort of. Daddy rounds 'em up. You aren't talking about money, their beady little eyes go dead.

SAM: You didn't—uhm—you didn't have one of your fires, did you? The stuff I left in the garage—some of it was my father's—

BUNNY: You watch the draft this year? 'Course you didn't, idiot question. They try to make it dramatic, like there's some big surprise who picks who in the first round? Only they been working it over with their experts and their computers for months. Doctor's reports, highlight reels, coaches' evaluations, psychological profiles—hell, I wouldn't be surprised if they collected stool samples on these boys, have 'em analyzed. All this stuff to pick a football player for your squad. Compared to that, what you know about the person you get married to doesn't amount to diddly, does it?

SAM: Suppose not.

BUNNY: You kind of bought yourself a pig in a poke, didn't you, Sam? All that time we were first seeing each other you didn't know I was tightly wound—

SAM: It wasn't just you, Bunny.

BUNNY: No, it wasn't, was it? You didn't exactly throw yourself into it heart and soul, did you?

She looks at him for an uncomfortably long moment—

BUNNY: Your shit's still in the garage if that's what you came for.

SAM nods, stands. BUNNY is in tears—

BUNNY: 350 pounds.

SAM: What?

BUNNY: This boy from West Side, plays tackle both ways. Bench-presses 350 pounds. You imagine having that much weight on top of you? Pushing down? Be hard to breathe. Hard to swallow.

SAM: I think they have another fella there to keep it off your chest. A spotter.

BUNNY: "I only got my little girl now," he says, "she's my lifeline." Then he tells me I can't be in the box anymore if I can't control myself. Sonofabitch don't even watch the damn game, just sits there drinking with his bidness friends, look up the the TV now and then. I'd do better to sit in the cheap seats with some real football people.

SAM: *(edging out)* You look good, Bunny. It's nice to see you.

BUNNY: *(smiles)* Thanks. I like it when you say that, Sam.

Love And Human Remains

(Sony Pictures Classics, 1995)

Screenplay by Brad Fraser
Directed by Denys Arcand
Characters: CANDY (Ruth Marshall)
           DAVID (Thomas Gibson)

NOTES: CANDY and DAVID are close friends, roommates, and ex-lovers. They live in a large city in Canada. DAVID is bisexual. Most of his lovers now are men. He is an actor, and has had some success, but he is not pursuing it right now. He works as a waiter. CANDY works as a book reviewer, and parties with DAVID sometimes, but she feels something missing from her life. They are both in their twenties.

INTERIOR. CANDY AND DAVID'S LIVING ROOM—NIGHT

DAVID sits on the futon watching One Flew Over the Cuckoo's Nest. *It is the "invisible baseball game" scene. CANDY is writing at her computer. The movie is replaced by a commercial for telephone sex. Two slightly dumpy blonde women in corsets touch one another and smile at the camera as a loud male voice-over is heard. CANDY and DAVID speak over the commercial.*

ANNOUNCER: *(on television)* Alone. Bored. Looking for friends? Have we got the line for you—five three zero Hott. That's H-O-T-T. Five three zero four six eight eight, where beautiful babes are waiting to talk to you.

CANDY: This bartender wants to take me out.

DAVID: Hold out for a brain surgeon.

CANDY: It's either him or the lesbian I met at the gym today.

DAVID: Take the bartender. Mixed marriages seldom work.

CANDY: I'm cereal.

DAVID: Darling, one doesn't seriously discuss changing their sexual orientation after thirty. People lose respect.

The commercials end and the movie resumes. CANDY's attention returns to her computer screen as they talk. DAVID watches the movie.

CANDY: I want more than just sex.

DAVID indicates the television.

DAVID: That's why God invented video.

CANDY: I need some tenderness in my life.

DAVID: Pick the lesbian.

CANDY: I'm nervous.

DAVID: Candy, you're talking about a date. Not a lifetime commitment.

DAVID grabs the remote and flips the channels. He stops at Imitation of Life. *Lana Turner is speaking to a fat black woman in a very insincere manner. CANDY forgets her computer screen and turns to DAVID.*

CANDY: Don't you ever wish you had a lover?

DAVID: I have many lovers.

CANDY: Not lover lovers.

DAVID: It didn't work for us.

DAVID flips back to One Flew Over the Cuckoo's Nest. *CANDY begins to type again.*

CANDY: That was different.

DAVID: I'm not into settling down.

CANDY: Deep down you want someone to be special for you.

DAVID: I'm quite capable of being special for myself.

CANDY: Were you in love with me?

DAVID flips back to **Imitation of Life.**

DAVID: I don't know.

CANDY: People do fall in love—for the rest of their lives.

DAVID: Not me.

CANDY: (*OS*) Look at my parents.

DAVID flips back to **One Flew Over the Cuckoo's Nest.**

DAVID: Your parents are the Munsters in normal clothes.

CANDY: You're wrong, David. Everyone needs to be loved.

DAVID: That's why we have friends.

DAVID flips back to **Imitation of Life.**

CANDY: It's not the same.

DAVID: You're saying my relationships with you and Bernie are invalid?

CANDY: I don't like him.

CANDY rises and paces around the room, agitated.

DAVID: (sarcastic) No.

CANDY: He's weird, David.

DAVID: He's not.

CANDY: What was that blood on my face cloth?

DAVID gives CANDY an annoyed look and flips back to **One Flew Over the Cuckoo's Nest.**

DAVID: He was in a fight.

CANDY: Were you in love with me?

DAVID frowns as he watches the movie. He doesn't like this sort of conversation.

DAVID: That's not the right phrase.

CANDY: It seemed like you were in love with me.

DAVID: There's no such thing.

CANDY: I know you were in love with me.

DAVID flips to **Imitation of Life**. *CANDY grabs the remote from his hand. She speaks with a lot more anger than the situation warrants.*

CANDY: For Christ's sake pick a channel!

DAVID gives her a confused look. He's not understanding this at all. CANDY's anger evaporates and she seems to become depressed.

CANDY: I'm going to bed.

CANDY begins to exit the living room.

DAVID: No kisses?

CANDY turns to DAVID and blows him two half-hearted kisses and leaves. DAVID's concentration returns to the movie. Lana Turner is speaking to an oily-looking man.

LANA TURNER: I know I've been away from it for a long time—but I really can act.

DAVID watches the movie with a lot more interest than it deserves.

Love And
Human Remains (2)
(Sony Pictures Classics, 1995)

Screenplay by Brad Fraser
Directed by Denys Arcand
Characters: DAVID (Thomas Gibson)
*   BERNIE (Cameron Bancroft)*

NOTES: BERNIE is also a longtime friend of DAVID's, in his twenties. He works in a typical white-collar office job and has an active straight sex life. He is actually psychotic, and has recently become a serial killer. Several women have been brutally murdered in the city, and it's in the news everywhere. BERNIE has a certain special attachment to DAVID. After one of his recent murders, he showed up at DAVID's apartment (*see previous scene*) drunk and bloody. Now he goes to DAVID for understanding, but can't seem to tell DAVID what the problem is.

EXTERIOR. THE ROOFTOP OF CANDY AND DAVID'S BUILDING—NIGHT
DAVID and BERNIE sit on the ledge of the rooftop sharing a bottle of scotch in a brown paper bag.

DAVID: You happy?

BERNIE: Sometimes. You?

DAVID shrugs.

DAVID: Everything's changed so much.

DAVID hands the bottle to BERNIE and contemplates the prairie sky.

DAVID: You can't see a sky that endless anywhere else. There's always something in the way, y'know?

BERNIE: Not all of us got to leave.

DAVID: You should've come to visit me.

BERNIE: I couldn't.

BERNIE turns away from DAVID, swinging his legs over the ledge of the roof so his feet dangle above the street. DAVID gives him a nervous look but says nothing.

DAVID: You okay?

BERNIE: Why's everything so fucking hard?

DAVID: Not everything. Just the important stuff.

BERNIE: It's always the same bullshit. Everyday. Go to work. Meet a babe. Get laid. Dump them.

DAVID: Who're you dumping now?

BERNIE: Linda.

DAVID: Who's Linda?

BERNIE: This chick I fuck sometimes.

DAVID: I hope you're playing safe.

BERNIE: I think you need to worry about that more than I do.

DAVID: It's the same for everyone, Bernie.

BERNIE: You think about it that much?

DAVID: I don't want to die.

BERNIE: Nothing's any fun if the possibility isn't there.

DAVID: You mean that?

BERNIE looks faraway for a moment, as if he is thinking of something very personal.

BERNIE: (*quietly*) Sure.

DAVID looks at BERNIE curiously.

DAVID: Jesus.

BERNIE rolls onto his stomach and looks over the ledge to the sidewalk below.

BERNIE: Y'know what I like best about coming up here?

DAVID: What?

BERNIE: You can spit on anyone walking by and they'll never know where it came from.

DAVID: (*laughs*) You're damaged.

BERNIE turns to DAVID and gives him an angelic smile. (CUT TO)

BERNIE sits on the ledge, once more dangling his legs over the edge. DAVID stands on the roof surface, leaning on the edge.

BERNIE: When are you gonna get a real job?

DAVID: Waiting tables is a respectable profession.

BERNIE: It's kid stuff, Bernie.

DAVID: At least I work hard for the money I earn.

BERNIE: Now.

DAVID: I always did.

BERNIE takes the last swig from the scotch bottle. He throws it out overhand. They both listen. After a moment there is the distant tinkle of breaking glass.

DAVID: Acting is hard work.

BERNIE: Is that why you don't do it anymore?

DAVID wanders away from the ledge. The sound of a distant siren is heard moving east on Jasper Avenue—toward them.

DAVID: Acting's not the problem. It's auditioning. I hate it.

BERNIE: Hard to act if you don't audition.

DAVID: I just need some time.

BERNIE: When're you gonna do something with your life?

DAVID: (*mildly*) Like you? Work at a job I hate and fuck women I can't stand?

BERNIE: It's a life.

DAVID: Not the kind of life I want.

BERNIE: When are you gonna grow up?

DAVID: What is this?!

BERNIE's anger has been growing steadily. He explodes.

BERNIE: I don't fucking know you anymore!

DAVID: What?

BERNIE checks his anger and speaks more reasonably, but there seems to be something else—a kind of pain or anger— underneath his words.

BERNIE: I used to know what you thought. You used to know what I thought. But we're not in touch like that anymore.

DAVID shrugs. BERNIE takes DAVID's head in his hands and presses his forehead against DAVID's. He looks into DAVID's eyes.

BERNIE: What's in your head, David?

DAVID isn't sure if BERNIE's being serious or not. He laughs nervously.

DAVID: What's in your head, Bernie?

BERNIE lets go of DAVID and pulls away. He seems disappointed.

BERNIE: It's all changed.

DAVID: We're not kids anymore.

BERNIE sighs, his body sags slightly. DAVID moves to BERNIE and puts his hand on his shoulder.

DAVID: Bern?

BERNIE violently pulls his shoulder away. DAVID recoils from BERNIE's anger. BERNIE seems to catch himself again. He speaks more reasonably.

BERNIE: It's fucked.

DAVID: (*confused*) What?

BERNIE gestures out at the city and the world beyond.

BERNIE: Everything.

DAVID is really having trouble keeping up. He lights a cigarette.

DAVID: You trying to tell me something?

BERNIE stands on the ledge. He moves out so the toes of his shoes protrude beyond the edge of the roof. DAVID watches him, horrified. BERNIE holds out his hand to DAVID.

BERNIE: Take my hand.

DAVID: Why?

BERNIE: Just do it.

DAVID takes BERNIE's hand and steps onto the ledge. They both look at the sidewalk below.

BERNIE: Let's jump.

DAVID carefully withdraws his hand from BERNIE's and steps off the ledge onto the roof. He stares at BERNIE. BERNIE steps back slightly from the edge and stares out over the city. DAVID butts his cigarette beneath his foot. BERNIE steps onto the roof.

DAVID: I'm going to the club.

BERNIE: Need a ride?

DAVID: No. Thanks.

DAVID walks to the ladder side of the rooftop and prepares to descend. He stares at BERNIE for a moment, as if he might say something, then decides not to and continues down the ladder. BERNIE moves to the ladder side of the rooftop and watches DAVID moving into the alley. He smiles a bit sadly.

Love Life
(Trimark, 1997)

Screenplay by Jon Harmon Feldman
Directed by Jon Harmon Feldman
Characters: MOLLY (Sherilyn Fenn)
ALAN (John Tenney)

NOTES: ALAN and MOLLY are a couple; they've been together for a few years. He is a professor of literature at a small college, and an unpublished writer, often arrogant, somewhat lost. She is his girlfriend, without her own goals or self-definitions, not highly educated, but a very kind and sensitive person. They live together and plan to marry. She is starting to feel a need to find her own creativity, and has begun a course in television writing. ALAN, meanwhile, has initiated an affair with another woman, Zoey, someone they both know in their circle of acquaintances. In this scene, ALAN has cheated on MOLLY only a few times. He is sitting on the sofa, dozing, dreaming of having sex with Zoey, when MOLLY's voice breaks into his dream. He imagines that she is walking in on him and Zoey. (This scene has been transcribed from the video.)

INTERIOR. ALAN AND MOLLY'S HOUSE—DAY
MOLLY comes into the house, where ALAN is asleep on the sofa.
MOLLY: Alan? Alan?
MOLLY walks into the living room.

MOLLY: Alan? Alaaan . . .

She sneaks up on him, kneels beside him and wakes him up playfully.

MOLLY: Alan! (*She laughs as he wakes up.*) Hi!

ALAN: Hi.

MOLLY: So what did you think? Did I write it well?

ALAN: (*picks up the pages on his lap*) Yeah, you know, it's um, hard—it's a start. It's two pages.

MOLLY: Come on, tell me. Really.

ALAN: It's hard to say. It's two pages. It's missing the, uh, middle and end. It's most of the beginning. What?

MOLLY: Wouldn't it be easier just to say you don't like it?

She stands and walks across him to the other end of the sofa.

ALAN: Honey, it's two pages! What do you think, you're gonna sit down the first time and write *Moby Dick*?

MOLLY: Well no, it's not a novel, it's for television.

She sits on the other end of the sofa and faces him.

ALAN: Well, okay, the television equivalent of *Moby Dick*. What is that, *The Jeffersons*?

MOLLY: (*laughing*) You're so funny, Alan.

ALAN: (*testy*) Honey, what do you think I do all day? Do you think I write two pages and pat myself on the back? I mean, it—no, I'm sorry. You know, you're right. Jesus. What was I thinking? This—you know, I think you should *retire* on these two pages. Really. Because I must have been out of my mind. 'Cause I think you have reached insights here that just have eluded the greatest—ah, (*reading from paper*) "I like being a kid. No one expects anything of me." Oh boy, that just really—

She stands, takes the paper from him, and starts to walk away.

ALAN: (*cont'd*) What do you want me to say? It's two pages! I can't—(*He starts to stand and stubs his toe on* *something.*) Ow! Fuck! Goddammit! Fucking lamp! (*He strikes at it.*)

MOLLY: (*returns to him*) You okay? You want me to get you some ice?

ALAN: I'm fine! It's just like this, fucking, like knitting needles, and just like, you stub your toe on everything around, it's like a little household, a household mine field of household disasters! (*sighs*) I should walk around on stilts in this place, really, it's like this fucking pigsty, lookit—

She starts to gather up the mess.

ALAN: (*cont'd*) Leave it there, it's my shirt, I'll pick it up.

MOLLY: Oh, it's just a few things. (*She takes shirts and boots and heads for the bedroom.*)

ALAN: Yeah, it's my mess. Don't pick it up! They're mine! You don't have to pick it up! You don't have to clean up!

MOLLY: I'm putting 'em in the hamper, okay?

ALAN: Well, *don't* put 'em in the fucking hamper! (*She goes into the bedroom.*) Jesus Christ, listen to me. No, don't listen to me! I—Why do you put up with me? Jesus Christ! I lecture you on your writing, like, I mean, what do I know? I mean, I can't con anyone into publishing *my* stuff! I come home late, I don't call you—this place is a fucking pigsty and it's my fault! It's my mess! And you clean it up!

MOLLY: (*in bedroom*) It's not that bad.

ALAN: (*getting up and going to her*) I mean, everything is my fucking fault! Why don't you get angry at me? Really! Why don't you just tell me, Alan, you are a real prick, you know that?

MOLLY: Because you're not! You're—why would I say that?

ALAN: I am a prick, you know that.

MOLLY: I wish you'd stop saying that.

ALAN: You know, sometimes I wonder what it would take for you to get angry at me? Really. (*He walks back into*

the living room and she follows him.) What it would take
for you to say Alan, you are a real prick. I mean, if there
is such a thing. If there is such an act that could be per-
petrated—(*He stops himself. Sighs.*)

MOLLY: Alan, do me a favor and tell me what it is you've
done.

ALAN: Done? No, I, I haven't—

MOLLY: Tell me!

ALAN: (*nods*) Okay. Okay. I met someone. You know,
someone else. I don't want you to think it's you. It's not,
you know, some shortcoming in you—Goddamn toe! Why
do you want to marry me? Why do you think I'd be better
at marriage than I am at anything else in my life? Oh, Jesus
Christ, I, I feel nothing but full of these horrible cliches
right now.

MOLLY: And what a crime to be unoriginal. Right, Alan?

ALAN: Look, I don't want you to worry. I'll move out. I
want you to keep the house, we're paid up through the end
of the month, and I'll, I'll get out. You know, I'll steer
clear.

MOLLY: I'll have a place by morning. I'll have a great fucking place.

Love Serenade
(Miramax, 1997)

Screenplay by Shirley Barrett
Directed by Shirley Barrett
Characters: VICKI-ANN (Rebecca Frith)
*   DIMITY (Miranda Otto)*

NOTES: VICKI-ANN and DIMITY are sisters living in a very small town in Australia. VICKI-ANN is outgoing to the point of overbearing, and constantly tries to push her sister into doing something with her life. She is a bustling, high-strung woman who desperately wants love, sex and companionship in her life but needs to relax a bit to receive it. DIMITY is very shy and introverted. She is younger than her sister and her social skills are quite underdeveloped. She doesn't have much interest in developing them, either. When the small town gets a new D.J. at the radio station (a very well-known radio personality who has mysteriously taken a job here), and he moves in next door, VICKI-ANN develops a major crush. But Ken Sherry, the D.J., seduces DIMITY instead. It has just happened this morning and DIMITY doesn't quite understand all the ramifications. She shows up at the place where she and her sister have lunch together.

EXTERIOR. SUNRAY ROTARY PARK—DAY
DIMITY sits waiting at the concrete picnic table. She is wearing one of Ken Sherry's shirts and looking extremely

233

self-conscious about it. She ties it at the waist, just above the elastic of her track suit pants. She unties it again. She crosses her legs, and affects a sophisticated womanly sort of pose, which she holds rigidly till suddenly VICKI-ANN is upon her, carrying their brown paper lunch bags.

VICKI-ANN: Hi.

DIMITY: Hi.

VICKI-ANN: What's wrong?

DIMITY: Nothing's wrong. Why?

VICKI-ANN: You're sitting funny.

She passes DIMITY her sandwich bag.

VICKI-ANN: Here you go.

DIMITY: Thanks.

They sit at either side of the table and begin to munch on their sandwiches.

VICKI-ANN: He was late today.

DIMITY: Who?

VICKI-ANN: Ken Sherry.

They continue munching for a few moments. VICKI-ANN is obviously deeply preoccupied. DIMITY gazes admiringly at Ken Sherry's shirt while she eats.

VICKI-ANN: I wonder if he's gone and got a girlfriend already.

DIMITY: Why do you say that?

VICKI-ANN: I don't know. Just something he said on the radio today.

The Rotary Park crow hops on the table between them, looking menacingly at their lunches.

DIMITY: (*to the crow*) Go away!

The crow ignores her.

VICKI-ANN: Maybe I'm reading too much into it.

The crow pecks hopefully at a bag containing buns.

DIMITY: (*to the crow*) Go away!

She shoos him vigorously till he flies off. They continue eating their sandwiches. VICKI-ANN's eyes fall on DIMITY's shirt. She stares at it as she chews.

VICKI-ANN: Whose shirt is that?

DIMITY: What, this shirt?

VICKI-ANN: Yes, that shirt.

DIMITY: This is my boyfriend's shirt.

VICKI-ANN: Your *boyfriend*?

DIMITY nods complacently. VICKI-ANN snorts.

VICKI-ANN: (*derisively*) Who's your boyfriend? Albert?

DIMITY shakes her head as she chews.

DIMITY: No.

VICKI-ANN: Who then?

DIMITY: Ken Sherry.

VICKI-ANN: Excuse me?

DIMITY: Ken Sherry.

VICKI-ANN: Um, excuse me very much, Dimity, but I don't think Ken Sherry is your boyfriend.

DIMITY: Well, we had sex this morning.

VICKI-ANN stares at her for about three solid minutes. Then, in rather a high-pitched, whiny tone:

VICKI-ANN: *What did you do that for?*

DIMITY: What?

VICKI-ANN: Have sex with Ken Sherry!

DIMITY: He wanted to!

VICKI-ANN: You threw yourself at him!

DIMITY: No, I didn't!

VICKI-ANN: *Don't you realize he's trying to get over a painful divorce? He doesn't want to be having sex with people!*

DIMITY: Yes, he does . . .

Suddenly VICKI-ANN seems to have stopped breathing. She is bright red, jaw agape, making a frightful strangled noise. Her eyes begin to bulge, the veins in her neck begin to pop. DIMITY throws down her sandwich in dismay.

DIMITY: Jesus, Vicki-Ann!

She gets up and begins to thump VICKI-ANN resoundingly on the back.

DIMITY: *Breathe! Come on, breathe, Vicki-Ann, breathe!*

With a dreadful gasping sound VICKI-ANN finally begins to breathe large, gulping, stertorous breaths.

DIMITY: (*briskly*) That's right, in, out. In, out. In, out.

Finally VICKI-ANN regains her composure. Her color recedes, her breathing restores. DIMITY returns to her side of the table, picks up her sandwich despondently and resumes her lunch. Slowly, a little shakily, VICKI-ANN stands up and points a finger at DIMITY.

VICKI-ANN: That's it. I wash my hands of you. You're no longer my sister. I've done nothing but care for you and look after you all my life and now you've betrayed me. You've betrayed my trust and you've betrayed Ken Sherry's trust. No longer speak to me.

She stomps off. DIMITY watches her go, then yells after her.

DIMITY: I'm allowed to have a boyfriend too, you know!

VICKI-ANN turns around and comes right back up to DIMITY.

VICKI-ANN: What did you say?

DIMITY seems to have lost a bit of conviction now that VICKI-ANN is standing right over her.

DIMITY: You heard.

VICKI-ANN: Having sex with someone does not mean they're your boyfriend, Dimity.

And with that, she trudges off.

Manhattan
(United Artists, 1979)

Screenplay by Woody Allen
Directed by Woody Allen
Characters: TRACY (Mariel Hemingway)
*   IKE (Woody Allen)*

NOTES: IKE and TRACY had a relationship which is now de-
funct. He is many years her senior; he's about forty and she is
eighteen. They have a certain honesty in their communication,
however. After a failed affair with MARY, IKE realizes that he
loves TRACY and shows up at her apartment, where she is preparing to leave for theater school in London.

EXTERIOR. MANHATTAN SIDEWALK—DAY

The camera shows the lobby of TRACY's apartment house,
looking outside from its interior. A limousine is parked at
the curb. The music changes to "But Not for Me" as IKE
runs onto the screen. He looks inside the glass doors,
breathing hard. He looks pleased. TRACY, in a trim suit, is
standing by the elevators, handing her luggage to a chauf-
feur. The driver leaves the building; TRACY takes a brush
out of her purse and begins to run it through her hair. She
brushes her hair for a moment, then stops, brush in hand,
as she sees IKE standing outside. IKE walks inside the lobby
while the chauffeur puts TRACY's suitcases into the lim-
ousine. IKE walks over to TRACY. The orchestrations of

"But Not For Me" are heard in the background. IKE looks at TRACY. She looks at him, playing with her brush's bristles.

IKE: (*sighing*) Hi.

TRACY: (*sighing*) Hi.

IKE: Tsch, I . . . (*he clears his throat*)

TRACY: What're you doing here?

IKE: Tsch. (*sighing*) Well, (*clearing his throat again*) I ran. (*catching his breath, sniffing*) Tsch, I-I tried to call you on the phone, but, uh . . . it was busy, so (*inhaling*) I know that was two hours worth of . . . (*TRACY chuckles*) So then I couldn't get a taxi cab, so I ran. (*breathing heavily*) Tsch . . . Where you going?

TRACY: London.

IKE: (*reacting, looking away for a moment*) You're going to London now? You mean if—What do you—what do you mean? If I—if I got over here two minutes later, you'd be—you'd be—you'd be . . . going to London? (*TRACY sighs and nods her head; IKE sighs too*) Well, I—let me get right to the point then. (*clearing his throat*) I don't think you oughta go. I think I made a big mistake. And I would prefer it if y-you didn't go.

TRACY: (*sighing*) Oh, Isaac.

IKE: I—I mean it. I know it looks real bad now (*chuckling*) but, uh . . . you know—it, uh, uh, are you—are you seeing anybody? Are you going with anybody?

TRACY: (*shaking her head*) No.

IKE: (*sighing and shrugging*) So . . . well . . . you st-st-st— Do you still love me or has that worn off or what?

TRACY: (*sighing, reacting*) Jesus, you pop up. You don't call me and then you suddenly appear. I mean . . . what happened to that woman you met?

IKE: Well—well, I'll tell you that—uh, it's—uh, Jesus, yeah, I don't see her anymore. I mean, you know, we say . . . Look, I made a mistake. What do you want me to say? (*pausing*) I don't think you oughta go to London. (*he sighs and takes a deep breath*)

TRACY: Well, I have to go. I mean, all the plans have been made, th-the arrangements. I mean, my parents are there now looking for a place for me to live.

IKE: (*sighing*) Tsch. W-well . . . uh, ah, do you still love me or—or what?

TRACY: Do you love me?

IKE: Well, yeah, that's what I—uh . . . well, yeah, of course, that's what this is all about . . . you know.

TRACY: Guess what? I turned eighteen the other day.

IKE: Did you?

TRACY: (*chuckling and nodding*) I'm legal, but I'm still a kid.

IKE: You're not such a kid. Eighteen years old. You know, you can—you can . . . they could draft you. You know that in some countries, you'd be . . . (*TRACY smiles, then laughs softly. IKE moves a strand of hair away from her face*) Hey . . . you look good.

TRACY: You really hurt me.

IKE: (*stroking TRACY's cheek*) Uh, it was not on purpose . . . you know. I mean, I—I . . . uh, you know, I was . . . yeah, I mean . . . you know, it was just—just the way I was looking at things then—

TRACY: (*interrupting*) Well, I'll be back in six months.

IKE: (*raising an eyebrow, reacting*) Six months—are you kidding?! Six months you're gonna go for?

TRACY: We've gone this long. Well, I mean, what's six months if we still love each other?

IKE: (*nodding his head*) Hey, don't be so mature, okay? I mean, six months is a long time. Six months. You know, you're gonna be i-in-in-in the— . . . working in the theatre there. You'll be with actors and directors. You know, you're . . . you know, you go to rehearsal and you—you hang out with those people. You have lunch a lot. And, and (*clearing his throat and frowning*) . . . well, you know, attachments form and—and, you know, I mean, you-you don't wanna get into that kind of . . . I mean, you—you'll change. You know, you'll be . . . in six months you'll be a completely different person.

TRACY: (*chuckling*) Well, don't you want me to have that experience? I mean, a while ago you made such a convincing case.

IKE: Tsch. Yeah, of course I do, but you know, but you could . . . you know, you—I mean, I—I just don't want that thing about you that I like to change.

An orchestration of "Rhapsody In Blue" begins in the background, the same music as in the beginning of the film.

TRACY: I've gotta make a plane.

IKE: Oh, come on, you . . . come on. You don't—you don't have to go.

TRACY: Why couldn't you have brought this up last week? Look, six months isn't so long. (*pausing*) Not everybody gets corrupted. (*IKE stares at TRACY, reacting. He pushes back his glasses.*) Tsch. Look, you have to have a little faith in people.

IKE continues to stare at TRACY. He has a quizzical look on his face. He breaks into a smile.

Marvin's Room
(Miramax, 1996)

Screenplay by Scott McPherson, adapted by John Guare
Directed by Jerry Zaks
Characters: BESSIE (Diane Keaton)
            HANK (Leonardo DiCaprio)

NOTES: BESSIE and Lee, two sisters in their forties, haven't had any contact for many years. BESSIE lives in Florida with her elderly, bedridden father, Marvin, and her Aunt Ruth, whom she lovingly cares for. She isn't married, and has never had her own family. When medical tests reveal she has leukemia, her doctor phones her sister, Lee, in Ohio. Lee, whose abusive husband left many years ago, is living with nuns in the convent temporarily because HANK, her seventeen-year-old son, has burned the house down. Since the fire, HANK has been in a mental institution. Lee, a beautician in training, travels to Florida with her sons, HANK and Charlie, because one of them might be a bone-marrow match for BESSIE. Now everyone is at BESSIE's house; HANK, however, has not yet agreed to be tested. HANK still deifies his missing father. He has found a box of old tools in Marvin's closet and has adopted them.

75. EXTERIOR. BESSIE'S HOUSE—BACKYARD—NIGHT
BESSIE has come to a place that has a feeling of isolation

because of the lay of the land and the placement of the trees. The houses seem to disappear and the sky commands our attention. HANK rests in the grass, barefoot. Near him is the old toolbox. Many of the tools have been laid out upon the lawn. BESSIE can barely make HANK out in the shadows.

BESSIE: Hank? What are you doing out here?

HANK: Nothing.

BESSIE: You gave me a scare. I'm not used to finding someone else out here.

HANK: Do you want me to go inside?

BESSIE: No. (*a beat*) We're all glad that you're here.

HANK: Yeah, we should do it again in seventeen years.

BESSIE: Your mom and I haven't always gotten along. That's why I haven't been in touch so much.

HANK: Uh-huh.

BESSIE: I wish you could have really known your grandfather. He'd have liked having a boy around.

HANK: Kind of gave me the creeps.

BESSIE: Well, he's been sick for a very long time.

HANK: Don't you ever wish he'd just die?

BESSIE: Hank . . . don't ask that.

HANK: Why not?

BESSIE: It's rude.

HANK: I haven't made up my mind about getting tested yet.

BESSIE: Is that what you were doing? Sitting out here thinking about that?

HANK: No.

BESSIE: Oh. (*pause*) What are you doing with the tools?

HANK: I'm just looking at them. I was going to put them back.

BESSIE: I didn't think you were stealing them, Hank. You can have them if you want.

HANK: Really?

BESSIE: Sure.

HANK: You're just giving them to me?

BESSIE: Sure, why not?

HANK: These are really cool tools.

BESSIE: They're your grandfather's. I think he'd like you to have them.

HANK: The hospital won't let me keep these, though.

BESSIE: Well, you won't be in there forever.

HANK: When I go back they're moving me to a place for adults.

BESSIE: Why?

HANK: I turn eighteen in three weeks.

BESSIE: Oh. Happy birthday.

HANK: Thanks. If the fire hadn't spread up the street it wouldn't be such a big deal. Now they want to be sure I'm not some kind of threat.

BESSIE: You're not a threat. I'm sure they'll see that. You're probably the best one there.

HANK: There's this one dude on my floor held a razor blade under his tongue for five hours. Talked to the orderlies and ate and everything.

BESSIE: Why on earth did he do that?

HANK: He was trying to break my record.

BESSIE: Hank. What do you want to be when you grow up?

HANK: I am grown up.

BESSIE: When I look at you I see a lost little boy. (*She reaches to touch his face.*)

HANK: (*slapping her hand away*) Then get your eyes checked.

Pause. BESSIE starts back toward the house.

Marvin's Room (2)
(Miramax, 1996)

*Screenplay by Scott McPherson, adapted by John
Guare
Directed by Jerry Zaks
Characters: BESSIE (Diane Keaton)
          HANK (Leonardo DiCaprio)*

NOTES: HANK has decided to get tested (*see notes for previous
scene*), but hasn't told anyone yet. He accompanies his brother
Charlie to the doctor's office.

113 INTERIOR. DR. WALLY'S OFFICE—DAY
BESSIE enters.

BESSIE: Hank. I thought you'd be at home.

HANK: No, I'm here.

BESSIE: Where's your mom?

HANK: She went over to the mall.

BESSIE: Where's Charlie?

HANK: He's in back already.

BESSIE: Are you here to be with Charlie?

HANK: I'll probably get tested too.

On BESSIE, as she reacts to this.

BESSIE: Nervous?

HANK: No.

BESSIE: (*looks around nervously*) These offices used to be infested with bugs.

HANK: Bugs don't bother me.

BESSIE: No?

HANK: They crawl out of the drain in the boys' shower. They hide in the junk pile in auto shop. They float in the soap basins on the sinks. You get used to them.

BESSIE: I wouldn't.

HANK: One dude in my room. There's twelve of us in this room and this one dude catches bugs and puts them on a leash.

BESSIE: A leash?

HANK: A hair leash. He pulls out a strand of his hair and ties it around the bug and the other end he tacks down under his bunk. He had this whole zoo of bugs walking in little circles under his bed.

BESSIE: Hank.

HANK: Till this other dude smashed them all with the back of his cafeteria tray. It was funny.

BESSIE: Why do you make up these stories?

HANK: What?

BESSIE: These stories. Razors under the tongue, hair leashes.

HANK: I'm not making anything up.

BESSIE: Why did you pretend you weren't going to get tested? Why did you put me through that?

HANK walks out of the doctor's office. BESSIE sits for a moment, then gets up and follows.

EXTERIOR. DR. WALLY'S OFFICE—DAY

HANK leans against the building, sulking. BESSIE catches up to him.

HANK: I haven't told you shit. You don't know anything about where they've got me.

BESSIE: Well, you can tell me if you want.

HANK: You don't know.

BESSIE: Then tell me.

Pause.

HANK: You don't know.

BESSIE: I was in the hospital. It was boring. I was scared and it was boring.

HANK: There's this one dude—

BESSIE: Hank, if this is another tall tale, I'm not interested.

Silence.

BESSIE: (*cont'd*) I'm going back, in case Charlie is done.

She waits a moment but still nothing from HANK. She leaves.

115. INTERIOR. DR. WALLY'S WAITING ROOM—DAY

BESSIE is reading a magazine. After a moment, HANK comes in and sits down. It is hard for him to start talking.

HANK: I played in a pool tournament in my ward. Did Mom tell you?

BESSIE: No.

HANK: I came in fourth. It's true. She doesn't think it's such a big deal.

BESSIE: That's great.

HANK: I got my toe broken in there.

BESSIE: How?

HANK: Guy threw a garbage can at me and it landed on my foot.

BESSIE: Why'd he do that?

HANK: No reason I know of. (*a beat*) A lot of drugs float around in there.

BESSIE: Do you take them?

HANK: Most of the time I keep to myself. I think about not being there. I think what it would be like to be someone else. I'd have this house with all this land around it. And

I'd get a bunch of dogs and I'd let them run wild. And I'd build a go-cart track. Those places pull in the bucks. I'd be raking it in. And nobody would know where I was. I'd be gone. Most of the time I just want to be someplace else.

BESSIE: Why aren't you?

HANK: Huh?

BESSIE: Why aren't you someplace else?

HANK: What do you mean?

BESSIE: You're the one who told me people only do what they want.

HANK: Yeah.

BESSIE: So you must want to be in there.

HANK: No. No way.

BESSIE: Then show them you don't need to be in there.

HANK: It's not easy like that. People start thinking of you a certain way and pretty soon you're that way.

BESSIE: I don't want you wasting your life in there.

HANK: Neither do I.

BESSIE: Then why are you still there?

HANK: They put me there.

BESSIE: Why did they put you there?

HANK: Because I burned down the house.

BESSIE: Why did you burn down the house?

Pause. Dr. Wally comes in from the examination area.

DR. WALLY: Hank, do you want to come on back? We can get you started while we're waiting for the anesthetic to start working on little Sammy.

HANK: Charlie.

DR. WALLY: I'm sorry. Did I call you Hank?

The doctor exits. HANK starts to follow, then stops.

HANK: Would you like to come back there with me?

BESSIE: Sure I would.

Marvin's Room (3)
(Miramax, 1996)

Screenplay by Scot McPherson, adapted by John Guare
Directed by Jerry Zaks
Characters: BESSIE *(Diane Keaton)*
LEE *(Meryl Streep)*

NOTES: BESSIE and LEE haven't really been sisters for quite some time (*see notes for previous scenes*). When their father Marvin had his first stroke, LEE decided she wasn't "giving up her life" to her father's caretaking. She's been living in Ohio and BESSIE has been living with Marvin and Aunt Ruth in Florida, caring for both of them for many years. BESSIE doesn't know her nephews, but she's getting into their hearts. LEE has been hardened by her difficult life, raising her two sons alone; sometimes she takes it out on the boys. She's been training for her cosmetology license and, despite HANK burning the house down, she feels like she's finally starting to get her life back together when she hears of BESSIE's leukemia, and must drop everything to come to Florida. LEE wants to put Marvin in a home; she doesn't want to care for him if BESSIE becomes too ill. The sisters' mutual guilt and resentment comes to the surface and they have blowups, but they are also rediscovering their love for each other.

116. INTERIOR. KITCHEN—NIGHT

BESSIE pours herself coffee. LEE enters in the dark. She turns on the kitchen light. BESSIE, not wearing her wig, covers her exposed scalp with her hands.

LEE: Oh.

BESSIE: I was just going to bed.

BESSIE quickly escapes to the privacy of her room. LEE stands still for a moment, then pours a glass of orange juice from the refrigerator. BESSIE comes back in wearing her wig.

BESSIE: (*cont'd*) Forgot my coffee.

LEE: Why are you drinking coffee so late?

BESSIE: I like it.

LEE: You have a way with Hank.

BESSIE: I don't.

LEE: You do.

BESSIE: He's a good boy.

LEE: Is he?

BESSIE: Sure he is.

LEE: I wish I knew your secret.

BESSIE: I just talk to him.

LEE: Are you saying I don't.

Slight pause.

BESSIE: I'm tired and we've got Disney World tomorrow.

BESSIE goes to her room. LEE swirls her juice in her glass, then goes into the living room. She takes a neglected bottle of vodka from the shelf, and adds a healthy shot to her juice.

118. INTERIOR. BESSIE'S ROOM—NIGHT

BESSIE is about to take off her wig and get into bed when LEE knocks on the door and comes in, carrying a case.

LEE: You know, I could fix your wig for you.

BESSIE: Does it look bad?

LEE: No, but if you've got a wig you should have fun with it. You never know when you might meet someone.

BESSIE: I haven't thought about a man in years.

LEE: You're lying.

She realizes BESSIE is not lying.

BESSIE: I'm sorry we haven't been seeing eye to eye. I don't want us to fight.

LEE: I don't think we have been.

BESSIE: I want us to get along.

LEE: We do get along.

BESSIE: I don't want us to just get along. I don't want us to be polite.

LEE: I've never had a problem with that.

BESSIE: I want us to . . . I want . . . Not much seems important to me right now.

LEE: (*not wanting to talk about it*) We're sisters.

BESSIE: The past is—

LEE: We're sisters.

BESSIE: I want you to know—

LEE: (*very uncomfortable with this situation*) I do know.

They are interrupted by the sound of Marvin stirring in his room.

LEE: (*cont'd*) Should we—

BESSIE: No. He scares himself sometimes, but then he goes right back to sleep.

The sound of Marvin settling back to sleep.

BESSIE: (*cont'd*) Are you seeing anybody now?

LEE: Usually.

BESSIE: I hope you have someone real in your life.

LEE: I don't have much trouble with that.

BESSIE: I'm not talking about "that."

LEE: You should be. There's no reason you haven't had love in your life.

BESSIE: I think I've—

LEE: There's no reason. You're not ugly, Bessie.

BESSIE: Thank you.

LEE: You're not. I know lots of boys were interested in you, they just thought you were stuck up.

BESSIE: Thank you.

LEE: Well, if you had given them any encouragement.

BESSIE: I had a true love.

LEE: You did?

BESSIE: Yes.

LEE: Did he know?

BESSIE: Yes.

LEE: How could I not have known about it?

BESSIE: It wasn't anyone you knew.

LEE: It's not like I'm going to tell anybody.

BESSIE: Clarence James.

LEE: Who?

BESSIE: He was only around in the summers.

LEE catches on.

LEE: You went with a carny worker!

BESSIE: He was a very nice person.

LEE: I didn't say anything.

BESSIE: This is why I kept it a secret.

LEE: Which one was he?

BESSIE: He mostly ran the Ferris wheel.

LEE: I remember him. He was cute.

BESSIE: He had the funniest laugh. He'd open his mouth real wide and no sound would come out.

LEE: What happened?

BESSIE: Nothing like you think.

LEE: (*teasing*) What happened?

BESSIE: They always have a last picnic down by the river and Clarence goes swimming. And he knows everybody is watching him. Everybody is there, his family, his friends, me. And he's laughing, making that monkey face, which gets all of us laughing, and he dunks under the water and pops up somewhere else laughing even harder. And he dives under again and then he doesn't come up and he doesn't come up and he doesn't come up. Laughing and choking looked the same on Clarence.

LEE: Bessie, you should have told me.

BESSIE: If I couldn't tell people I had a carny boyfriend, I couldn't tell them my carny boyfriend drowned.

LEE: You should have told me anyway.

BESSIE: We were never that close.

LEE: Weren't we?

BESSIE: No.

Pause.

LEE: Do you want me to do something with that wig?

BESSIE: What?

LEE: I don't know. Let me look at it.

BESSIE turns her head giving LEE a look.

LEE: (*cont'd*) No, you have to take it off.

BESSIE: Oh.

LEE: I won't hurt it.

BESSIE is reluctant.

LEE: (*cont'd*) This is a nice wig, Bessie. It's nicely ventilated. We can do something with this. Do you want me to?

BESSIE: Sure.

BESSIE takes off her wig and gives it to LEE. LEE tries to hide her reaction from BESSIE.

LEE: I'm glad we made this trip. I only wish we could stay longer. This is a nice weave. (*not wanting BESSIE to see she is upset*) Let me get my brush.

LEE leaves. Alone, BESSIE wraps a scarf around her head.

INTERIOR. BATHROOM—NIGHT

LEE steadies herself, looking in the mirror. She doesn't want to cry. She takes her hairbrush, which she had all the time, from the pocket of her robe. She opens the bathroom door and, in a loud whisper—

LEE: Found it.

Moonstruck
(MGM, 1987)

Screenplay by John Patrick Shanley
Directed by Norman Jewison
Characters: LORETTA (Cher)
RONNY (Nicholas Cage)

NOTES: LORETTA is going to marry Johnny. She doesn't really love him. She has been dating him for some time, and he finally proposed. Then he suddenly had to leave the country. He asks LORETTA to invite his estranged brother, RONNY, to the wedding. LORETTA visits the Brooklyn bakery that RONNY runs, and finds a very angry, passionate man. RONNY blames JOHNNY for his missing hand and his ruined life. Years ago, he caught his hand in a bread slicer, and his fiancée left him. He reacts strongly to the news of JOHNNY's wedding. They both end up in RONNY's apartment above the bakery.

62. INTERIOR. RONNY'S APARTMENT—DAY

It's a two-bedroom apartment. The decor reflects RONNY's love of the opera. The furniture is overstuffed, fringed in the colors of Italian passion. But it is all a bit faded, the remains of an old flamboyance. The walls are decorated with opera posters; over the fireplace there is a painting depicting a scene from "La Boheme": Mimi standing in the snow. RONNY stares at the picture of Mimi in the La Boheme poster. LORETTA comes in from the kitchen and sets down a cup of coffee.

LORETTA: You ready for the coffee?

LORETTA moves back into the kitchen. RONNY turns and watches as she walks down the hall.

RONNY: What's that smell?

LORETTA: I'm making you a steak.

RONNY: You don't have to help me.

LORETTA: I know that. I do what I want.

RONNY: I like it well done.

LORETTA: You'll eat this bloody to feed your blood.

63. INTERIOR. RONNY'S APARTMENT—DINING ROOM—DAY

Close-up of RONNY's artificial hand, holding a fork stuck in a steak. He switches hands and eats hungrily. LORETTA watches.

RONNY: This is good. Uhhh . . .

LORETTA: Loretta.

RONNY: Where'd Johnny find you?

LORETTA: He knew my husband who died.

RONNY: How'd he die?

LORETTA: Bus hit him.

RONNY: Fast.

LORETTA: Instantaneous.

RONNY: When you get engaged?

LORETTA: Yesterday.

RONNY drops his knife and fork and turns away. LOR-ETTA is not surprised and doesn't move.

RONNY: Why?

LORETTA: Why what?

RONNY: I don't know.

LORETTA: (*smiles*) So. Five years ago your hand got cut off and your woman left you for another man. No woman since then?

RONNY: No.

LORETTA: Stupid.

RONNY: When did your husband get hit by the bus?

LORETTA: Seven years ago.

RONNY: How many men since then?

LORETTA: Just Johnny.

RONNY: Stupid yourself.

LORETTA: No. Unlucky. I have not been lucky.

RONNY: I don't care about luck, you understand that? It ain't that.

LORETTA: What? Do you think you're the only one ever shed a tear?

RONNY: Why you talking to me?

LORETTA: You got any whiskey? How 'bout giving me a glass of whiskey?

64. INTERIOR. LORETTA AND RONNY AT THE TABLE WITH A BOTTLE OF WHISKEY

Camera is close on Scotch being poured into two glasses. LORETTA picks up her glass and swallows a healthy dose.

RONNY: She was right to leave me.

LORETTA: You think so?

RONNY: Yes.

LORETTA: You really are stupid, you know that.

LORETTA pours herself another shot.

RONNY: You don't know nothing about it.

LORETTA: I was raised that a girl gets married young. I didn't get married until I was twenty-eight. I met a man. I loved him. I married him. He wanted to have a baby right away. I said no. Then he got hit by a bus. No man. No baby. No nothing! I did not know that man was a gift I could not keep. I didn't know . . . You tell me a story and you think you know what it means, but I see what the true story is, and you can't. (*she pours them both another drink*)

She didn't leave you! You can't see what you are. I can see everything. You are a wolf!

RONNY: I'm a wolf?

LORETTA: The big part of you has no words and it's a wolf. This woman was a trap for you. She caught you and you could not get away. (*she grabs his wooden hand*) So you chewed off your foot! That was the price you had to pay to be free. (*throws his hand down*) Johnny had nothing to do with it. You did what you had to do, between you and you, and I know I'm right, I don't care what you say. And now you're afraid because you found out the big part of you is a wolf that has the courage to bite off its own hand to save itself from the trap of the wrong love. That's why there has been no woman since that wrong woman. You are scared to death what the wolf will do if you make that mistake again.

RONNY: What are you doing!

LORETTA: I'm telling you your life!

RONNY: Stop it!

LORETTA: No!

RONNY: Why are you marrying Johnny? He's a fool!

LORETTA: Because I have no luck!

RONNY: (*pounding on the table*) He made me look the wrong way and I cut off my hand. He could make you look the wrong way and you could cut off your whole head!

LORETTA: I am looking where I should to become a bride!

RONNY: A bride without a head!

LORETTA: A wolf without a foot!

RONNY stiff-arms everything off the dining table and grabs LORETTA. They kiss passionately. He pulls her up on the table and over the table to him. They are in each other's arms. They are on fire. LORETTA pushes him away, gasping for air.

LORETTA: Wait a minute! Wait a minute!

She changes her mind and lunges into another kiss. They stop again after a long moment. They really haven't breathed. They both suck in air and look at each other in wonder and fear and passion.

RONNY: It's like I'm falling! It's like I'm in the ocean!

They kiss again. When they pull apart, LORETTA is crying.

LORETTA: I have no luck!

He picks her up in his arms.

RONNY: Son of a bitch!

LORETTA: Where are you taking me?

RONNY: To the bed.

LORETTA: Oh. Oh god. I don't care about anything! I don't care about anything! Take me to the bed.

He carries her away, into the bedroom.

Naked
(Fine Line, 1993)

Screenplay by Mike Leigh
Directed by Mike Leigh
Characters: SOPHIE (Katrin Cartlidge)
　　　　　　JOHNNY (David Thewlis)

NOTES: This scene takes place in London, but JOHNNY comes from Manchester. He has arrived at the house of his old girl-friend from Manchester, Louise; she has moved to London. It is never explained why JOHNNY comes to London—he doesn't ever appeal to Louise to get back together—but something in his life has gone wrong, and throughout the film he has a persistent, unexplained cough. Louise isn't home when JOHNNY gets there (she doesn't expect him) and it is very cold. Her roommate, SO-PHIE, arrives. SOPHIE is typical London Cockney trash, very thin, dyed jet black hair, raggedy miniskirt and leather jacket. She is not well educated or intelligent, but she is sexy. It's easy for JOHNNY to toy with her—he has a sharp wit and a sharper tongue.

EXTERIOR. LOUISE AND SOPHIE'S HOUSE—DAY
Later in the day. An old inner-city residential district of Lon-don. Surrounded by decaying houses, JOHNNY is standing in the middle of the road. He is holding a piece of paper. He looks lost. Shortly after this, JOHNNY is sitting on a low wall at the top of a long flight of steps leading up to

259

*the front door of a large Victorian Neo-Gothic house.
SOPHIE ambles toward the house. She climbs the steps. At
the top . . .*

SOPHIE: Oh, shit—sorry! I didn't see you there.

JOHNNY: Do you live 'ere?

SOPHIE: Yeah . . . I do, unfortunately.

JOHNNY: Do you know Louise Clancy?

SOPHIE: Yeah. Are you a friend of 'ers?

JOHNNY: Know where she is?

SOPHIE: She's at work.

JOHNNY: What time does she get back?

SOPHIE: Dunno. About seven or something.

JOHNNY: Fuckin' hell!

Pause.

SOPHIE: D'you wanna come in for a cuppa tea?

JOHNNY: Is that all right with you, love? It's just . . . you
know . . . cold.

*Moments later, inside. JOHNNY is following SOPHIE up
the stairs of the flat.*

JOHNNY: Listen, have you got anything for a headache?

SOPHIE: Ah . . . yeah, we 'ave as it 'appens.

JOHNNY: You know, like a monkey wrench or somethin'.

*SOPHIE laughs, and opens the bathroom door. JOHNNY
stops at a wall-diagram of the human skeleton.*

JOHNNY: What's all this about?

SOPHIE: Oh, yeah . . . that's Sandra, that is.

JOHNNY: Hallo, Sandra!

SOPHIE laughs.

SOPHIE: This is 'er place. She's a fuckin' nurse. That's 'er
idea of interior design.

JOHNNY: Oh, yeah—it's a skeleton.

SOPHIE: (*she opens a large medicine chest*) And this is 'er cocktail cabinet, an' all. (she takes out a pill bottle) There you go . . . that should do it.

She gives him the bottle. He puts it in his mouth.

JOHNNY: No, it's too big.

She laughs and walks away. He returns his attention to the skeleton.

SOPHIE: D'you want a cuppa tea?

JOHNNY: Yeah.

A few minutes have passed. SOPHIE is standing in the middle of her kitchen. JOHNNY is leaning against a cupboard. He pops a headache pill into his mouth.

SOPHIE: So, are you Louise's boyfriend?

JOHNNY: No.

SOPHIE: Oh, right. What, you're just like a mate?

JOHNNY: Primate. (*he takes his bag off his shoulder and drops it on the floor*)

SOPHIE: You must be the missing link, then?

JOHNNY: Yeah, that's me.

SOPHIE: You're not gonna tell me your name?

JOHNNY: No.

SOPHIE: I'm not gonna tell you mine either.

JOHNNY: All right . . . We'll be strangers.

A little while later, in the living room. Close-up of a boomerang, sitting amongst other assorted ethnic artifacts on a shelf.

JOHNNY: I see your boomerang came back then, love.

The camera tilts to a set of ebony elephants on the shelf below.

JOHNNY: What about the old diminishing pachyderm formation there?

SOPHIE: No, that's all Sandra's collection. She's in Zimbabwe at the moment. And fuck knows what she's gonna bring back from there.

SOPHIE is sitting on a floor cushion. She passes a joint to JOHNNY, who is sitting close by in an armchair.

JOHNNY: Pellagra or hepatitis B or something.

SOPHIE: She's with her boyfriend.

SOPHIE pulls down her already skimpy garment to reveal bare shoulders, throwing JOHNNY a moody glance as she does so. Pause.

JOHNNY: So, how is Louise?

SOPHIE: I dunno . . . I don't know 'er as well as you.

JOHNNY: D'you get on with 'er?

SOPHIE: We've been out a couple 'o times.

JOHNNY: Does she like you?

SOPHIE: I dunno—you'd better ask 'er. Most people don't.

JOHNNY: D'you find that she's at all jealous of you?

SOPHIE: No.

JOHNNY: So . . . I dunno . . . Would you describe yourself as a . . . happy little person?

SOPHIE: Yeah . . . I'm the life and soul.

JOHNNY: Have you ever thought, right . . . I mean, you don't know, but you might already 'ave had the happiest moment in your whole fuckin' life, and all you've got to look forward to is sickness and purgatory?

SOPHIE: Oh, shit! Well . . . I just live from day to day, meself. (*she takes back the joint*)

JOHNNY: I tend to skip a day now and again—you know what I mean? I used to be a werewolf, but I'm all right NOW!! (*"Now" comes out as a werewolf howl*)

SOPHIE: Oh, fuckin' 'ell! I bet they're 'appy, eh? All they gotta do is sit round, howlin' at the moon.

JOHNNY: It's better than standin' on the cheesy fuckin' thing. Know what I mean? I mean, tossin' all these satellites and shuttles out into the cosmos—what do they think they're gonna find up there that they can't find down 'ere? They think if they piss high enough, they're gonna come across the monkey with the beard and the crap ideas, and it's like, "Oh, there you are, Captain! I mean . . . are you busy, because I've got a few fundamental questions for you!" Are you with me?

SOPHIE: Yeah . . .'cos let's face it, right, what are rockets? I mean, they're just . . . big metal pricks! You know, I mean, the bastards aren't satisfied with fuckin' the earth up—they've gotta fuck space an' all.

JOHNNY: (*takes back the joint*) Will you tell me something love? Are you aware of the effect you have on the average mammalian, Mancunian, x-y-ly-chromosome, slavering, lusty male member of the species?

SOPHIE: Er . . . yeah.

JOHNNY: I thought so.

Naked (2)
(Fine Line, 1993)

Screenplay by Mike Leigh
Directed by Mike Leigh
Characters: LOUISE (Lesley Sharp)
  JOHNNY (David Thewlis)

NOTES: JOHNNY has been in LOUISE's house in London since the previous afternoon (*see previous scene*). He has had sex with LOUISE's roommate, Sophie, and LOUISE suspects it. LOUISE is JOHNNY's old girlfriend from Manchester; she doesn't know why JOHNNY has appeared, and he's not telling. In fact, he's belligerent toward her. He has a persistent, unexplained cough.

INTERIOR. LOUISE AND SOPHIE'S HOUSE—DAY

Downstairs, in the living room, a little after daylight. JOHNNY is sitting in an armchair, reading a book (James Gleick, Chaos*). He is wearing only his overcoat and he is smoking. LOUISE hands him a mug of tea. He takes it without looking at her. She sits on the sofa and takes one of his cigarrettes.*

JOHNNY: Oh. 'Ave a fag.

LOUISE: Yeah. Thanks. I will. (*she lights it and settles back on the sofa*) What're you readin'?

Pause. She picks up SOPHIE's bodice and examines it.

264

JOHNNY: Will you stop fuckin' about and fidgetin' in my peripherals—I'm tryin' to concentrate.

LOUISE is holding the bodice in front of her face.

LOUISE: She's got a very little waist, Sophie, an't she? (*she peeps at him over the top of the bodice*) She's got little tits an' all. (*she throws down the bodice*) Are you not cold?

JOHNNY: I'm readin' about the Butterfly Effect.

LOUISE: What's the Butterfly Effect?

JOHNNY: Every time a butterfly flaps its wings in Tokyo, this old granny in Salford gets a bilious attack.

LOUISE: What happens if a butterfly flaps its wings in Salford?

JOHNNY: That's not the point.

LOUISE: Oh, is it not? What are you doin' in London, Johnny?

JOHNNY: What are you doin' in London?

LOUISE: I've told you what I'm doin' in London.

JOHNNY: You've told me nothing.

LOUISE: The last time I saw you, I told you—

JOHNNY: (*he throws down the book*) Fuckin' hell! Were you born irritatin'? What have you come downstairs for anyway?

LOUISE: I fell asleep with the window open. I was cold. I came down. I 'ad a pee. I've made some tea. I'm 'ere. All right?

JOHNNY: What was that? The greatest story ever told?

LOUISE: I live 'ere. (*pause*) So what 'appened? Were you bored in Manchester?

JOHNNY: Was I bored? No, I wasn't fuckin' bored. I'm never bored. That's the trouble with everybody—you're all so bored. You've 'ad nature explained to you and you're bored with it. You've 'ad the living body explained to you and you're bored with it. You've 'ad the universe explained to you and you're bored with it. So now you just want cheap thrills and like plenty of 'em, and it dun't matter 'ow tawdry or vacuous they are as long as it's new, as long as it's new, as long as it flashes and fuckin' bleeps in forty fuckin' different colors. Well, whatever else you can say about me, I'm not fuckin' bored!

LOUISE: Yeah, all right.

JOHNNY: So, 'ow's it goin' for you?

LOUISE: It's a bit borin', actually.

JOHNNY: Are you not enjoyin' yourself? (*LOUISE shakes her head*) Have you made many friends?

LOUISE: No.

JOHNNY: 'Ave you got, erm, a goblet or something, because me heart's bleedin'.

LOUISE: When are you goin' back to Manchester?

JOHNNY: When are *you* goin' back to Manchester?

LOUISE: I'm not goin' back.

JOHNNY: Why not?

LOUISE: You know why not.

JOHNNY: Do I?

LOUISE: I thought you said you never wanted to see me again.

JOHNNY: I don't ever wanna see you again, so will you fuck off back upstairs?

LOUISE: Why are you such a bastard, Johnny?

JOHNNY coughs.

JOHNNY: Monkey see, monkey do.

LOUISE: And what does that mean?

JOHNNY has a short bout of coughing.

JOHNNY: Oh, this fuckin' cough.

LOUISE: Mm. A butterfly must 'ave flapped its wings.

He coughs again.

JOHNNY: So, have you got to get up for work now, yeah?

LOUISE: No. It's too early. I'm going back to bed.

He coughs. LOUISE gets up and leaves the room. His cough continues.

Night And The City
(20th Century Fox, 1992)

Screenplay by Richard Price
Directed by Irwin Winkler
Characters: PHIL (Cliff Gorman)
HARRY (Robert DeNiro)

NOTES: HARRY FABIAN is a fast-talking New York lawyer—an ambulance chaser, a loser. He has concocted a scheme to become a boxing promoter, kicking it off with a big local "fight night" event. He's convinced it will be a hit, but he's digging a hole for himself borrowing the money for it, and making enemies. PHIL, HARRY's sometime friend, a local restaurant owner, has promised to lend HARRY half of the money, saying he'll give it to HARRY the night of the fight. But it's a false promise; PHIL knows that HARRY has been having an affair with his wife, Helen. PHIL also knows that Helen plans to leave him and open her own restaurant with a phony liquor license that HARRY procured for her. He sets HARRY up for a fall.

76. INTERIOR. WOLFE TONE—DAY
PHIL at the bar. Only a few customers. Dead hour. HARRY comes down the stairs. PHIL pours him a drink.

HARRY: It's not good, Phil.

PHIL: What . . .

HARRY: (*cagey*) It's off . . . I appreciate the loan but ah . . . save your coin there, Pops.

PHIL: What . . .

HARRY: I need twelve grand if I need a dime . . . the disco I was gonna use? They wanna hold me up for *nine* now . . . it's over . . . I tried to raise a few more dollars . . . it's very tight out there . . . cheers.

PHIL: (*with uncharacteristic mildness*) OK . . . so we'll make it twelve.

HARRY: (*stunned*) You're shittin' me.

PHIL: Not at all . . . I want fourteen five back.

HARRY: (*light-voiced in disbelief*) Phil . . . you're OK, you know that?

PHIL: You still gotta wait until the day before or so . . . it's a lot of money.

HARRY: Phil . . . they broke the mold with you.

PHIL: You hear the news?

HARRY: What . . .

PHIL: (*studying him*) Helen walked out on me.

HARRY: Aw Jesus! What a cunt!

PHIL: You know what else? She's opening the Blue Dolphin . . . that place on Hudson Street?

HARRY: Fuck her! It's better, you know? It's better that . . . if she's that kind of person to be*gin* with, you know? Aw Christ, man I am really sorry . . . sorry for her *more* because hey . . . a person like that *you* can always leave *them* but *they*, they have to live with themselves all their lives . . . you know what I mean? You have to live with yourself.

PHIL: (*studying him*) You make your own bed, right, Harry?

HARRY: (*animated*) Ex*act*ly . . . now *lie* in it.

PHIL: (*casual, dry*) Hey Harry . . . how did Helen get a liquor license?

HARRY: (*shrugging*) They're so fucked up down there— God knows. She lucked out I guess, you know? When you're hot you're hot, when you're not, you can't give it away.

PHIL stares at HARRY for a beat. He smiles; a rictus of a grin.

PHIL: Harry . . . I'm gonna throw you a good luck party . . . how many kids are fighting. Ten?

HARRY: Twelve.

PHIL: OK . . . twelve . . . I'm gonna blow you to a dinner party here the night before . . . you know, prefight night . . . it'll be nice publicity . . . you, Al, the kids.

HARRY: Yeah?

PHIL: Why not . . . protect my investment . . . get some publicity maybe . . . good for the place, too . . . no booze 'cause of the kids . . . so . . . well . . . look, come in with them Monday night early . . . they got the weigh-in Tuesday, right? Say six . . . I'll throw dinner for them, and I'll have the dough for you.

HARRY is buggy with joy, snapping and clapping.

HARRY: Mister *Phil!*

PHIL: *De nada.*

HARRY makes for the door and splits. PHIL is alone smoking a cigarette. He picks up the phone.

PHIL: Yeah . . . State Liquor Authority, please.

Nina Takes A Lover
(Triumph, 1995)

Screenplay by Alan Jacobs
Directed by Alan Jacobs
Characters: NINA (Laura San Giacomo)
              PHOTOGRAPHER (Paul Rhys)

NOTES: NINA and the PHOTOGRAPHER both live in San Francisco. They are both married and are having an affair with each other. He is British; she's American. He travels the world; she owns a shoe boutique. They have been seeing each other for a short time when this scene takes place.

INTERIOR. NINA'S BEDROOM / PHOTOGRAPHER'S STUDIO—NIGHT

NINA and the PHOTOGRAPHER are talking on the phone to each other. NINA's room is lit with just the lamp beside her bed. She's lying on the bed, wearing brown sweatpants and a tee shirt.

NINA: Hi. Where are you?

PHOTOGRAPHER: I'm in the studio.

NINA: So late?

PHOTOGRAPHER: Well, sometimes I sleep here, you know.

NINA: You should go home, it's late. Your wife is probably wondering where you are.

PHOTOGRAPHER: You want me to go?

NINA: Not really.

PHOTOGRAPHER: So I'll go.

NINA: No, talk to me a little. Then you can go.

PHOTOGRAPHER: Alright.

NINA: Hmm.

PHOTOGRAPHER: What should we talk about?

NINA: Whatever you want to talk about.

PHOTOGRAPHER: Where are you?

NINA: In my bedroom. Lying in bed. There's just one light on in the room. It's the only one on in the whole apartment.

PHOTOGRAPHER: What are you wearing?

NINA: A black silk nightgown.

PHOTOGRAPHER: What color?

NINA: Black, silk.

PHOTOGRAPHER: Just a nightgown.

NINA: Don't you believe me?

PHOTOGRAPHER: No.

NINA: Why not?

PHOTOGRAPHER: You just don't seem like the silk nightgown type.

NINA: Oh really? What type do I seem?

PHOTOGRAPHER: If you're alone, going to bed alone, then you . . . I think you're wearing sweat pants.

NINA: What color?

PHOTOGRAPHER: White.

NINA: Gray.

PHOTOGRAPHER: Well, gray alright. But I was right, wasn't I?

NINA: How did you know?

PHOTOGRAPHER: I just guessed.

NINA: What are you wearing?

PHOTOGRAPHER: Nothing. I'm absolutely naked.

NINA: I don't believe you.

PHOTOGRAPHER: You don't.

NINA: No.

PHOTOGRAPHER: Ask my assistant. Phyllis . . . what am I wearing? (*mock female voice*) Nothing. (*normal voice*) You see?

NINA: Let me talk to Phyllis.

PHOTOGRAPHER: She can't come to the phone now.

NINA: Let me talk to Phyllis.

PHOTOGRAPHER: She can't come to the phone now.

NINA: Why not?

PHOTOGRAPHER: She's putting her clothes on.

NINA: No wonder you're there so late.

PHOTOGRAPHER: Yeah, well, Phyllis has discovered, you know, that she works best when she's in her birthday suit.

NINA: That's the name of a band, you know.

PHOTOGRAPHER: What is?

NINA: The Birthday Suits. I saw them once at the Paradise Lounge.

PHOTGRAPHER: Were they really in their birthday suits?

NINA: Well, they had plungers over their private parts. Other than that they were in their birthday suits. The leader had a fine ass.

PHOTOGRAPHER: What kind of music?

NINA: I don't really remember.

PHOTOGRAPHER: But you remember he had a nice ass.

NINA: I have a selective memory.

PHOTOGRAPHER: Are you going to remember me when this is over?

NINA: It depends what you do.

Nina Takes A Lover (2)
(Triumph, 1995)

Screenplay by Alan Jacobs
Directed by Alan Jacobs
Characters: NINA (Laura San Giacomo)
PHOTOGRAPHER (Paul Rhys)

NOTES: NINA and the PHOTOGRAPHER are two married people having an affair (*see previous scene*). NINA has spent the night at the PHOTOGRAPHER's studio. She gets up and goes through his slides, not expecting to find what she finds.

INTERIOR. STUDIO—EARLY MORNING

The PHOTOGRAPHER is still sleeping in bed. NINA is looking through a box of slides. She holds them up to the light. She looks a little bored, looks at the PHOTOGRAPHER once in a while to see if he's up yet. After looking at the slides for a while, she finds a few that interest her. She studies them, moving her hand towards the light to see them better. The PHOTOGRAPHER wakes. Nina gets into bed and shows him the slide.

NINA: Who is she?

PHOTOGRAPHER: Someone I worked with.

NINA: She's a model?

PHOTOGRAPHER: She's a makeup artist.

NINA: She looks like a model. What's her name?

PHOTOGRAPHER: Alicia.

NINA: It looks like you guys were pretty close.

PHOTOGRAPHER: Yeah. You want some coffee?

He gets up, hoping to change the subject.

NINA: Did you sleep with her?

PHOTOGRAPHER: What?

NINA: You heard me.

PHOTOGRAPHER: Why are you asking?

NINA: I'm just curious.

PHOTOGRAPHER: What makes you think I slept with her?

NINA: The way you're holding each other. It looks like you did.

NINA returns to the table.

NINA: You're not going to answer me, are you?

PHOTOGRAPHER: Why are you so interested?

NINA: I'm interested in everything about you. It doesn't matter, I know the answer already.

The PHOTOGRAPHER joins her at the table with a cup of coffee.

PHOTOGRAPHER: If you know the answer, then why are you asking?

NINA: I want to hear you say it.

PHOTOGRAPHER: What's the question?

NINA: Did you sleep with her?

PHOTOGRAPHER: Yes.

NINA looks surprised, and a little hurt. It hasn't registered with her yet.

NINA: You did?

PHOTOGRAPHER: That's what you want me to say, isn't it?

NINA: Did you?

PHOTOGRAPHER: What difference does it make?

NINA: Then just say it.

PHOTOGRAPHER: I slept with her. Okay?

NINA: Did she come on to you?

PHOTOGRAPHER: It sort of just happened.

NINA: It just happened.

PHOTOGRAPHER: I didn't expect you . . .

NINA: What?

PHOTOGRAPHER: Nothing. Nothing.

NINA: You didn't expect I would care?

PHOTOGRAPHER: I knew you would care, I didn't expect you would ask.

NINA: Do you still see her sometimes?

PHOTOGRAPHER: Nina, why do you want to know this?

NINA: Were there any others?

PHOTOGRAPHER: There were two others.

NINA: There were?

NINA gets up and walks to the door.

NINA: Do you have pictures of them, too? I'd love to see pictures of them, too.

PHOTOGRAPHER: No, I don't have pictures. What do you think I am?

NINA comes back.

NINA: Alright. Who were the other two?

PHOTOGRAPHER: One was a waitress I met in Martinique.

NINA: While you were working there?

PHOTOGRAPHER: Yes.

NINA: And the other?

PHOTOGRAPHER: The other was a photographer.

NINA: Where did you meet her?

PHOTOGRAPHER: At a show in London.

NINA: Are you still in touch with her?

PHOTOGRAPHER: No. Not very often.

NINA: Do you love her?

PHOTOGRAPHER: No, not at all.

NINA: What's the photographer's name?

PHOTOGRAPHER: Her name is Simone.

NINA: And the waitress?

PHOTOGRAPHER: I don't remember.

NINA: You don't remember?

NINA heads for the door.

PHOTOGRAPHER: Wait.

NINA: Please . . . don't.

PHOTOGRAPHER: Nina.

No Looking Back
(Gramercy Pictures, 1998)

Screenplay by Edward Burns
Directed by Edward Burns
Characters: CHARLIE (Ed Burns)
*   CLAUDIA (Lauren Holly)*

NOTES: CLAUDIA still lives in the small working class Long Island town where she grew up. She works as a waitress in the local diner. She's never acted upon her dreams of getting out and doing something better with her life. CHARLIE is her ex-boyfriend; he has returned home after an absence of three or four years. He left CLAUDIA (and left town) while she was having an abortion after getting pregnant with his child. Now he wants her back; he wants her to leave with him on his next adventure. CLAUDIA, however, is now living with CHARLIE's friend Michael. Michael wants to marry her, stay where they are, and raise a family, but CLAUDIA is not ready to marry him. She's been resisting CHARLIE's attempts to break up her relationship, but now her resolve is weakening. CHARLIE's old charm (despite his appalling behavior) is starting to make her dream of escape. This scene takes place in a laundromat; CHARLIE takes off his lunch hour from his job as a mechanic to find CLAUDIA. She's seen him the night before at the local bar with a very young girl. He tells the truth when he says nothing happened between him and the girl, but it's not because he didn't try. It's wintertime, a cold and rainy day.

INTERIOR. LAUNDROMAT—DAY

CLAUDIA looks up as CHARLIE enters. She shakes her head and smiles.

CHARLIE: What are you smiling at?

CLAUDIA: You just come back from the junior high school?

CHARLIE: Hey. She was in college. Besides, I just drove her home.

CLAUDIA: Yeah, I'm sure you did.

CHARLIE: I brought you some lunch. You want half a meatball hero?

CLAUDIA: No, thanks.

CHARLIE: How about a beer, then? I got some beers.

CLAUDIA: A beer I'll take.

CHARLIE: Yeah, I figured as much.

CHARLIE pulls out two cans of beer and pops them open. She is smiling at him again.

CHARLIE: I'm telling you the truth, nothing happened. I just drove her home, a little kiss, and that was it. What? Are you jealous or something?

CLAUDIA: Why would I be jealous?

CHARLIE: No reason. I'm just saying if you are jealous, it's okay. I can understand. I'm sure it was weird for you to see me with another woman. Especially a fine young little thing like that.

CLAUDIA: If I thought there was a chance she might be out of the tenth grade, then maybe I might be jealous.

CHARLIE: I told you, she was in college.

CLAUDIA: I hope so for your sake.

CHARLIE goes over to the radio and raises the volume.

CHARLIE: Oh, I know this song. You like this song, don't you?

CLAUDIA: You know I like all his stuff.

CHARLIE: You want to dance?

CLAUDIA: What? Here?

CHARLIE: Yeah, come on. A little slow dance.

CLAUDIA: What are you talking about? You don't know how to dance.

CHARLIE: What? It's a slow dance. Any retard knows how to do a little slow dance. Besides, you don't remember our prom? We did some dancing that night, didn't we?

CLAUDIA: I don't think so.

CHARLIE playfully grabs her arms and tries to sway her.

CHARLIE: Come on, one dance.

CLAUDIA: I'm sorry. I can't.

They stand there, looking at each other.

CHARLIE: You hate me, don't you?

CLAUDIA: No, I'm just not dancing with you.

CHARLIE: All right. I guess I should probably be getting back to work now anyhow, huh?

CLAUDIA shrugs, suggesting that he should. CHARLIE grabs his bag and heads out.

CHARLIE: All right, I'll see you around. Enjoy the beer.

He stops at the door.

CHARLIE: Hey.

CLAUDIA: What?

CHARLIE: (*with a smile*) I told you you'd be cleaning his dirty underwear.

CLAUDIA smirks and gives him the finger. He smiles and turns and exits.

Outbreak
(Warner Bros., 1995)

Screenplay by Laurence Dworet & Robert Ray Pool,
revised draft by Neal Jimenez
Directed by Wolfgang Petersen
Characters: ROBBY (Renee Russo)
       SAM (Dustin Hoffman)

NOTES: ROBBY and SAM used to be married. They also used to work together fighting rare infectious diseases. Now there has been an outbreak of ebola in Zaire; SAM has been there working. He has asked ROBBY to stay with the dogs. But she was supposed to leave for her new job in Atlanta at the Center for Disease Control on Friday and SAM hasn't returned until today. It's Sunday and ROBBY expresses her anger and frustration as she leaves for the airport.

44. EXTERIOR. ROBBY'S HOUSE—DAY

For just a moment, the exterior of the house looks serene. ROBBY comes out, lugging a pair of well-worn suitcases. SAM is right behind her.

ROBBY: I am through talking about this.

SAM: Okay.

ROBBY: You've never understood the concept of real time. What day is it?

SAM: Sunday.

RONNY: When did you say you'd be back?

SAM: Friday.

ROBBY: Thursday, Sam—Thursday.

SAM: Right, Thursday. I meant Thursday.

ROBBY: Thursday—Friday—They're so close together—even I confuse them. Christ, why didn't I just go to Atlanta when I said I would.

SAM: Because you're a decent human being. If you put the big pieces in first . . .

ROBBY: Fuck you, Sam. You were going to be home Thursday, I was going to fly Friday and see my new apartment . . . go to my new job on Saturday, meet my new staff, buy a new toaster . . . maybe have Sunday to rest . . .

As she's talking, controlling her anger, she throws her luggage into the trunk.

ROBBY: (*cont'd*) Now I'm rushing to make a two o'clock flight, I won't get to the apartment until seven; if I'm lucky I can buy the toaster but it will be nine before I even have a chance to unpack . . . No, I can't unpack, cuz I have a nine o'clock hello-how-do-you-do staff party . . . Louis, move over, move over!

SAM: You're scaring him. (*nods*) Louis—

The dog moves immediately. ROBBY glances at SAM, angry that he has such firm control over this one.

ROBBY: That's because you let him on the couch.

ROBBY gets in the cab, looks to Neal, the cabdriver, who's keeping a straight face as the couple argues.

ROBBY: Let's go—

SAM: Wait. How long are you keeping the dogs?

ROBBY looks at SAM—what is he thinking?

ROBBY: They are going with me, Sam. To Atlanta.

SAM: They're my dogs, too. I'll miss 'em.

ROBBY, just now, is out of patience.

ROBBY: Do you want the dogs, Sam? Either they go with me or they stay here with you. We are not going to split them up and we are not going to share them. Decide.

SAM does not respond. ROBBY opens the cab door.

ROBBY: Okay . . .

SAM: Wait . . .

As he gently closes the door . . .

SAM: You keep 'em.

ROBBY: (to the driver) You can go now.

SAM: Wait, wait a second. There's something I've got to say. Now I'm forgetting . . .

ROBBY: Sam, I can't miss this plane.

SAM: No, right, I remember now. When you go to the pet store, remember they like those medium-sized bones—

ROBBY: —barbeque flavored. I know. (*a beat*) You look tired. It was bad in Zaire.

SAM: Could have been better.

ROBBY: What's the mortality?

SAM: About the same as our relationship.

ROBBY: You be careful.

SAM: I will. (*beat*) Good luck in Atlanta.

She forces a smile, nods to the driver, and the cab takes off down the street. SAM stands, alone, watching the cab move off into the distance. The dogs look to him out the back window, as if saying goodbye . . .

Out Of Africa
(Universal, 1985)

Screenplay by Kurt Luedtke
Directed by Sydney Pollack
Characters: KAREN (Meryl Streep)
DENYS (Robert Redford)

NOTES: *Out of Africa* is based on the memoirs of Karen Von Blixen, who moved to Kenya from her native Denmark and eventually ran a farm in Africa on her own. Her husband mostly absent, eventually gone altogether, KAREN has an affair with DENYS, an adventurer who can't be tied down. He "lives with" her—when he's not on a trip. He is at the farm for a few days when this scene occurs. She loves him and wants him to prove his love for her. (The last line of dialogue was cut during rehearsal.)

260. INTERIOR. DRAWING ROOM—NIGHT

DENYS sits leaning over a map spread out on the floor. KAREN's in a chair with clothes to mend.

DENYS: I flew as far as Narok: You can see the ruts where the lorries have been. The Serengeti's still good . . .

KAREN: It would take a week just getting there.

DENYS: More like ten days . . . Samburu still seems good. (*then*) I havn't seen Belknap.

KAREN: He must be in America by now. (*at his look*) I let him go . . . I had to. (*then*) But you don't really want to know about the farm, do you.

285

He's silent. She finishes mending her trousers, picks up his shirt.

KAREN: (*continuing*) Have you got buttons anywhere?

DENYS: What are you doing?

KAREN: Mending your shirt.

DENYS: I have that done in town.

She stares. He returns to the map. A beat.

DENYS: I'll try Samburu. Day after tomorrow.

KAREN: (*quietly*) You just got back.

DENYS: (*a beat*) Felicity's asked to come along. I started to say no . . . because I thought *you* wouldn't like it. (*silence*) There's no reason for her not to come.

KAREN: Yes there is. I *wouldn't* like it. (*silence*) Do you want her to come along?

DENYS: I want things that don't matter not to matter.

KAREN: Tell her no. Do it for me.

DENYS: And then? What else will there be?

KAREN: Why is your freedom more important than mine?

DENYS: I've *never* interfered with you.

KAREN: I'm not allowed to need you. Rely on you. Expect anything at all. I'm only free to leave. (*then*) But I *do* need you.

DENYS: There's no answer to that, Karen. Suppose I died? Would you die? You don't *need* me. You mix up need with want. You always have.

KAREN: My God. In the world you make, there'd be no love at all.

DENYS: Or the best kind. The kind we wouldn't have to prove.

KAREN: You'll live on the moon, then—

DENYS: —Why? Because I won't do it your way? Are we assuming there's one *proper* way to do all this? (*beat*) Do you think I care about Felicity?

KAREN: No.

DENYS: Then there's no reason for this, is there?

KAREN: I want you to give it up. For me.

He holds her gaze.

KAREN: (*continuing*) I've learned a thing you haven't. There *are* things worth having—they come at a price. I want to be one of them. (*beat*) I won't allow it, Denys.

DENYS: (*beat*) You've no idea, have you—the effect that language has.

KAREN: I used to think there was nothing you really wanted. But that's not it, is it? You want it all.

DENYS: I want it . . . a better way. (*then*) I'm going to Samburu. She can come or not.

KAREN: Then you'll be living elsewhere.

DENYS: . . . All right.

She gets up. As she goes:

KAREN: I didn't want your soul, Denys—I was only trying to mend your shirt.

The Player
(Fine Line, 1992)

Screenplay by Michael Tolkin
Directed by Robert Altman
Characters: JUNE (Greta Scacchi)
               GRIFFIN (Tim Robbins)

NOTES: GRIFFIN is the quintessential, sharklike Hollywood producer. Things are going well for him and it looks like he may be in line for an even higher position at the studio, until he starts getting threatening postcards and faxes from a disgruntled writer whom he had once blown off. He thinks the writer is David Kahane, so he tracks him down where he lives and phones from his car. He gets David's girlfriend, JUNE, who tells him David is at the movies. GRIFFIN watches June through the window as they talk. GRIFFIN then finds David at the movie theater and, in a confrontation that leads to a fist fight, accidentally kills him. He formally meets JUNE at David's funeral. Then the threats start again and GRIFFIN realizes he got the wrong man. When he finds a rattlesnake in his car he is truly shaken and goes to JUNE.

INTERIOR. JUNE'S HOUSE—NIGHT
JUNE is painting. GRIFFIN's Polaroid image is in the painting. She works for a while and then goes to get something near a window. She sees GRIFFIN's face staring at her. It startles her.

288

JUNE: Oh, My God! You gave me such a scare. What are you doing here? You gave me such a fright. Come in. Come on in.

(He leaves the window, and she goes to open the front door. She lets him in.)

JUNE: What's the matter? You look terrible. What's up? Sit down, I'll get you a drink.

He sits as she goes to the fridge and takes out a bottle of vodka. She pours him a drink.

JUNE: What happened?

GRIFFIN: Is it too late? I'm sorry . . .

JUNE: No, no, no. It's not too late. No.

GRIFFIN: I don't even know what time it is.

JUNE: What's wrong?

GRIFFIN: What are you painting? Is that me?

JUNE: Yes. That's you. See?

GRIFFIN: Do they have snakes in Iceland?

JUNE: Snakes? I don't think so.

GRIFFIN: Are you afraid of snakes?

JUNE: I don't know. I've never been close to a real one.

GRIFFIN: They scare the shit out of me.

JUNE: Have another.

GRIFFIN: I don't usually drink.

She pours him another drink.

JUNE: Did something happen tonight?

GRIFFIN: Yes, but, there's something else I have to tell you.

JUNE: Yes?

GRIFFIN: This isn't easy for me.

They stare at each other for a moment. Finally, she speaks.

JUNE: Yes . . . How about if I get on with my work, and you just talk to me when you feel like it? Okay?

She goes back to her work.

GRIFFIN: I came very close to dying tonight. (*she listens*) All I thought about was you. I don't even know you, and you came into my mind, and I couldn't, I couldn't think of anything else. Remember that first night we spoke . . . on the phone? Well, I was outside these windows watching you, you know. It was so exciting and so new and strange. I can't get you out of my mind.

JUNE: Are you making love to me?

He hadn't thought of that.

GRIFFIN: Yes. I guess I am. I guess I am. I want to make love to you. I want to make love to you.

She doesn't move for a bit.

JUNE: It's too soon. It's too soon. Isn't it? It's so strange how things happen. So strange. David was here, then he left, you arrived. Maybe it's the timing, but I feel like I would go anywhere with you, if you asked. But we mustn't hurry things. We can't hurry things, any more than we can stop them. (*She is close to tears.*) You'd better go now. I think I'm going to cry now. Better go. Quick.

She opens the door.

GRIFFIN: I'm sorry.

JUNE: No, no, no. Don't be sorry. Just go home and get some sleep, and call me, tomorrow. Invite me on a proper date. I'd like that . . .

He leaves, and she closes the door.

The Player (2)
(Fine Line, 1992)

Screenplay by Michael Tolkin
Directed by Robert Altman
Characters: GRIFFIN (Tim Robbins)
*   KAHANE (Vincent D'Onofrio)*

NOTES: This is the confrontation that leads to KAHANE's murder (*see notes for previous scene*).

INTERIOR. KARAOKE BAR—NIGHT

GRIFFIN and KAHANE are at a table. There are Asian men in suits, a slew of hostesses, and a karaoke machine. A drunk Japanese man holds a microphone and sings.

KAHANE: You ever been to Japan?

GRIFFIN: Yeah, once, on a location scout with Steven . . . Spielberg.

KAHANE: I lived there for a year. Student year abroad.

GRIFFIN: Great. I wish, I wish I'd done that.

KAHANE: I think about it alot. I'll never forget it.

GRIFFIN: You should write about it.

KAHANE: I did. Don't you remember?

GRIFFIN: What?

The drinks arrive.

KAHANE: *Arigato.* My idea. About an American student who goes to Japan. That was my pitch. The one you were supposed to get back to me on.

GRIFFIN is confused.

KAHANE: You don't remember, do you?

The song is over. GRIFFIN applauds briefly.

GRIFFIN: Of course, I remember.

KAHANE: You never got back to me.

GRIFFIN: Listen, I was an asshole. All right? It comes with the job. I'm sorry. I really am. I know how angry it must have made you. I'll make it up to you, that's what I'm here for. I'm gonna give you a deal, David. I'm not going to guarantee I'll make the movie, but I'm gonna give you a shot. Let's just stop all the postcard shit, all right? I'm here to say that I would like to start over. Friends?

GRIFFIN offers his hand, but KAHANE doesn't shake. KA-HANE watches him, and finally GRIFFIN puts his hand down without saying a word.

KAHANE: Fuck you, Mill. You're a liar.

GRIFFIN: You're stepping over the line, David.

KAHANE: You didn't come out here to see *The Bicycle Thief.* You came in five minutes before the picture ended. You nearly tripped over my feet. What'd you do, call my house? Speak to the ice queen? You'd like her, Mill. She's a lot like you. All heart. You're on my list, pal, and nothing's going to change that.

KAHANE gets up and walks.

KAHANE: See you in the next reel, asshole.

KAHANE leaves.

EXTERIOR. STREET—NIGHT

GRIFFIN leaves the bar. He walks past the theatre and around the corner to his car and unlocks it. Just as he is about to get in, KAHANE speaks from the shadows.

KAHANE: That's a nice boat you got there, Movie Exec . . . It's me. The writer. Still wanna buy my story?

GRIFFIN: I told you . . . I'd give you a deal. Stop by the studio first thing in the morning, and we'll work something out.

KAHANE: And who'll I ask for? Larry Levy?

GRIFFIN starts to follow KAHANE down the sidewalk.

GRIFFIN: What's Larry Levy got to do with this? How do you know about Larry Levy?

KAHANE: Don't you read the trades? The *New York Times* Business Section? He's moving in . . . you're moving out. You can't make a deal, that's what they say. Yesterday's news.

GRIFFIN: (*calling to him*) Wait a minute. Wait a minute.

Proof
(Fine Line Features, 1992)

Screenplay by Jocelyn Moorhouse
Directed by Jocelyn Moorhouse
Characters: MARTIN (Hugo Weaving)
*   ANDY (Russell Crowe)*

NOTES: MARTIN lives in Melbourne; he is in his thirties, and he is blind. He has a housekeeper, Celia; she does his cleaning, cooking, laundry, grocery shopping, bills. She is young, thirty. MARTIN and Celia have a relationship of deliberate mutual cruelty. MARTIN doesn't trust her—perhaps a leftover from his youth, when he didn't trust his mother, didn't even believe she had died, thought she'd "gotten away" from him—but Celia has certainly done things to earn that distrust. She moves furniture and hides things from MARTIN in order to control him. She wants him and doesn't hide it. MARTIN knows this. He says, "if I continue to deny her, she can't pity me." Their relationship is a complex mixture of hate, love and dependence. MARTIN takes photographs as a hobby. He then asks Celia to describe the photos and he labels them—for proof, he says. When MARTIN meets ANDY—he accidently injures a cat in the alley behind the restaurant where ANDY works as a dishwasher—the two men become friends and MARTIN starts to trust ANDY. He gets ANDY to describe his photos. This is the first time ANDY—a kind, down to earth, but directionless young man—has been to MARTIN's home. They've just been to the movies and gotten into a brawl that involved a brush with the cops.

40. INTERIOR. MARTIN'S HOUSE—NIGHT—DAY 4

One of MARTIN's classical records is spinning on his record player. ANDY wanders about the lounge room, fascinated by the details of MARTIN's home. He passes MARTIN's desk. A typewriter, complete with a half-typed classical record review, sits amongst the various paraphernalia of MARTIN's employment: a Walkman, a taperecorder with microphone, records with Braille labels. ANDY looks at the heading of the review. It is a review of a recording of Beethoven's 7th Symphony by the London Philharmonic Orchestra.

ANDY: (*calling out*) This what you do for a crust? Review records?

MARTIN is busy in the kitchen, opening and closing cupboard doors.

MARTIN: Yes. For a couple of magazines, and one or two radio programs.

ANDY: Not a bad job. Listening to records all day.

ANDY walks over to the couch. BILL, the dog, dominates most of it. ANDY squeezes in next to the dog.

ANDY: (*calling out to MARTIN again*) This your blind dog?

MARTIN: Bill isn't blind. He can see quite well.

ANDY: Na, I meant . . . guide dog.

ANDY has his eyes closed. He passes his fingertips over the braille letters of one of MARTIN's books, trying to imagine . . .

MARTIN: He was. He's retired now. I didn't want to get a new dog. I've already had five. I got sick of saying goodbye . . . Besides, a cane is better for mobility. Damn!

ANDY gets up off the couch and walks into the kitchen.

ANDY: What's the matter?

MARTIN: Celia. She's moved the liquor glasses again. She does it once a month. Moves everything just to remind me I'm blind.

ANDY sees the glasses hidden on top of a cupboard. He grabs two glasses.

ANDY: Found 'em. On top of the cupboard. I've got two.

ANDY and MARTIN walk back into the lounge area. ANDY and MARTIN sit down on opposite chairs in the lounge-room. MARTIN unscrews the top from a bottle of port. Ugly, the one-eyed cat, sits on the arm of his chair, while Bill sits on the couch next to ANDY.

ANDY: I suppose you must depend on Celia for a lot of things.

MARTIN: Oh far from it. I only keep her on because she needs the money. I can't imagine anyone else employing her if I dismissed her.

ANDY: I'd like to meet her.

MARTIN: I'd rather you didn't.

ANDY watches MARTIN pour port into both glasses to exactly the same level.

ANDY: How do you know when to stop?

MARTIN: The sound.

ANDY: Fuckin' amazing.

MARTIN laughs.

MARTIN: Here you are.

MARTIN hands a glass of port to ANDY. ANDY sips from his glass, and looks at a photo on the mantelpiece.

ANDY: Who's that in the photograph?

MARTIN: Which photograph?

ANDY: The old one. On the mantelpiece.

MARTIN: How do you know it's old?

ANDY: It looks old. Black and white. The lady in it has old-fashioned clothes. Is that your mum?

MARTIN: (*quiet a moment*) Yes.

ANDY stands up and walks over to the photograph. He picks it up and brings it back to where they sit.

ANDY: Is the kid you?

MARTIN: I've always supposed so.

ANDY: You've never seen your own mum. Want me to describe her to you?

MARTIN: All right.

ANDY looks closely at the photograph.

ANDY: She doesn't look like you.

MARTIN: (*surprised*) Really? People always said she did.

ANDY: (*matter of factly*) Na. They were probably just saying that.

ANDY looks up at MARTIN, realizing what he just said.

ANDY: She's sitting down. She's got long white legs with little black shoes. She's got her arms around you, but your head's turned away. Her fingers are long and white too, like a statue, you know.

MARTIN listens, absorbed.

ANDY: She's only young—maybe twenty-eight, nine. Her hair is dark and she's got it up at the back.

ANDY traces the loose strands of her hair across her faded white face.

ANDY: Your hair's short.

MARTIN: She always cut it herself. I never went to a barber. I never went out with my mother at all. She was embarrassed by me, you see. She always wanted an ordinary child that she could do ordinary things with. She got me.

There is a pause. After a while MARTIN speaks.

MARTIN: Thank you, Andy.

MARTIN holds out his hand for the photograph. ANDY passes it to him. MARTIN feels the frame, almost caressing it. MARTIN listens to the classical music, holding the photograph.

MARTIN: One day, I might show you a photograph. It was the first photograph I ever took. I was twelve years old. It's not much of a photograph really. Just a garden that was visible through one of the windows in our flat. But it's the most important photograph I've ever taken.

ANDY listens to MARTIN, curious.

MARTIN: Every morning and every afternoon, my mother would describe this garden to me. Through her eyes I saw the seasons come and go. I questioned her so thoroughly, always trying to catch her in a lie. I never did. But by taking the photo, I knew I could, one day.

ANDY: Why would your mother lie to you?

MARTIN: To punish me. For being blind.

ANDY: Does it really matter if she lied about some garden?

MARTIN: Yes. (*pause*) It was my world.

Proof (2)
(Fine Line Features, 1992)

Screenplay by Jocelyn Moorhouse
Directed by Jocelyn Moorhouse
Characters: CELIA (Genevieve Picot)
MARTIN (Hugo Weaving)

NOTES: CELIA, MARTIN's housekeeper, (*see notes for previous scene*) is aware of MARTIN's friendship with Andy and threatened by it. She pursues her agenda to seduce MARTIN even more vigorously. She takes a polaroid of MARTIN on the toilet and threatens to post it in public unless he goes out with her for one night. MARTIN knows her threat is real—CELIA is cold, capable of almost anything—and so he agrees. CELIA takes him to the symphony, which he truly enjoys and thanks her for, but she still won't return the photograph. She makes him return to her house for dinner.

56. INTERIOR. CELIA'S HOUSE—NIGHT—DAY 7

The light comes on, revealing CELIA's modest house. CELIA and MARTIN enter the lounge room.

CELIA: I prepared a light supper.

MARTIN: (*uncomfortable*) Will this take long?

CELIA guides MARTIN towards an armchair.

CELIA: You can sit here.

It should gradually become obvious that the walls are covered in photographs, and every photograph is of MARTIN:

299

MARTIN in the park, MARTIN asleep, MARTIN walking.
MARTIN sits in the chair, and CELIA sits in one nearby.
Just above MARTIN's head, on the wall, is a framed photo
of MARTIN and Bill. All the photos are telephoto, or blown
up. None of them are posed—MARTIN has been photo-
graphed without his knowledge on all occasions. CELIA re-
moves her sweater and sits down.

CELIA: I'm a bit of a photographer myself, Martin.

MARTIN: Really? What do you photograph?

CELIA: Things I love. (*pause*) I don't think you know how
    fond I am of you.

MARTIN: I'm getting a fair idea.

CELIA pours a glass of port for MARTIN, and hands it to
him.

CELIA: Your favorite.

MARTIN takes the port and sniffs it, while CELIA exits
briefly. MARTIN sits alone a moment, surrounded by photos
of himself. CELIA enters the room again. She brings food
on a tray. MARTIN smells the food.

CELIA: Your favourite cold meats.

She begins to undo her blouse. She is braless beneath it.
CELIA walks closer to MARTIN.

CELIA: For so long I wanted you in my house. And now
    you're here. I would have preferred to begin the night with-
    out the photograph—but it was clear you wouldn't ask me
    out of your own volition. But the photo doesn't matter now.
    Tonight's been all I hoped for and more. (*She unbuttons*
    her blouse and moves closer to MARTIN.) Hopefully more.

She moves closer to MARTIN.

CELIA: Hopefully more.

MARTIN shifts uncomfortably.

MARTIN: Is supper self-serve?

CELIA: I never knew my father. And my mother died ten
    years ago. Now there's only me. (*She looks around at the*
    photos.) And you.

MARTIN looks uneasy. He takes a bite to eat.

CELIA: You and I have a lot in common. We're both moth-
erless. Both alone. Do you ever get the feeling of being
watched?

MARTIN: All my life.

CELIA walks a little closer to MARTIN. He senses her.

CELIA: You never knew when it was me.

MARTIN clears his throat.

MARTIN: Celia. Why don't we get to the point?

CELIA: Have you ever wondered why I've stayed working
for you all these years, when you're so deliberately cruel
to me?

MARTIN: I have asked myself that question.

CELIA: And what was the answer?

MARTIN: (*hesitant*) You . . . like it?

CELIA: I don't like it. I hate it. Ask the question again.

MARTIN: What quest—

CELIA: Why do I stay with you?

MARTIN: I don't know.

CELIA: Yes you do, Martin. No more game playing. Games
are over. Time for truth.

MARTIN: All right, Celia. I know why you stay.

CELIA: Can I ask you something?

MARTIN: Yes.

CELIA: I get the feeling that you've never been with a
woman, am I right?

MARTIN: I think we're getting a little personal here.

CELIA: You're thirty-two years old, Martin. Isn't it about
time we did? There's no need to be afraid. Have you ever
touched a woman . . . ?

*CELIA touches MARTIN's hand. He flinches and goes to
pull away, but she grabs him around the wrist.*

MARTIN: Please Celia—

CELIA: Feel this.

CELIA places MARTIN's hand over her heartbeat. MARTIN doesn't struggle to pull away.

CELIA: Feel it thumping in there? It's beating fast. Faster than usual. That's where the music got you, isn't it? That's where you get me.

CELIA slides MARTIN's fingers onto one of her breasts. MARTIN is breathing quickly, in a mixture of fear, repulsion and desire. CELIA takes off MARTIN's glasses and, leaning forward into the chair, brushes a breast against MARTIN's cheek. The sparkling brooch on CELIA's blouse casts a myriad of colors onto MARTIN's face.

CELIA: I'm greedy, Martin. I want you all to myself. I used to have that, but things have changed. I have to change them back.

MARTIN doesn't move. He is mesmerized.

CELIA: Take this opportunity, Martin. It may not come again.

CELIA slowly reaches down and begins to undo MARTIN's fly. She reaches inside. MARTIN gasps. MARTIN reaches for CELIA's face. He finds it. He pulls her down so that he can kiss her on the mouth. They kiss passionately. CELIA slips her hand beneath MARTIN's shirt and strokes his skin. MARTIN strokes CELIA's breasts. Suddenly MARTIN panics.

MARTIN: No. I can't.

CELIA: Trust me.

MARTIN: I can't.

CELIA: Don't be scared.

MARTIN: I'm not scared.

CELIA: You want me.

MARTIN: I don't. I don't want anyone. Leave me alone!

MARTIN stumbles to his feet and lurches for the door, crashing into things.

MARTIN: Where's the door? Where's the door?

CELIA: Don't go. Don't leave me.

CELIA calls out to him. He finds the door and runs outside.

CELIA: Your fly's undone!

Pulp Fiction
(Miramax, 1994)

Screenplay by Quentin Tarantino
Directed by Quentin Tarantino
Characters: VINCENT (John Travolta)
             JULES (Samuel L. Jackson)

NOTES: **VINCENT and JULES work together in Los Angeles; their boss is Marcellus, a relatively major drug dealer. They have been sent to "take care of" some guys who are trying to cheat Marcellus out of a deal. They know that it will probably involve killing them. This is a typical day for VINCENT and JULES.**

2. INTERIOR. '74 CHEVY (MOVING)—MORNING

An old gas guzzling, dirty, white 1974 Chevy Nova barrels down a homeless-ridden street in Hollywood. In the front seat are two young fellas—one white, one black—both wearing cheap black suits with thin black ties under long green dusters. Their names are VINCENT VEGA (white) and JULES WINNFIELD (black). JULES is behind the wheel.

JULES: —okay now, tell me about the hash bars?

VINCENT: What do you want to know?

JULES: Well, hash is legal there, right?

VINCENT: Yeah, it's legal, but it ain't a hundred percent legal, I mean you can't walk into a restaurant, roll a joint, and start puffin' away. You're only supposed to smoke in your home or certain designated places.

JULES: Those are the hash bars?

VINCENT: Yeah, it breaks down like this: it's legal to buy it, it's legal to own it and, if you're the proprietor of a hash bar, it's legal to sell it. It's legal to carry it, which doesn't really matter 'cause—get a load of this—if the cops stop you, it's illegal for them to search you. Searching you is a right that the cops in Amsterdam don't have.

JULES: That did it, man—I'm fuckin' goin', that's all there is to it.

VINCENT: You'll dig it the most. But you know what the funniest thing about Europe is?

JULES: What?

VINCENT: It's the little differences. A lotta the same shit we got here, they got there, but there they're a little different.

JULES: Example?

VINCENT: Well, in Amsterdam, you can buy beer in a movie theater. And I don't mean in a paper cup either. They give you a glass of beer, like in a bar. In Paris, you can buy beer at McDonald's. Also, you know what they call a Quarter Pounder with Cheese in Paris?

JULES: They don't call it a Quarter Pounder with Cheese?

VINCENT: No, they got the metric system there, they wouldn't know what the fuck a Quarter Pounder is.

JULES: What'd they call it?

VINCENT: Royale with Cheese.

JULES: (*repeating*) Royale with Cheese. What'd they call a Big Mac?

VINCENT: Big Mac's a Big Mac, but they call it Le Big Mac.

JULES: What do they call a Whopper?

VINCENT: I dunno, I didn't go into a Burger King. But you know what they put on french fries in Holland instead of ketchup?

JULES: What?

VINCENT: Mayonnaise.

JULES: Goddamn!

VINCENT: I seen 'em do it. And I don't mean a little bit on the side of the plate, they fuckin' drown 'em in it.

JULES: Uucch!

3. INTERIOR. CHEVY (TRUNK)—MORNING

The trunk of the Chevy opens up, JULES and VINCENT reach inside, taking out .45 Automatics, loading and cocking them.

JULES: We should have shotguns for this kind of deal.

VINCENT: How many up there?

JULES: Three or four.

VINCENT: So there could be five guys up there?

JULES: It's possible.

VINCENT: We should have fuckin' shotguns.

They close the trunk.

4. EXTERIOR. APARTMENT BUILDING COURTYARD— MORNING

VINCENT and JULES, their long matching overcoats practically dragging on the ground, walk through the courtyard of what looks like a hacienda-style Hollywood apartment building. We track alongside.

VINCENT: What's her name?

JULES: Mia.

VINCENT: How did Marcellus and her meet?

JULES: I dunno, however people meet people.

VINCENT: She ever do anything I woulda saw?

JULES: I think her biggest deal was she starred in a pilot.

VINCENT: What's a pilot?

JULES: Well, you know the shows on TV?

VINCENT: I don't watch TV.

JULES: Yeah, but you're aware that there's an invention called television, and on that invention they show shows?

VINCENT: Yeah.

JULES: Well, the way they pick the shows on TV is they make one show, and that show's called a pilot. And they show that one show to the people who pick the shows, and on the strength of that one show, they decide if they want to make more shows. Some get accepted and become TV programs, and some don't, and become nothing. She starred in one of the ones that became nothing.

They enter the apartment building.

5. INTERIOR RECEPTION AREA (APARTMENT BUILD-ING)—MORNING

VINCENT and JULES walk through the reception area and wait for the elevator.

JULES: You remember Antwan Rockamora? Half-black, half-Samoan, usta call him Tony Rocky Horror.

VINCENT: Yeah, maybe. Fat, right?

JULES: I wouldn't go so far as to call the brother fat. He's got a weight problem. What's the nigger gonna do, he's Samoan.

VINCENT: I think I know who you mean, what about him?

JULES: Well, Marcellus fucked his ass up good. And word around the campfire, it was on account of Marsellus Wallace's wife.

The elevator arrives, the men step inside.

6. INTERIOR. ELEVATOR—MORNING

VINCENT: What'd he do, fuck her?

JULES: No no no no no no no, nothin' that bad.

VINCENT: Well what then?

JULES: He gave her a foot massage.

VINCENT: A foot massage?

JULES nods his head yes.

VINCENT: That's all?

JULES nods his head yes.

VINCENT: What did Marcellus do?

JULES: Sent a couple of guys over to his place. They took him out on the patio of his apartment, threw his ass over the balcony. Nigger fell four stories. They had this garden at the bottom, enclosed in glass, like one of them greenhouses—nigger fell through that. Since then, he's kinda developed a speech impediment.

The elevator doors open, JULES and VINCENT exit.

VINCENT: That's a damn shame.

7. INTERIOR. APARTMENT BUILDING HALLWAY—MORNING

Steadicam in front of JULES and VINCENT as they make a beeline down the hall.

VINCENT: Still I hafta say, play with matches, ya get burned.

JULES: Whaddya mean?

VINCENT: You don't be givin' Marcellus Wallace's new bride a foot massage.

JULES: You don't think he overreacted?

VINCENT: Antwan probably didn't expect Marcellus to react like he did, but he had to expect a reaction.

JULES: It was a foot massage, a foot massage is nothing, I give my mother a foot massage.

VINCENT: It's laying hands on Marcellus Wallace's new wife in a familiar way. Is it as bad as eatin' her out—no, but you're in the same fuckin' ballpark.

JULES: Whoa . . . whoa . . . whoa . . . stop right there. Eatin' a bitch out, and givin' a bitch a foot massage ain't even the same fuckin' thing.

VINCENT: Not the same thing, the same ballpark.

JULES: It ain't no *ballpark* either. Look maybe your method of massage differs from mine, but touchin' his lady's feet, and stickin' your tongue in her holiest of holies, ain't the same ballpark, ain't the same league, ain't even the same fuckin' sport. Foot massages don't mean shit.

VINCENT: Have you ever given a foot massage?

JULES: Don't be tellin' me about foot massages—I'm the fuckin' foot master.

VINCENT: Given a lot of 'em?

JULES: Shit yeah. I got my technique down man, I don't tickle or nothin'.

VINCENT: Have you ever given a guy a foot massage?

JULES looks at him a long moment—he's been set up.

JULES: Fuck you.

He starts walking down the hall. VINCENT, smiling, walks a little bit behind.

VINCENT: How many?

JULES: Fuck you.

VINCENT: Would you give me a foot massage—I'm kinda tired.

JULES: Man, you best back off, I'm gittin' pissed—this is the door.

The two men stand in front of a door numbered "49." They whisper.

JULES: What time is it?

VINCENT: (*checking his watch*) Seven-twenty-two in the morning.

JULES: It ain't quite time, let's hang back.

They move a little way from the door, facing each other, still whispering.

JULES: Look, just because I wouldn't give no man a foot massage, don't make it right for Marcellus to throw Antwan off a building into a glass-motherfuckin-house, fuckin' up the way the nigger talks. That ain't right, man. Motherfucker do that to me, he better paralyze my ass, 'cause I'd kill a motherfucker.

VINCENT: I'm not sayin' he was right, but you're sayin' a foot massage don't mean nothin', and I'm sayin' it does. I've given a million ladies a million foot massages and they all meant somethin'. We act like they don't, but they do. That's what's so fuckin' cool about 'em. This sensual thing's goin' on that nobody's talkin' about, but you know it and she knows it, fuckin' Marcellus knew it, and Antwan shoulda known fuckin' better. That's his fuckin' wife, man. He ain't gonna have a sense of humor about that shit.

JULES: That's an interesting point, but let's get into character.

VINCENT: What's her name again?

JULES: Mia. Why you so interested in big man's wife?

VINCENT: Well. Marcellus is leavin' for Florida and when he's gone, he wants me to take care of Mia.

JULES: Take care of her? (*making a gun out of his finger and placing it to his head*)

VINCENT: Not that! Take her out. Show her a good time. Don't let her get lonely.

JULES: You're gonna be takin' Mia Wallace out on a date?

VINCENT: It ain't a date. It's like when you and your buddy's wife go to a movie or somethin'. It's just . . . you know . . . good company.

JULES just looks at him.

VINCENT: It's not a date.

JULES just looks at him.

VINCENT: I'm not gonna be a bad boy.

JULES shakes his head and mumbles to himself.

JULES: Bitch gonna kill more niggers than time.

VINCENT: What was that?

JULES: Nothin'. Let's get into character.

VINCENT: What'd you say?

JULES: I didn't say shit. Let's go to work.

VINCENT: Don't play with me, you said somethin', now what was it?

JULES: (*referring to the job*) Do you wanna do this?

VINCENT: I want you to repeat what you said.

JULES: That door's gonna open in about thirty seconds, so git yourself together—

VINCENT: —my self is together—

JULES: —bullshit it is. Stop thinkin' 'bout that Ho, and get yourself together like a qualified pro.

Raising Arizona
(20th Century Fox, 1987)

Screenplay by Ethan Coen and Joel Coen
Directed by Joel Coen
Characters: ED (Holly Hunter)
*   HI (Nicholas Cage)*

NOTES: ED and HI are married and live in Tempe, Arizona. Their courtship took place over the course of time; each time HI was sent back to prison for another petty crime, ED, an officer of the law, was there to take his mug shot. Finally HI proposed, went straight, and they set about trying to have a family. But ED found that she couldn't have children. On the news they see the story of the Arizona quintuplets—furniture king Nathan Arizona has hit the jackpot—and they decide to "adopt" one of the quints for their own. ED waits in the driver's seat as HI breaks into the Arizonas' home and steals a baby.

INTERIOR. CHEVY—NIGHT

ED sits anxiously waiting in the driver's seat, peering intently through the windshield. As she catches sight of something she breaks into a broad smile, unlocks the door, and slides over to the passenger seat. HI is opening the door with one hand, cradling a baby in the other.

ED: Which one ya get?

HI: *(as he gets into the driver's seat)* I dunno. Nathan Jr., I think.

ED: Gimme here.

He hands her the infant, then hands her the copy of Dr. Spock's Baby and Child Care.

HI: Here's the instructions.

ED: Oh, he's beautiful!

HI nods as he pulls away from the curb.

HI: He's awful damn good. I think I got the best one.

ED is gushing and kissing the baby through the rest of the conversation.

ED: I bet they were all beautiful. All babies are beautiful!

HI: Yeah. This one's awful damn good though.

ED: Don't you cuss around him.

HI: He's fine, he is. I think it's Nathan Jr.

ED: We are doin' the right thing, aren't we Hi?—I mean, they had more'n they could handle.

HI: Well now honey, we been over and over this. There's what's right and there's what's right, and never the twain shall meet.

ED: But you don't think his momma'll be upset? I mean overly?

HI: Well a course she'll be upset, sugar, but she'll get over it. She's got four little babies almost as good as this one. It's like when I was robbin' convenience stores—

ED suddenly bursts out crying.

ED: I love him so much!

HI: I know you do, honey.

ED: (*still sobbing*) I love him so much!

TRAILER LIVING ROOM

ED is entering with NATHAN JR.

HI: This is it young Nathan Jr. Just feast your eyes about, old boy!

ED: Don't be so loud around him, Hi.

HI: (*softly*) Damn, I'm sorry honey.

ED: And don't you cuss around him.

HI: Aw, he don't know a cuss word from shinola.

ED: Well see that he don't.

HI: (*jovially*) He's all right, he is. (he reaches for the child) . . . Come on over here, Nathan Jr., I'll show you around.

He takes the baby in both hands and holds him out at arm's length, pointing him at the various places of interest. The baby looks goggle-eyed at each one.

HI: (*cont'd*) . . . Lookahere, young sportsman. That-there's the kitchen area where Ma and Pa chow down. Over there's the TV, two hours a day maximum, either educational or football so's you don't ruin your appreciation of the finer things. This-here's the divan, for socializin' and relaxin' with the family unit. Yessir, many's the day we sat there and said wouldn't it be nice to have a youngster here to share our thoughts and feelin's—

ED: (*impatient with the nonsense*) He's tired, Hi.

HI: Well, we'll just sit you right there, boy . . . (*He is propping Nathan Jr. up in the corner of the couch. HI sits at the other corner and ED sits in a facing chair.*) . . . Just put those dogs up'n take a load off.

HI beams at NATHAN JR. ED smiles at NATHAN JR. NATHAN JR. looks from one to the other, deadpan. They seem to be waiting for him to contribute to the conversation. Silence. Suddenly HI slaps his knee.

HI: What are you kiddin'?! We got a family here! (*ED is getting up*) . . . He's a scandal, honey! He's a little outlaw!

ED: (*as she picks up the baby*) He's a good boy.

HI: He ain't *too* good! You can tell by that twinkle in his eye!

ED: Don't you think we should put him to bed?

HI: Hang on, honey . . . (*he is frantically reaching for a Polaroid camera*) . . . Let's us preserve the moment in pictures!

ED: Just one, okay? . . .

She sits down on the couch with NATHAN JR. as HI starts screwing the camera into a tripod.

ED: (*cont'd*) . . . I gotta tell ya, I'm a little scared Hi.

HI: (*absently, as he sets up the camera*) How come is that, honey?

ED: Well we got a baby, Hi. It's an awful big responsibility.

HI: (*as he peers through the lens*) Honey, could ya slide over a tad and raise the nipper up?

ED: (*as she complies*) I mean we never done this before and I'm kinda nervous.

HI: You're doin' real good, sugar.

HI sits on the couch, holding the camera's cable release. He puts his arm around ED and smiles at the offscreen camera. ED nestles her head against HI's shoulder.

ED: I love you, Hi.

HI: We're set to pop here, honey.

ED: You're gonna help, aren't ya?

HI: (*through his teeth as he continues to grin at the offscreen camera*) How's that, honey?

ED: Give Nathan Jr. a normal family background, just quiet evenings at home together . . .

We begin to hear distant thunder.

HI: You can count on it, honey.

ED: . . . Everything decent'n normal from here on out.

HI: Uh-huh.

As he squeezes the cable release—FLASH—the image momentarily freezes on HI beaming, NATHAN JR. staring, and ED looking at HI with a little bit of concern.

The Return Of The Secaucus 7
(Columbia, 1981)

Screenplay by John Sayles
Directed by John Sayles
Characters: J.T. (Adam Lefevre)
*   MAURA (Karen Trott)*

NOTES: This group of friends named themselves the Secaucus
7 when they were arrested ten years earlier in Secaucus, N.J., on
their way to a war protest in Washington. Now they're all at a
weekend reunion at Mike and Katie's house in New England.
They all knew each other, and some of them dated each other,
when they were in high school and college in the seventies.
MAURA has just broken up with JERRY, J.T.'s best friend;
she's known J.T. many years. She comes to the reunion alone.
J.T. is a singer, and the only one in the group that didn't go to
college and get a "real job." He drifts around, never has any
money, borrows from his friends here and there. He's decided
to hitchike to L.A. to take a real stab at his music. He's like a
big puppy dog, still young at heart. MAURA is fresh off her
breakup; in fact, she was supposed to marry Jeff. (He shows up
at the reunion later.) The "single people" are sleeping in Mike
and Katie's living room. MAURA is on the sofa, J.T. is on the
floor in front of the sofa, and Frances is across the room on a
cot. This scene has been transcribed from the video.

316

INTERIOR. MIKE AND KATIE'S LIVING ROOM—
NIGHT

MAURA props herself up on the sofa and whispers to J.T.

MAURA: J.T.?

J.T.: (*he sits up and faces her*) Can't sleep?

MAURA: No.

J.T.: Me neither. (*pause*) How're you feelin'?

MAURA: I dunno. Funny. It's so different not to be . . . attached to Jeff. I feel like a different person.

J.T.: You don't seem so different. Just a little sad.

MAURA: Did you ever . . . before when you knew me . . . (*sighs*) I can't get this out.

J.T.: You can't what?

MAURA: Never mind. (*she smiles at him*) You really goin' to L.A.?

J.T.: I think so. It's time to either shit or get off the pot with my music.

MAURA: You involved with anybody right now?

J.T.: Involved? . . . No. (*pause*) You cold?

MAURA: No. I keep thinking about sleeping with you.

J.T.: . . . Oh. (*pause*) Wow.

MAURA: I mean, I've never been in this position before where I've really considered it—

J.T.: Uh—(*nervous laugh*)

MAURA: What I was goning to ask you before was, did— did you ever consider it? I mean, when I was with Jeff . . . did you ever wonder what it would be like? Not that you'd make any moves while Jeff was still in the picture but—

J.T.: Uh-huh.

MAURA: Uh-huh what? J.T., don't make me do all the work.

J.T.: Uh—sorry. It's just that uh—I don't know if you're, like, bein', you know, rhetorical or, if you're makin' an offer.

MAURA: You could ask.

J.T.: You wanna sleep with me?

MAURA: I think so. Do you wanna sleep with me?

J.T.: Uh-huh. (*nervous laugh*) I mean, if things had been different—I mean, I always liked you, it's that I never considered that you—

MAURA: —I wasn't available.

J.T.: Right, right. I—I always liked you—

They look at each other for a long moment.

J.T.: So—so you think we should?

MAURA: What do you think? (*pause*) I mean, I mean if it's Jeff, it's been over for months, really.

J.T.: Do you think . . . c-could we now? I mean, would you like to?

MAURA: (*looks across the room*) . . . Is Frances asleep?

J.T.: Oh, she must be.

MAURA: We have to be quiet.

They look at each other, then come together for a long kiss. They break apart just a little—

MAURA: Ooh, I like you so much.

J.T.: I am so excited. My stomach's all tight.

MAURA: Me, too. I never thought we'd get to do this. Do you wanna come up, or should I come down?

J.T.: It's an old couch. You better come down.

They kiss again.

Scandal
(Miramax, 1989)

Screenplay by Michael Thomas
Directed by Michael Caton-Jones
Characters: MANDY (Bridget Fonda)
*   CHRISTINE (Joanne Whaley-Kilmer)*

NOTES: MANDY and CHRISTINE first met while they were both dancing in a tawdry floor show in London. They had an immediate competition that became a friendship. It's the sixties; the sexual revolution and the drug culture are beginning to bud. CHRISTINE meets a charismatic man, Stephen, a well-connected doctor who introduces her into the circles of the aristocracy and Parliament. Stephen's high-placed friends come to him for drugs and girls. It is not an official arrangement, but the girls do end up sleeping with some of Stephen's friends, and do take gifts and money from them. These "connections" eventually blossom into the famous Profumo scandal, in which several members of Parliament are exposed. The girls, however, are in the early thrilling stages of playing with fire. MANDY is American; CHRISTINE, British.

INTERIOR. MANDY'S BEDROOM—NIGHT

MANDY's improving herself. She's concentrating on the spinning 45 on the turntable, parlez-vousing. The phrase the Marie-Claire's working on is: Amusez-vous bien. *The bathroom door opens, and CHRISTINE drifts in, wrapped in towels. She pulls the plug.*

MANDY: Do you mind?

CHRISTINE: I have to dry my hair.

MANDY: I have to brush up. What's wrong with that? I don't want to find myself in Paris standing there like an idiot not knowing what to say to a taxi driver.

CHRISTINE: Is that what you're going to say to a taxi driver? *Amusez-vous bien?* You say that to a taxi driver and he'll have you for lunch.

MANDY's stung.

MANDY: What's wrong with you? What's happened?

CHRISTINE: Nothing's happened.

MANDY: Where's the Persian?

CHRISTINE: He's gone to Scotland.

But there's something troubling her. She's restless, distracted, she can't find the hair dryer. MANDY can see it, but she's not saying anything.

CHRISTINE: I saw Nina Gadd at the hairdresser's. You know Nina.

MANDY: No.

CHRISTINE: Yes you do. She knows you. What's that thing on your head?

It's like a Pan Am sleep mask, worn over the fevered brow.

MANDY: It's a frown-pad.

CHRISTINE: A what?

MANDY: It stops you frowning. Everybody wears them in America. It stops you getting lines.

CHRISTINE: Mandy. You're sixteen.

MANDY: Seventeen next month. Can't be too careful.

Her impish grin. She's still a kid at heart, but she's growing up fast. CHRISTINE can't help smiling—

CHRISTINE: You'll get on, you will. When I'm selling matches in Picadilly Circus, you'll be driving round in a Bentley.

It's meant in jest of course, but it has fatal ring. MANDY has been wanting to ask, girl to girl—

MANDY: Tell me. When you were with Peter. Did he ever kiss you?

CHRISTINE: Never. No kissing. No going down. Sit up straight and face the wall. All very hygienic.

MANDY makes a face. She knows just what she means. But she tries to make alllowances—

MANDY: He's had a terrible life, you know.

Found it! CHRISTINE plucks the hair dryer from its hiding place, unrolls the cord, and plugs it in. She switches it on, and begins playing it through her hair. MANDY watches, struck as we all are, by her effortless angular sensuality: despite anything, MANDY is always that little bit in thrall of the older girl.

MANDY: Where are you going?

She can't hear her. She switches it off.

MANDY: Where are you going?

CHRISTINE: I'm having dinner.

MANDY: Where?

CHRISTINE: The 21 Club.

It's said with studied nonchalance. But MANDY knows better—

MANDY: I know all about the 21 Club. Jackie told me. The 21 Club's a knocking shop.

CHRISTINE's shy grin.

CHRISTINE: It's a free meal.

True. MANDY's on the spot. This is actually a critical moment between these two: They are about to lead each other one more step astray.

CHRISTINE: Do you want to come? You can come if you like. You don't have to if you don't want to. That's what Nina says.

MANDY: Nina Gadd's on the game.

She said it. But CHRISTINE's a step ahead.

CHRISTINE: What's the harm in it? We're all flesh. That's what Stephen says.

MANDY: Not me.

CHRISTINE: Suit yourself. *Amusez vous bien.*

And she switches on the dryer, full throttle, blowing her hair in a sheet of thrilling copper.

Sea of Love
(Universal, 1989)

Screenplay by Richard Price
Directed by Harold Becker
Characters: FRANK (Al Pacino)
DENICE (no original actress)

NOTES: FRANK and DENICE work at the same police pre-cinct. They are divorced, and DENICE has remarried FRANK's partner, GRUBER. FRANK drinks too much and lately has been going through a bad time; he's been calling DENICE at home at all hours, drunk. DENICE has moved on, but FRANK is stuck in his lonely life. Here DENICE confronts him the day after a three-a.m. call. All day, FRANK has been interviewing suspects and acquaintances of victims, trying to get a lead on a particu-larly elusive serial killer. This scene did not appear in the final film.

INTERIOR. SQUAD ROOM—5:00 P.M.—CLOSE ON FRANK'S DESK

FRANK is going over a handwritten list of women's names, checking them against the address book he found on the coffee table. The squad clerk escorts another woman over to Frank's desk. The woman is attractive, thirty-five, staring straight at Frank all business. It's DENICE.

FRANK: *(rises, thrown)* You looking for Gruber?

DENICE: For you.

FRANK: For me? You want to get some coffee or something? Cappuccino? Espresso? Double Espresso?

DENICE: Frank, you have to leave me alone from now on . . .

FRANK: Hey, Denice.

DENICE: (*sitting down*) You beat up my husband . . .

FRANK: Beat up . . . hey . . . he started . . .

DENICE: (*shaking her head sadly*) "He started." That's what a *kid* says.

FRANK: Well he did.

DENICE: You know what else a kid does?

She produces the ringed picture of herself that Gruber ripped out of Frank's locker. Frank looks at it, embarrassed.

DENICE: (*in a childish sing song*) Nyah nyah nyah nyah . . . real clever, Frank.

FRANK: (*mortified*) I dunno, I was hurt . . . it was stupid . . . (*beat*) You know, Denice . . . I waited until I was thirty-nine years old before I got married. Why'd I do that? You know why? (*FRANK tries to look cagey, wise, but he can't answer his own question*)

DENICE: (*laughing*) Frank . . . We get married, all you do is hang out with the guys, drink, screw those . . . cop *pig*lets up at the bars . . . lot of fun for me . . . lots of center . . . I cut you loose, nothing stopping you. All of a sudden you're lonely, you want me . . . woof . . . too much . . . too much.

FRANK: Hey . . . I'm in the trenches here every night . . .

DENICE: C'mon . . . don't give me that "trench" bullshit . . . you're not in a squad car . . . it's *you*, Frank . . . you're one of the boys . . . good for you, enjoy it . . . you don't have to make excuses. You hate to go home, that's that.

FRANK: (*tense, confused, heated*) I *can't* go home! (*awkward beat*) Something's up with me now. (*whispering*) The nights are real *bad*.

DENICE: (*studying him*) Yeah, well, I know about bad nights. (*beat*) Look . . . I just need another kind of man than you, you know what I mean?

FRANK: (*dryly*) Donald Gruber . . . a man among men.

DENICE: (defensive, heated) You *bet* . . . he's *there* . . . he's steady like a mountain . . . he don't screw around, he don't drink and he sleeps like a *rock*.

FRANK: Denice . . . do you have any *ink*ling of how *bor*ing a *sum*mary of a human being that was?

DENICE shrugs, stares at him, grins sheepishly. It looks like FRANK just scored. FRANK grins. He puts his hand over DENICE's, leans forward.

FRANK: (*whispering, confidential*) Straight up . . . how's making love with him compared to making love with us. You tell me it's as good, I'll call you a liar to your face.

DENICE stares at him deadpan for a long beat then breaks out in a radiant grin. FRANK beams in triumph.

DENICE: (*leaning forward*) I'm pregnant.

FRANK: (*stunned, whipped*) How do you know it's yours?

sex, lies and videotape
(Miramax, 1989)

Screenplay by Steven Soderbergh
Directed by Steven Soderbergh
Characters: CYNTHIA (Laura San Giacomo)
ANN (Andie MacDowall)

NOTES: ANN is married to John and living what seems to be the perfect upper-middle-class suburban life. But something is wrong, and she is in therapy trying to find out what it is. Her husband, John, meanwhile, is having an affair with her sister, CYNTHIA. Now John's old college friend, Graham, has appeared in town and is staying with John and ANN while he looks for a place. ANN finds herself drawn to him and tells her sister about him.

19. INTERIOR. CYNTHIA BISHOP'S APARTMENT—DAY

ANN stands watching CYNTHIA get dressed for work.

CYNTHIA: So where's he from?

ANN: I don't know. He went to school here, then he was in New York for a while, then Philadelphia, and then just kind of traveling around.

CYNTHIA: Must be nice. So, what's he like, is he like John?

ANN: No, not at all. Actually, I don't think John likes him much anymore. He said he thought Graham had gotten strange.

CYNTHIA: Is he? Strange, I mean?

ANN: Not really. Maybe if I just saw him on the street I'd have said that, but after talking to him . . . he's just kind of . . . I don't know, unusual.

CYNTHIA: Uh-huh. So what's he look like?

A pause.

ANN: Why?

CYNTHIA: I just want to know what he looks like, is all.

ANN: Why, so you can go after him?

CYNTHIA: Jesus, Ann, get a life. I just asked what he looked like.

ANN says nothing.

CYNTHIA: Besides, even if I decided to fuck his brains out, what business is that of yours?

ANN: Do you have to say that?

CYNTHIA: What?

ANN: You know what. You say it just to irritate me.

CYNTHIA: I say it because it's descriptive.

ANN: Well, he doesn't strike me as the kind of person that would go in for that sort of thing, anyway.

CYNTHIA: Ann, you always underestimate me.

ANN: Well, I wonder why.

CYNTHIA: I think you're afraid to put the two of us in the same room together. I think you're afraid he'll be undeniably *drawn* to me.

ANN: Oh, for God's sake. Really, Cynthia, really, I don't think he's your type.

CYNTHIA: ''My type''? What is this bullshit? How would you know what ''my type'' is?

ANN: I have a pretty good idea.

CYNTHIA: Ann, you don't have a clue. Look, I don't even know why we're discussing this, I'll just call him myself.

ANN: He doesn't have a phone.

CYNTHIA: Well, I'll call him when he does.

ANN: But he won't.

CYNTHIA: What are you talking about?

ANN: He's not getting a phone, he doesn't like talking on the phone.

CYNTHIA: Oh, *please*. Okay, so give me the Zen master's address, I'll think of a reason to stop by.

ANN: Let me talk to him first.

CYNTHIA: Why? Just give me the address, you won't even have to be involved.

ANN: I don't feel right just *giving* you the address so that you can go over there and . . .

CYNTHIA: And what?

ANN: And . . . do whatever it is you do.

CYNTHIA laughs loudly. ANN, not happy, watches her dig through the jewelry box.

ANN: Lost something?

CYNTHIA: That goddam diamond stud earring that cost me a fucking fortune.

ANN: Are you getting Mom something for her birthday?

CYNTHIA: I don't know, I'll get her a card or something.

ANN: A *card*? For her fiftieth birthday?

CYNTHIA: What's wrong with that?

ANN: Don't you think she deserves a little more than a card? I mean, the woman gave birth to you. It's her fiftieth birthday—

CYNTHIA: Will you stop? Jesus.

ANN: I just thought it might—

CYNTHIA: Okay, *Ann*, okay. How about this: you buy her something nice, and I'll pay for half. All right?

ANN: Fine.

CYNTHIA: Good. Now, if you'll pardon me, *I* have to go to work.

sex, lies and videotape (2)
(Miramax, 1989)

Screenplay by Steven Soderbergh
Directed by Steven Soderbergh
Characters: CYNTHIA (Laura San Giacomo)
                GRAHAM (James Spader)

NOTES: Ann has told her sister CYNTHIA about GRAHAM, her husband's old friend who has come to town. (*see notes from previous scene*) CYNTHIA is intrigued and comes to GRAHAM's apartment to find out for herself.

24. INTERIOR. GRAHAM'S APARTMENT—DAY

GRAHAM sits smoking a cigarette. There is a knock at his door.

GRAHAM: It's open.

CYNTHIA enters. GRAHAM looks up at her.

GRAHAM: Who are you?

CYNTHIA: I'm Cynthia Bishop.

GRAHAM: Do I know you?

CYNTHIA: I'm Ann Milaney's sister.

GRAHAM: The extrovert.

CYNTHIA: (*smiles*) She must have been in a good mood when she said that. She usually calls me loud.

GRAHAM: She called you that, too. May I ask why you're here?

CYNTHIA: You want me to leave?

GRAHAM: I just want to know why you're here.

CYNTHIA: Well, like I said, Ann is my sister. Sisters talk. You can imagine the rest.

GRAHAM: No, I really can't. I find it healthy never to characterize people I don't know or conversations I haven't heard. I don't know what you and your sister discussed about me or anything else. Last time I saw Ann she left here very . . . confused, I would say. And upset.

CYNTHIA: She still is.

GRAHAM: And are you here to berate me for making her that way?

CYNTHIA: Nope.

GRAHAM: She didn't tell you why she was upset?

CYNTHIA: Nope.

GRAHAM: She didn't give you my address?

CYNTHIA: Nope.

GRAHAM: How did you find me?

CYNTHIA: I, uh, know a guy at the power company.

GRAHAM: I don't understand. Why did you want to come here? I mean, I can't imagine Ann painted a very flattering portrait of me.

CYNTHIA: Well, I don't really listen to her when it comes to men. I mean, look at John, for crissake. Oh, you went to school with him, didn't you? You're probably friends or something.

GRAHAM: Nope. I think the man is a liar.

CYNTHIA: (*smiles*) I think you're right. So come on, I came all the way over here to find out what got Ann so spooked, tell me what happened.

GRAHAM: (*smiles*) Spooked.

He motions to the box of videotapes.

GRAHAM: That box of tapes is what got Ann so "spooked."

CYNTHIA goes over to the box and looks inside for a long moment, studying the labels.

CYNTHIA: Oh, okay. I think I get it.

GRAHAM: What do you get?

CYNTHIA: Well, they must be something sexual, because Ann gets freaked out by that shit. Are these tapes of you having sex with these girls or something?

GRAHAM: Not exactly.

CYNTHIA: Well, either you are or you aren't. Which is it?

GRAHAM: Why don't you let me tape you?

CYNTHIA: Doing what?

GRAHAM: Talking.

CYNTHIA: About what?

GRAHAM: Sex. Your sexual history, your sexual preferences.

CYNTHIA: What makes you think I'd discuss that with you?

GRAHAM: Nothing.

CYNTHIA: You just want to ask me questions?

GRAHAM: I just want to ask you questions.

CYNTHIA: And that's all?

GRAHAM: That's all.

CYNTHIA: (*a crooked smile*) Is this how you get off or something? Taping women talking about their sexual experiences?

GRAHAM: Yes.

CYNTHIA: Would anybody else see the tape?

GRAHAM: Absolutely not. They are for my private use only.

CYNTHIA: How do we start?

GRAHAM: I turn on the camera. You start talking.

CYNTHIA: And you ask questions, right?

GRAHAM: Yes.

CYNTHIA: How long will it take?

GRAHAM: That depends on you. One woman only used three minutes. Another filled up three two-hour tapes.

CYNTHIA: Can I see some of the other tapes to get an idea of what—

GRAHAM: No.

CYNTHIA: (*thinks*) Do I sit or stand?

GRAHAM: Whichever you prefer.

CYNTHIA: I'd rather sit. Are you ready?

GRAHAM: Just a moment.

GRAHAM grabs his 8mm video camera, puts in a new tape, and puts it on.

GRAHAM: I am now recording. Tell me your name.

CYNTHIA: Cynthia Patrice Bishop.

GRAHAM: Describe for me your first sexual experience.

CYNTHIA: (*thinks*) I was ... eight years old. Michael Green, who was also eight, asked me if he could watch me take a pee. I said he could if I could watch *him* take one, too. He said okay, and then we went into the woods behind our house. I got this feeling he was chickening out because he kept saying, "Ladies first!" So I pulled down my underpants and urinated, and he ran away before I even finished.

GRAHAM: Was it ever a topic of conversation between the two of you afterward?

CYNTHIA: No. He kind of avoided me for the rest of the summer, and then his family moved away. To Cleveland, actually.

GRAHAM: How unfortunate. So when did you finally get to see a penis?

CYNTHIA: When I was fourteen.

GRAHAM: Live, or in a photograph or film of some sort.

CYNTHIA: Very much live.

GRAHAM: What did you think? Did it look like you expected?

CYNTHIA: Not really. I didn't picture it with veins or ridges or anything, I thought it would be smooth, like a test tube.

GRAHAM: Were you disappointed?

CYNTHIA: No. If anything, after I looked at it awhile, it got more interesting. It had character, you know?

GRAHAM: What about when you touched it? What did you expect it to feel like, and then what did it really feel like?

CYNTHIA: It was warmer than I thought it would be, and the skin was softer than it looked. It's weird. Thinking about it now, the organ itself seemed like a separate thing, a separate entity to me. I mean, after he pulled it out and I could look at it and touch it, I *completely* forgot that there was a guy attached to it. I remember literally being startled when the guy spoke to me.

GRAHAM: What did he say?

CYNTHIA: He said that my hand felt good.

GRAHAM: Then what happened?

CYNTHIA: Then I started moving my hand, and then he stopped talking.

sex, lies and videotape (3)
(Miramax, 1989)

Screenplay by Steven Soderbergh
Directed by Steven Soderbergh
Characters: CYNTHIA (Laura San Giacomo)
            ANN (Andie MacDowall)

NOTES: Ann has told her sister CYNTHIA about her husband's friend Graham, who has appeared in town, and CYNTHIA has gone to Graham's house (*see two previous scenes*) and made an interview tape, on which she masturbated. ANN has already made a connection with Graham and now reacts to the news of what CYNTHIA's done.

31. INTERIOR. JOHN AND ANN MILANEY'S HOUSE—DAY

ANN is talking to CYNTHIA on the phone. ANN looks very morose.

CYNTHIA: He just asked me questions.

ANN: What kinds of questions?

CYNTHIA: Questions about sex.

ANN: Well, like what did he ask, exactly?

CYNTHIA: Well, like, I don't want to tell you, exactly.

ANN: Oh, so you'll let a total stranger record your sexual life on tape, but you won't tell your own sister?

CYNTHIA: Apparently.

334

ANN: Did he ask you to take your clothes off?

CYNTHIA: Did he ask me to take my clothes off? No, he didn't.

A pause.

ANN: *Did* you take your clothes off?

CYNTHIA: Yes, I did.

ANN: (*floored*) Cynthia!

CYNTHIA: What?

ANN: Why did you do that?

CYNTHIA: Because I wanted to.

ANN: But why did you want to?

CYNTHIA: I wanted him to see me.

ANN: Cynthia, who knows where that tape may end up? He could be . . . bouncing it off some satellite or something. Some horny old men in South America or something could be watching it.

CYNTHIA: He wouldn't do that.

ANN: You don't know that for sure.

CYNTHIA: Well, it's too late now, isn't it?

ANN: Did he touch you?

CYNTHIA: No, but I did.

ANN: You touched *him*?

CYNTHIA: No, I touched *me*.

ANN: Wait a minute. Do you mean . . . don't tell me you . . . in front of him.

CYNTHIA: In front of him, Ann, yes.

ANN: (*serious*) You are in trouble.

CYNTHIA: (*laughs*) Listen to you!! You sound like Mom. What are you talking about?

ANN: I can't believe you did that!!

CYNTHIA: Why?

ANN: I mean, I couldn't do that in front of *John*, even.

CYNTHIA: You couldn't do it, period.

ANN: You know what I mean, you don't even *know* him!

CYNTHIA: I feel like I do.

ANN: That doesn't mean you *do*. You can't *possibly* trust him, he's . . . perverted.

CYNTHIA: He's harmless. He just sits around and looks at these tapes. What's the big deal?

ANN: So he's got this catalogue of women touching themselves? That doesn't make you feel weird?

CYNTHIA: No. I don't think they *all* did what I did.

ANN: You are in serious trouble.

CYNTHIA: Ann, I don't understand why this freaks you out so much. *You* didn't do it, *I* did, and if it doesn't bother me, why should it bother you?

ANN: I don't want to discuss it.

CYNTHIA: Then why do you keep asking about it?

sex, lies and videotape (4)
(Miramax, 1989)

Screenplay by Steven Soderbergh
Directed by Steven Soderbergh
Characters: CYNTHIA (Laura San Giacomo)
          JOHN (Peter Gallagher)

NOTES: CYNTHIA has been having an affair with her sister's husband, JOHN. When JOHN's old friend Graham shows up in town, not only is JOHN's wife Ann drawn to him, but so is CYNTHIA and she goes to his house and makes an "interview" tape on which she masturbates (see previous scenes). Ann is appalled, and so is JOHN, for a different reason. He shows up at CYNTHIA's to fool around, full of judgment.

41. INTERIOR. CYNTHIA BISHOP'S—DAY

JOHN sits on the edge of CYNTHIA's bed, slowly undressing.

JOHN: It's just so blatantly stupid, I have a hard time believing you did it.

CYNTHIA: What's so stupid about it?

JOHN: That you . . . you don't even know the guy.

CYNTHIA: Well, *you* know him, he's a friend of *yours*, do you think he can be trusted?

JOHN: Shit, after what you've told me, I don't know. I *should've* known, when he showed up dressed like some arty brat.

CYNTHIA: I *like* the way he dresses.

JOHN: What if this tape gets into the wrong hands?

CYNTHIA: "The wrong hands"? We're not talking about military secrets, John. They're just tapes that he makes so he can sit around and get off.

JOHN: Jesus Christ. And he doesn't have sex with *any* of them? They just talk?

CYNTHIA: Right.

JOHN: Jesus. I could almost understand it if he was screwing these people, *almost*. Why doesn't he just buy some magazines or porno movies or something?

CYNTHIA: Doesn't work. He has to know the people, he has to be able to interact with them.

JOHN: Interact, fine, but did you have to masturbate in front of him, for God's sake? I mean . . .

CYNTHIA: I felt like it, so what? Goddam, you and Ann make such a big deal out of it.

A pause.

JOHN: You told *Ann* about this?

CYNTHIA: Of course. She *is* my sister. I tell her *almost* everything.

JOHN: I wish you hadn't done that.

CYNTHIA: Why not?

JOHN: It's just something I'd prefer she didn't know about.

CYNTHIA: She's a grown-up, she can handle it.

JOHN: I just . . . Ann is very . . .

CYNTHIA: Hung up.

JOHN: It just wasn't a smart thing to do. Did you sign any sort of paper, or did he have any contract with you saying he wouldn't broadcast these tapes?

CYNTHIA: No.

JOHN: You realize you have no recourse legally? This stuff could show up anywhere.

CYNTHIA: It won't. I trust him.

JOHN: (*disbelieving*) You trust him.

CYNTHIA: Yeah, I do. A helluva lot more than I trust you.

JOHN: What do you mean?

CYNTHIA: Exactly what I said. I'd trust him before I'd trust you. How much clearer can I be?

JOHN: It hurts that you would say that to me.

CYNTHIA: (*laughs*) Oh, *please*. Come on, John. You're fucking your wife's sister and you've hardly been married a year. You're a liar. But at least I *know* you're a liar. It's the people that *don't* know, like Ann, that have to watch out.

JOHN: By definition you're lying to Ann, too.

CYNTHIA: That's right. But I never took a vow in front of God and everybody to be "faithful" to my sister.

JOHN: Look, are we going to do it or not?

CYNTHIA: Actually, no, I've changed my mind. I shouldn't have called.

JOHN: (*ingratiating*) Well, I'm here now. I'd like to do something . . .

CYNTHIA: How about straightening up the living room?

JOHN doesn't smile.

CYNTHIA: Come on, John. You should be happy, we've gone this far without Ann finding out. I'm making it real easy on you. Just walk out of here and I'll see you at your house for a family dinner sometime.

JOHN: Did he put you up to this?

CYNTHIA: Who?

JOHN: Graham.

CYNTHIA: No, he didn't put me up to this. Jesus, I don't need people to tell me what I should do. I've just been thinking about things, that's all.

JOHN: I can't believe I let him stay in my house. Right under my nose. That deviant fucker was right under my nose and I didn't see him.

CYNTHIA: If he had been under your prick you'd have spotted him for sure.

JOHN: (*looks at her*) God, you . . . you're mean.

CYNTHIA: I know. Will you please leave now?

JOHN: Maybe I don't want to leave. Maybe *I* want to talk.

CYNTHIA: John, we have *nothing* to talk about.

JOHN: I knew it, I knew it. Things are getting complicated.

CYNTHIA: No, John, things are getting real simple.

She's The One
(Fox Searchlight, 1995)

Screenplay by Edward Burns
Directed by Edward Burns
Characters: HEATHER (Cameron Diaz)
*   MICKEY (Ed Burns)*

NOTES: MICKEY and Francis, the Fitzpatrick brothers, couldn't be more different. MICKEY leads an unstable life as a New York cabbie. After he found his fiancee, HEATHER, cheating on him, he took off and spent three years driving around the country. Then he returned and lived with his father in Brooklyn until he met a waitress, fell in love, and impulsively married her. They live in a small apartment in the Village. MICKEY's brother Francis works on Wall Street, has a beautiful wife, a nice apartment, and is jeopardizing everything by having a secret affair with HEATHER, who also works on Wall Street. What Francis doesn't know (and MICKEY does) is that HEATHER put herself through school by working as a call girl. One day, MICKEY picks up HEATHER in his cab and asks for his TV back, the one he bought shortly before they broke up. They end up at her apartment.

INTERIOR. HEATHER'S APARTMENT—DAY
HEATHER steps into the room, removing her suit jacket.

HEATHER: Okay. I've made up my mind. I can't go through with this. If you're going to take the TV, I think

341

it's only fair that you give me back the watch. I mean, it *is* the watch I gave you, right?

MICKEY appears opposite her, carrying his old TV. He looks ridiculous.

MICKEY: Yeah, it is. But like you said, the watch was a gift. And the TV wasn't.

HEATHER: (*smiling*) But if you recall correctly, I did pay for part of that TV. I mean, it's not like you could afford it on your own.

MICKEY laughs. He puts the TV down and takes off the watch.

MICKEY: Okay. You want the watch, you can have the watch. It doesn't really mean that much to me anyhow.

HEATHER: (*grabbing his hand*) It's not the watch I want, Mickey.

MICKEY pulls away, hands her the watch, and grabs his TV.

MICKEY: Yeah, why don't we just give that a break already, okay, Heather?

HEATHER: Give you a break? You mean to tell me that you actually came up here for the TV?

MICKEY: Yeah. Why do you think I came up here?

HEATHER: You're so full of shit.

MICKEY: Oh, yeah? And how do you figure that?

HEATHER: You can honestly say that you don't even think of me anymore?

MICKEY: Yeah, sure, of course I think about you. I think, what could have possibly possessed you to take that dirtbag home to my apartment?

MICKEY exits past her and heads up the spiral staircase, still carrying the television. HEATHER follows.

HEATHER: Come on, Mickey. We both knew the relationship was over before that. I wanted a career and you wanted

. . . who the hell knows what you wanted? Did you ever figure that out?

MICKEY: Yeah, you know what? As a matter of fact, I did.

MICKEY steps into the living room. HEATHER walks right past him and sits down on her couch. MICKEY follows and stands above her. The TV is getting heavier.

HEATHER: Oh, that's right. Your brother told me you got married.

MICKEY: What do you mean, my brother? Since when do you speak to Francis?

HEATHER hesitates and then smiles.

HEATHER: Well, you know, he and his friends have real jobs, so occasionally I run into him.

MICKEY finally takes a seat opposite her, resting the television on his knees.

MICKEY: You know, it's a shame he's married. You two probably would have hit it off.

HEATHER: Maybe. (*pause*) Anyhow, I'm just sorry you had to find out the way you did. I would have liked to have been friends.

MICKEY: Friends? Really? You know what, Heather? I don't think that would have worked, actually, because I have this thing that I try to keep the number of friends who lie and cheat me to a minimum.

HEATHER: Oh, please, Mickey. Put your fucking sanctimonious bullshit to rest already.

MICKEY: I'm sorry. I guess the fact that I've always tried to behave like a decent human being has rubbed you the wrong way, hasn't it?

HEATHER: Well, look where your decency has gotten you. You're the only English-speaking white guy driving a cab in New York. That should tell you something.

MICKEY looks long and hard at her. He stands up and heads to the door.

MICKEY: You know what, Heather? I've got to imagine it beats sucking dick for a living, though, huh?

HEATHER: Depends on whose dick it is.

MICKEY just shakes his head as he walks out the door.

She's The One (2)
(Fox Searchlight, 1995)

Screenplay by Edward Burns
Directed by Edward Burns
Characters: MICKEY (Ed Burns)
FRANCIS (Michael McGlone)

NOTES: FRANCIS has found out from Heather that MICKEY got his TV back from her (*see notes for previous scene*). He shows up at MICKEY's apartment, for the first time, for a "spontaneous" visit, but really to find out if MICKEY had sex with Heather. MICKEY still doesn't know that FRANCIS and Heather are lovers. Meanwhile, MICKEY has been having some difficulties in his marriage, and FRANCIS and Heather have been having spats of their own. FRANCIS has also been feeling guilt and pressure about his own marriage; he hasn't had sex with his wife for months. He wants to divorce his wife and marry Heather, but Heather is not too keen on the idea. Tensions are high all around.

INTERIOR. HOPE'S APARTMENT—DAY
A knock on the door. MICKEY answers and FRANCIS, wearing a double-breasted suit, walks in.
MICKEY: Hey, Fran. What are you doing here?
FRANCIS: What? I can't come by to see my big brother?
MICKEY: Yeah, sure.
FRANCIS steps into the apartment and looks around as he lights a cigarette.

FRANCIS: Jesus Christ! What a fucking dump! Hey, I like the pink walls, though. Finally comfortable with that part of yourself, huh?

MICKEY: You can't just come in, sit down and keep your mouth shut, right moneybags? I mean that would just be to difficult for you, huh?

FRANCIS: Oh, sorry. I forgot Mr. Summer Breeze is so *sensitivo*. Hey, I like the TV, though. How did you swing that one, man? I thought you said you two were broke.

MICKEY: Yeah, we still are. But you actually won't believe this. I picked Heather up in my cab last week and we got to talking, and she said she still had my old TV. So I went up to her place and I took it. It was kind of strange seeing her again, you know?

FRANCIS: So you went back and took your TV?

MICKEY: Well, you see it sitting there, don't you?

FRANCIS: You didn't feel like a loser?

MICKEY: Why would I feel like a loser?

FRANCIS: Oh, I don't know. Three years go by and you scurry back for a TV? It's like admitting you're a failure and you can't afford a new TV.

MICKEY: How the hell do we have the same blood pumping through our veins? Do you really think I give a shit what Heather thinks about me? I mean, come on, Franny.

FRANCIS: So, did you fuck her.

MICKEY: Did I what?

FRANCIS: When you were up at the apartment? Did you put it to her? Did you bang her?

MICKEY: What do you think, I'm some kind of degenerate? You think I'm some sort of immoral skell who cheats on his wife? Listen, I don't cheat on my wife, okay?

FRANCIS: Oh, so you didn't fuck her?

MICKEY: It just dawned on me, Franny. You haven't fully evolved yet, have you?

FRANCIS: Mick, come on. I mean, you almost married this woman. Then you're going to be alone in her apartment to get a TV? I don't buy it.

MICKEY: What do you want to hear? Do you want to hear that I had sex with her? I mean, would that make you happy? All right, yeah, I did her. I did her on the kitchen table, we did it on the couch, we even did it on the friggin' TV; it was beautiful. I mean, I think you would have been proud of me.

FRANCIS: Hey, play all the games you want to play, Mick, but I'm a man. I know what I know.

MICKEY: You know what you know. Listen, you know what, Franny? I don't need this shit from you, okay? I don't need you to come over to my apartment and bust my hump. Why don't you just do me a favor and get the hell out of here, okay?

FRANCIS: Sure. I'll do you that favor.

FRANCIS takes another drag from his cigarette and heads past MICKEY toward the door. He then stops before exiting and slouches against the wall.

FRANCIS: I'm sorry, Mick. I'm feeling so guilty about this fucking divorce. I shouldn't feel guilty about that, right?

MICKEY: No, you shouldn't. What you should feel guilty about, though, is fucking that other woman for six months. That's what you should feel guilty about.

MICKEY picks up his newspaper and turns his back on FRANCIS.

Short Cuts
(Fine Line, 1993)

Screenplay by Robert Altman and Frank Barhydt
Directed by Robert Altman
Characters: MARIAN (Julianne Moore)
RALPH (Matthew Modine)

NOTES: RALPH and MARIAN are married. He is a doctor, she is a painter; they have a "nice" life in a comfortable home in Los Angeles, but their relationship is distant and lacks intimacy and compassion. We have never seen them kiss. They are expecting guests for dinner, people they barely know. Yesterday RALPH walked in on MARIAN painting her sister Sherri nude and was dismissed by the two women. Today RALPH lost a patient, a small boy who had been hit by a car. Tonight the thin veneer of their daily life snaps.

INTERIOR. WYMAN HOUSE / STUDIO—LATE DAY
RALPH is in the studio sitting in a chair with a drink. MARIAN is straightening up. He looks at Marian's painting of Sherri.

RALPH: Why are they naked? Why does naked make it art?

MARIAN: Did you make me a drink?

RALPH: It's in the blender.

She goes to the bar.

MARIAN: Smells strong. I'm gonna have some wine.

RALPH: Is that what you're wearing?

MARIAN: Yes.

RALPH: I thought we were cooking out.

MARIAN: Stuart's bringing fish, remember?

RALPH: If it's a barbeque, why're you getting so dressed up?

MARIAN: This isn't dressed up.

RALPH: I'm not changing.

MARIAN: She'll probably dress up.

RALPH: Are you competing?

MARIAN: Competing with who?

RALPH: Claire, honey. We're talking about Claire. Are you competing with Claire?

MARIAN: For what?

RALPH: What women compete for, I guess.

MARIAN shrugs it off. She has other things to do.

RALPH: Do you think he's attractive?

MARIAN: Who?

RALPH: The husband.

She's noncommittal. She doesn't want to pursue this.

MARIAN: Stuart, it is.

RALPH: He's the kind of guy that women find attractive, isn't he? The outdoorsman type.

MARIAN: We don't know alot about them. I hope they like something other than chamber music.

RALPH: Isn't it wonderful, Marian, how we can skate around an issue. Always playing our little game.

MARIAN: That's a good idea, a game. It might help break the ice. Jeopardy maybe.

RALPH: I'm talking about us. I'm talking about now.

MARIAN: What about us?

RALPH: You know.

MARIAN: Know what?

RALPH: Let's forget it.

MARIAN: Forget what? What are you talking about?

RALPH: Nothing. It's ancient history.

MARIAN: No, something's on your mind.

RALPH: That party.

MARIAN: What party?

RALPH: You know what party I'm talking about, Marian. The one with Mitchell Anderson.

MARIAN: Jesus, Ralph. That was three years ago.

RALPH: You kissed him, didn't you?

MARIAN: No.

RALPH: Your lipstick was smeared when you came back.

MARIAN: How would you know? You were drunk.

MARIAN spills the wine all over her skirt. She grabs a cloth, but she's soaked.

MARIAN: Goddammit! Look at this! Jesus Christ! Look at this. Look what you made me do.

She hurries off to the kitchen. RALPH watches.

MARIAN: Goddammit, I wanted to wear this. Shit.

RALPH: That's the way you looked that night with Mitchell Anderson when you were out necking.

MARIAN removes her skirt and rinses it under the faucet. She has no panties on.

RALPH: He did kiss you, didn't he?

MARIAN: Oh, come on, Ralph. I thought we were through with that.

RALPH: I want you to tell me about that night with Mitchell Anderson.

MARIAN: There's nothing to tell.

RALPH: All right, then tell me about nothingness. I'd like to hear a complete account of nothing. What you didn't do for two and a half hours.

MARIAN: Why, Ralph? What's so important? It was three years ago.

MARIAN lays out the skirt on a table as if to dry.

RALPH: All right it's not important. It's water under the bridge. But what irritates me, Marian, if that's the right word for it, is that you won't tell me the truth. You can't say the obvious. You won't admit that you lied. That's what I don't like—having to play this charade.

MARIAN comes down the steps in front of RALPH to her studio.

MARIAN: God, Ralph, how did this start? Do you know how this started? Because I really . . . I really don't know how this started.

She gets a hair dryer from her art supplies.

RALPH: Marian! Look at me, Marian! You don't have any panties on. What do you think you are? One of your goddam paintings?

MARIAN finds the hair dryer, crosses in front of RALPH, and goes back up the stairs. She finds a plug.

RALPH: I'm giving you the chance to come clean. Clear the slate. On to a higher consciousness. And then don't ever lie to me again, Marian.

MARIAN: This is not like you, Ralph.

MARIAN starts the dryer.

RALPH: What? To demand? You're right, Marian, but I want to know. I want to know the truth.

MARIAN: We're just talking, right?

RALPH: Yes, Marian. We're just talking.

MARIAN: You want me to tell you the truth.

RALPH: That's all I've ever asked, Marian.

She continues to dry her skirt with the hair dryer.

MARIAN: Okay, he kissed me. Does that satisfy you?

RALPH: Did that satisfy you?

MARIAN: Everybody was pretty far gone, as you may or may not remember.

RALPH: I don't really need all this perspective. Just the facts.

MARIAN picks up the skirt in one hand and the hair dryer in the other. She stands in front of RALPH naked from the waist down, drying her skirt.

MARIAN: All right. All right Ralph. Okay. Somehow the two of us were elected to go out and get liquor. We drove to Foremost, which was closed, and then Cappy's, which was also closed. In fact, everything was closed. And I was beginning to wonder whether anything would be open. All I could think of were those all-night supermarkets. I wondered whether anyone would even be in the mood for a drink if we had to drive around half the night looking for an open market.

She continues drying her skirt.

MARIAN: He was really drunk. I hadn't even realized how drunk he was until we started driving. He was terribly slow and all hunched over the wheel and we were talking about a lot of things, a lot of things that didn't make sense . . . about religious images and this painter named Larry Rivers and then he said something about Norman Mailer and about how Norman Mailer stabbed his wife in the breast. And he said he'd hate it if anybody did that to me. He said he'd like to kiss my breast. And then he pulled the car over to the side of the road and then he kissed me.

MARIAN finishes drying her shirt and shuts off the hair dryer. She walks back to the table and spreads out the skirt.

RALPH: How long?

MARIAN: How long, what?

RALPH: How long did he kiss you?

MARIAN is either thinking or doesn't want to answer.

RALPH: Then what?

MARIAN: Then he said do you want to have a go at it?

RALPH: Jesus, Marian. Do you want to have a go at it? Do you want to have a go at it? Do you want to have a go at it?! What does that mean, Marian? Do you want to have a go at it? Did he kiss your tits? Did you touch him?

MARIAN: Touch him? Touch him? Okay, Ralph, do you want to know what happened? He kissed me and I kissed him back.

MARIAN pulls on her skirt furiously.

MARIAN: And then we did it. We just did it right there in the car. He fucked me right there in the car. I was drunk. It didn't mean anything to me. I wish it hadn't happened, but it did. Is that all you want to know? Is that all? Is that all?

RALPH: Yes, Marian. That's all.

RALPH gets up and begins walking out of the room.

MARIAN: Ralph, he didn't come in me. I swear to God, he didn't come in me.

RALPH: Okay.

MARIAN: Where are you going, Ralph?

RALPH: Well, Marian, we have guests coming. I'm gonna go and light the barbecue.

Short Cuts (2)
(Fine Line, 1993)

Screenplay by Robert Altman and Frank Barhydt
Directed by Robert Altman
Characters: DOREEN (Lily Tomlin)
          EARL (Tom Waits)

NOTES: DOREEN and EARL are an unhappy, blue collar couple in their forties. They live in a small trailer-type house in a bad section of Los Angeles. DOREEN works at a diner as a waitress. EARL works a string of dead-end jobs, his current one being a limo driver. He's an alcoholic, and although DOREEN insists she won't put up with his drinking, she stays with him. And he stays with her. She's just had a close brush with disaster; on her way home from work, she suddenly braked to avoid hitting a small boy who crossed the street in front of her. She tapped him with her car, and he fell to the ground, but he was apparently unscathed, and she tried to take him home, but he wouldn't get in the car with a stranger. She left the scene without getting his phone number or address, or giving hers to him. She arrives home shaken.

INTERIOR. PIGGOT TRAILER—DAY
EARL is watching bowling. He's stripped down to his undershirt and he's had a few drinks. When he hears DOREEN's car outside he goes to the window. DOREEN slams the door shut. EARL takes his glass to the sink and rinses

it out. He sniffs to be sure there's no liquor smell. He re-turns to his chair and starts playing with the stethoscope casually. DOREEN closes the porch door.

DOREEN: What's the door standin' wide open? Hey, you hungry, honey? What are you doin' anyway? How come you're not workin'? You're not gonna lose your job again are you? You better give that back, some doctor's gonna be lookin' for it.

EARL continues to fiddle with the stethoscope without both-ering to answer DOREEN.

DOREEN: I got London Broil from the Greek. Want me to fix it? Want me to freeze it?

EARL: Doreen, Doreen, the question queen, stole a London Broil thick and lean.

DOREEN: How about a fruit plate? Something light.

EARL: How bout a short skirt, Doreen. Short enough so I can see every inch of your ass. How'd that be?

DOREEN: What are you talking crazy for?

DOREEN walks to the bedroom, unzipping her uniform.

EARL: Well we don't want to talk about that, do we? We just want to talk about Earl. Let's hear more about Earl. How 'bout cops, baby, I bet they love those short skirts. I know fishermen like 'em.

DOREEN gives EARL the finger from the bedroom. She walks in to the other room.

DOREEN: Listen, honey, today something terrible hap-pened. I hit this little kid with my car.

EARL: Oh, God.

DOREEN: Oh he didn't get hurt, I swear to God he's okay, but Jesus it scared the hell out of me.

EARL: Oh, Jesus, all right, were the cops there?

DOREEN: I told you, he wasn't hurt.

EARL: Okay, all right, listen. Did they get your name?

DOREEN: I told you. Nobody was there. He's all right.

EARL: Okay, all right, I just don't want to get sued.

DOREEN: Earl, it was just a stroke of luck that I didn't kill him.

EARL: Well, I'm glad somebody's luck is holding out.

Camera pulls back to reveal EARL watching TV. DOREEN is in the kitchen taking some aspirin.

DOREEN: He's eight years old, I asked him. Tomorrow's his birthday. Such a close call. Everything could have changed. Our whole lives could have changed.

EARL: Yeah, well, I wish something would come along and change our lives.

DOREEN: What's that supposed to mean?

EARL: Oh, nothin', but maybe I'm just sick and tired of watchin' you show off your ass at work. You know.

DOREEN: Oh, you're drunk, and you lied to me. Get the hell out of here.

EARL: You want me outta here? You got it.

EARL is on his feet. He goes to the bedroom.

DOREEN: You told me you weren't gonna lie no more. That was the deal. No more lies.

EARL: Okay watch me go, baby.

EARL comes out putting on a shirt and tie.

EARL: You know a lotta guys don't like a big ass in their face when they're tryin' to eat.

DOREEN: Ah, pick a fight. Go ahead, pick a fight.

EARL: Tell you something, you know, I don't know who you think'd want to look at your sad, middle-aged ass anyway.

DOREEN: Don't you talk to me like that and don't you come back. I'm not takin' you back no more. You understand?

EARL: Oh yeah?

DOREEN: No more. No more. I'm not takin' you back.

EARL: I'm not comin' back.

EARL is collecting his things working his way to the door.

DOREEN: Slobbering all over Honey like that. It was so embarassing.

EARL: I didn't touch Honey!

DOREEN: I didn't say you touched her. I said you slobbered on her.

EARL yanks open the flimsy screen door.

EARL: How come you don't wear your wedding ring to work anymore?

DOREEN: Oh you're such a bullshit artist.

EARL storms out.

EARL: You're the one chippin' away at our mansion of love, baby, not me.

DOREEN: Why don't you go get drunk and pee on Irmadine's drapes again?

EARL: I'm gonna get drunk. I'm gonna get drunk right now, goddammit.

EARL pulls out a miniature, guzzles some and throws the empty on the ground.

DOREEN: Look how stupid you're acting.

EARL guns the engine of the limo and drives out.

DOREEN: What if I killed him, then what?

The limousine disappears. DOREEN looks around and sees her neighbor Pat has been watching the whole fight. DOREEN turns around to go back inside.

DOREEN: Oh, Pat, what are you lookin' at? It's nothin' new. Have a nice day.

Sleep With Me
(MGM/UA, 1994)

Screenplay by Roger Hedden, Neal Jimenez, Rory Kelly, Duane Dell'Amico, Joe Keenan, Michael Steinberg
Directed by Rory Kelly
Characters: JOSEPH (Eric Stoltz)
FRANK (Craig Sheffer)

NOTES: JOSEPH and FRANK are close friends since college. They have both known Sarah that long. Now they are all in their late twenties. JOSEPH and Sarah are married, but lately their marriage has been on the rocks. FRANK has been in love with Sarah for years. He finally got around to telling her so at a recent party they all attended. Sarah was upset at JOSEPH for encouraging the passes of a bimbo, and FRANK seized the opportunity. Sarah slept with FRANK, and it was wonderful, and she's very confused about what to do. FRANK shows up at a party where he knows she'll be, to see her and convince her to leave JOSEPH. He gets kicked out. Now he's sitting in his car outside the house.

55. INTERIOR. FRANK'S CAR—NIGHT

Somebody leans over from the passenger seat giving him a start. It's Joseph.

JOSEPH: I thought this was your car but I didn't see you at the party.

FRANK: Deborah wouldn't let me in.

JOSEPH: I like Deborah but she gets a little shrill sometimes, don't you think? I don't know how Duane puts up with her.

FRANK: How does she put up with him?

JOSEPH: I guess that's what marriage is. Putting up.

JOSEPH pulls out the flask from the wedding rehearsal, opens it, and holds it up for a toast.

JOSEPH: To old friends.

He takes a drink and hands it to FRANK who takes a long pull.

JOSEPH: I'm glad you're here. There's something I need to talk to you about.

FRANK: What's that?

JOSEPH: It's Sarah.

FRANK: Yeah.

JOSEPH: She's been so distant. Ever since that damn tea party.

FRANK: She was pretty upset.

JOSEPH: She thinks I fucked that girl.

FRANK: Did you?

JOSEPH: No.

FRANK: Did you tell Sarah that?

JOSEPH: She doesn't believe me. I don't know what to do. You got any advice?

FRANK: You know I'm not much of a marriage expert.

JOSEPH: No. You're not, are you?

FRANK doesn't respond.

JOSEPH: You know, I can't help wondering if there's something else to this distance thing.

FRANK: What do you mean, Joe?

JOSEPH: Like maybe there's something else that happened— with her.

JOSEPH looks FRANK in the eyes. FRANK can't respond. But JOSEPH already has his answer.

JOSEPH: So what was it like, Frank?

FRANK: What?

JOSEPH: Finally nailing Sarah.

FRANK looks at him, frozen.

JOSEPH: It's okay.

Tears sting FRANK's eyes. JOSEPH looks away.

FRANK: I love her.

JOSEPH: I know. You've made that very clear.

FRANK: Look at me. I'm a fucking crybaby on top of everything else. I didn't know this about myself.

JOSEPH: You're reaching new lows almost every passing minute.

FRANK: You'd like to kill me right now, wouldn't you?

JOSEPH: I don't know. You got a gun. We can find out.

FRANK straightens up.

FRANK: I'm sorry.

JOSEPH: Shut up, Frank.

FRANK, recovered completely now, returns Joseph's glare.

FRANK: It was her choice.

JOSEPH: Is that so? I thought she chose me. But maybe I'm wrong. Maybe I should go ask her.

JOSEPH gets out of the car and begins marching toward the house. FRANK jumps out and follows, not sure what to do.

FRANK: Don't do this.

JOSEPH: Were you able to stop yourself, Frank?

Strictly Ballroom
(Miramax, 1993)

Screenplay by Baz Luhrmann and Craig Pearce,
from a Screenplay by Baz Luhrmann and Andrew
Bovell
Directed by Baz Luhrmann
Characters: SCOTT (Paul Mercurio)
*   FRAN (Tara Morice)*

NOTES: SCOTT KENDALL is an exceptional young ballroom dancer in Australia. His parents were ballroom dancers before him, and they now own a ballroom dance studio. Les is his mother's dance partner of many years, since his father long ago gave up dancing. FRAN is a beginning dancer; she's studied at the studio for only two years. She feels clumsy and inadequate, but she approaches SCOTT anyway because she feels a kinship to him; they both dance passionately, from the heart. SCOTT has recently lost his dance partner, Liz. She left him at the last competition, after SCOTT started dancing his own non-federation steps. The crowd loved it but the judges didn't. SCOTT wants to dance his way, but he was also raised to win, so he is conflicted. He needs a partner for the upcoming Pan Pacific competition, but FRAN is not what he had in mind.

43. INTERIOR. KENDALL'S STUDIO—MAIN SALON—NIGHT
It is later that night and the studio is empty. Only the light

from the record player illuminates SCOTT's face. He stares through himself into the mirror and strikes a ballroom pose.

SCOTT: (*softly*) Bullshit. Bullshit!

SCOTT's eyes snap shut in disgust. His body sways to the driving, insistent rhythm that beats in his brain. For a moment Les's words intrude . . .

[**LES:** Well, to pick what was actually wrong with the steps, you'd have to be an experienced professional, like myself.]

. . . but they are banished by a primeval explosion of music and energy as SCOTT leaps into an inspired and savage solo. SCOTT is unaware that FRAN, concealed behind the change room door, is secret witness to this dance of dark and passionate beauty. The rhythm drives him on and on, spinning, spinning, spinning—suddenly in the mirror a face, it is FRAN. SCOTT stops, startled.

FRAN: That's looking good.

SCOTT: Uh. What are you doing here?

FRAN: I uh, I, I, I just . . .

SCOTT: How long have you been here?

FRAN: Two years—I'm just looking for someone.

SCOTT: Everyone's gone home.

FRAN: Yeah I know. It's just that I've got this idea. Like, like, I mean, it's, it's um, it's um, I wanna try to . . . I want to dance with you. I want to dance with you. I want to dance with you your way at the Pan Pacifics.

SCOTT: The Pan Pacifics? You want to dance my way at the Pan Pacifics?

FRAN: Yeah.

SCOTT: You can't dance my way. You don't win.

FRAN: It's just because you've been overdoing it. If you, if you kept it simpler, and danced from the heart.

SCOTT: And had the right partner?

FRAN: And had the right partner.

SCOTT: Oh, I see, that's you, is it?

FRAN: When you dance your steps, I understand how you feel, 'cause I make up my own steps too.

SCOTT: You make up your own steps?

FRAN: Yeah—and now we both haven't got partners.

SCOTT: Look, what are you carrying on about? You've never had a partner. You've been dancing with a girl for two years, haven't you?

FRAN: Yeah . . .

SCOTT: Yeah . . .

FRAN: . . . but—

SCOTT: . . . and now you've come up to me who's been dancing since I was six years old . . . and you want to dance non-Federation, and convince the judges at the Pan Pacific Grand Prix with three weeks to train?

FRAN: Yeah.

SCOTT: I don't think so.

FRAN: Just give me a try-out.

SCOTT: Look. Go home.

FRAN: Just one hour.

SCOTT: This is very embarrassing.

FRAN: I, I just need a chance.

SCOTT: You're going to wake up tomorrow and feel like a real idiot about this.

FRAN: Do you want to dance your own steps or not?

SCOTT: It's none of your business.

FRAN: Well, do you?

SCOTT: Look. A beginner has no right to approach an Open Amateur.

FRAN: Yeah. Well an Open Amateur has no right to dance non-Federation steps . . . but you did, didn't you?

SCOTT: But that's different.

FRAN: How is it different? You're just like the rest of them. You think you're different, but you're not because you're just, you're just really scared, you're really scared to give someone new a go because you think, you know, they might just be better than you are. Well, you're just pathetic and you're gutless. You're a gutless wonder. Vivir con miedo, es como vivir a medias. (*After this angry outburst, she starts to cry.*)

SCOTT stops, startled.

SCOTT: What's your name again?

FRAN: Fran.

SCOTT: Yeah. Fran what?

FRAN: Just Fran.

SCOTT: All right then, just Fran. Don't push me. Rumba.

SCOTT spins FRAN into dance position. She stumbles.

SCOTT: Great, you can't even do a basic.

FRAN: You said one hour.

He takes her up again.

Swingers
(Miramax, 1996)

Screenplay by Jon Favreau
Directed by Doug Liman
Characters: MIKE (Jon Favreau)
     ROB (Ron Livingston)

NOTES: *Swingers* is about a group of guys in L.A. who are not really big swingers. They are mostly struggling actors and struggling to get dates. MIKE has just buzzed in his friend ROB, who's come to check up on him. MIKE has been in a funk, holed up in his apartment for days. He moons over pictures of his ex-girlfriend. It was a six-year relationship, and they've been broken up for six months. After the breakup, MIKE moved from New York to L.A. and has been trying to get his career as an actor/comedian going, but both his career and personal life are not really happening. He's at the bottom of his depression. ROB has even less to be happy about, but right now he has a better perspective on life.

INTERIOR. MIKE'S APARTMENT

A knock at the door. MIKE opens it, and ROB walks in with a brown bag. He surveys the scene. He's seen this before. He moves some laundry off an armchair and sits down. He pulls a pepperoni and a loaf of semolina out of the bag. He hands Mike a pint of orange juice.

MIKE: Thanks, man.

ROB: No problem, buddy. You eat anything today?

MIKE shakes his head "no."

ROB: Yesterday?

MIKE shakes his head again.

ROB: You haven't been drinking, have you?

MIKE: No. Just O.J.

ROB cuts into the pepperoni with his Swiss army knife. MIKE drinks his juice.

MIKE: Sorry about what happened at the Dresden. I had no idea . . .

ROB: Don't sweat it. Now I got an L.A. gun story. You should hear the way I tell it to the guys back home. He had an Uzi.

MIKE half-smiles. Beat.

ROB: You want to talk about it?

MIKE: What's the point?

ROB: It's been two days. You should call that girl Nikki . . .

MIKE grabs his head in pain.

MIKE: Uuuuugh!

ROB: Oh boy.

MIKE: I'm such an asshole.

ROB: She wasn't your type anyway.

Beat.

MIKE: I think I'm gonna move back East.

ROB: Well, *that's* dumb.

MIKE: What's dumb about it?

ROB: Well, you're doing so well . . .

MIKE: How am I doing well? I host an open mike and I played a fuckin' bus driver in a movie. Big fuckin' deal. I'm with an agency that specializes in fuckin' magicians. How *good* am I doing?

ROB: At least you didn't get turned down for Goofy . . .

MIKE: They turned you down?

ROB: They went for someone with more theme park experience. I woulda killed for that job.

MIKE lets it sink in.

ROB: See, it's all how you look at it. If your life sucks, then mine is god-awful. I mean, I moved out here partially because I saw how well you were doing. You got in the union, you got an agent. I thought if you could make it, maybe I could too . . .

MIKE: I didn't make it . . .

ROB: That's your problem, man. You can't see what you've got, only what you've lost. Those guys are right. You are money.

MIKE smiles, then . . .

MIKE: (*starting to cry*) Then why won't she call?

ROB: Because you left, man. She's got her own world to deal with in New York. She was a sweet girl, but fuck her. You gotta move on. You gotta let go of the past. The future is so beautiful. Every day is so sunny out here. It's like Manifest Destiny, man. I mean, we made it. What's past is prologue. That which does not kill us makes us stronger. All that shit. You'll get over it.

MIKE: How did you get over it? I mean, how long till it stopped hurting?

ROB: Sometimes it still hurts. You know how it is, man. I mean, each day you think about it less and less. And then one day you wake up and you don't think of it at all, and you almost miss that feeling. It's kinda weird. You miss the pain.

We see that MIKE has been gnawing away at ROB's pepperoni and semolina as he listens intently.

MIKE: You *miss* the pain?

ROB: . . . for the same reason you miss her. You lived with it so long.

MIKE: Wow. (*finishing the loaf*) You wanna grab a bite?

ROB: Sure.

Thelma & Louise
(MGM, 1991)

Screenplay by Callie Khouri
Directed by Ridley Scott
Characters: THELMA (Geena Davis)
     LOUISE (Susan Sarandon)

NOTES: THELMA and LOUISE are old friends. They started out on a road trip, a little vacation just for themselves, away from work for THELMA, away from her husband for LOUISE. Then things went horribly wrong. As they were leaving a bar, a man attacked THELMA and tried to rape her. LOUISE shot him, and they have been on the run since, driving through the desert. NOTE: Scenes 180, 183, and 185 have been tacked together here and can be performed as one scene with very little adjustment.

180. INTERIOR. CAR—NIGHT

THELMA is sipping on a little Wild Turkey.

THELMA: Now what?

LOUISE: Now what what?

THELMA: Whaddo we do?

LOUISE: Oh. I don't know, Thelma. I guess maybe we could turn ourselves in and spend our lives trading cigarettes for mascara so we can look nice when our families come to visit on Saturdays. Maybe we could have children with the prison guards.

THELMA: I'm not suggestin' that! I'm *not goin'* back. No matter what happens. So don't worry about me.

LOUISE speeds up. Thelma hands LOUISE a little bottle of Wild Turkey and she drinks it down. THELMA has one, too.

THELMA: Can I ask you a kind of weird question?

LOUISE: Yeah.

THELMA: Of all the things in the world that scare you, what's the worst thing that scares you the most?

LOUISE: You mean now or before?

THELMA: Before.

LOUISE: I guess I always thought the worst thing that could happen would be to end up old and alone in some crummy apartment with one of those little dogs.

THELMA: What little dogs?

LOUISE: You know those little dogs you see people with?

THELMA: Like a chihuahua?

LOUISE: Those, too, but you know those little hairy ones? Those flat-faced little fuckers with those uglygoddamned teeth?

THELMA: Oh yeah. you mean Peek-a-poos.

LOUISE: Yeah. Those. Those always put the fear of God in me. What about you?

THELMA: Well, to be honest, the idea of getting old with Darryl was kinda startin' to get to me.

LOUISE: I can see that.

THELMA: I mean, look how different he looks just since high school. It's bad enough I have to get old, but doin' it with Darryl around is only gonna make it worse. (*quieter*) I mean, I don't think he's gonna be very nice about it.

LOUISE: Well, now, maybe you won't have to.

THELMA: Always lookin' on the bright side, aren't ya?

183. INTERIOR. CAR—LOUISE AND THELMA'S POV THROUGH THE WINDSHIELD—NIGHT

The sky is bright and expansive and the road goes on forever.

THELMA: This is so beautiful.

LOUISE: Gosh. it sure is.

THELMA: I always wanted to travel. I just never got the opportunity.

LOUISE: Well, you got it now.

They both look forward for another moment. And then, at the same time, they look at each other, each taking the other one in completely, in this moment. They're saying everything to each other in this moment, but their expressions don't change and they don't say a word. Music plays on the radio.

184. EXTERIOR. DESERT HIGHWAY—NIGHT

A semi-gas tanker is up ahead on the road. It looks like the one they saw earlier. It's got the same mud flaps . . .

INTERIOR. CAR—NIGHT

LOUISE: Look! Look who it is, Thelma. I'll be darned. What's he doin' way out here?

THELMA: Just ignore him.

LOUISE passes him and, as she does, he honks. They look up and he is wildly pointing to his lap.

LOUISE: Oh, Christ. I hate this guy.

THELMA: We should have just ignored him.

199. INTERIOR. CAR—DESERT HIGHWAY—DAWN

They are quiet for a moment, then THELMA starts quietly laughing to herself. She is trying to stop but cannot.

LOUISE: What?

THELMA: (*shaking with laughter*) Nothing. It's not funny.

LOUISE: What? What's not funny. Thelma!

THELMA is trying to compose herself but cannot.

THELMA: Okay, but . . . (*she can barely speak*) I can't say.

THELMA isn't making a sound. She is stuck in a convulsion of laughter.

LOUISE: What?!

THELMA: (*gasping for air*) Harlan.

LOUISE: What?! What about him?!

THELMA: Just the look on his face when you . . . (*she is falling apart again*) . . . it's not funny!

LOUISE: (*shocked*) Now, Thelma, that is not . . .

THELMA is still trying to get a grip on herself.

THELMA: Boy, he wasn't expecting that!

LOUISE: (*scolding*) Thelma!

THELMA: (*impersonating Harlan*) Suck my dick . . . *Boom!*

THELMA is laughing wildly.

LOUISE: (*quietly*) Thelma. It's not funny.

THELMA has just crossed the line from laughing to crying.

THELMA: (*trying to catch her breath*) I know!

They both get quiet. THELMA leans back just watching LOUISE. She studies her as if she's never really seen her before. All of a sudden a look of shocked realization comes over THELMA's face. She jerks upright and startles LOUISE.

THELMA: (*cont'd*) (*carefully*) It happened to you . . . didn't it?

LOUISE knows what she is talking about. She becomes immediately agitated.

LOUISE: I don't want to talk about it! Thelma, I'm not kidding! Don't you even . . .

THELMA: . . . in Texas . . . didn't it? That's what happened . . . Oh my God.

LOUISE looks as if she is looking for a way to flee.

LOUISE: (*fighting hysteria*) I'm warning you, Thelma. You better drop it right now! I don't want to talk about it!

THELMA: (*gently*) Okay, Louise . . . It's okay.

LOUISE's eyes are wild, not seeing, while THELMA now seems completely serene.

Tom and Viv
(Miramax, 1994)

Screenplay by Michael Hastings and Adrian Hodges
Directed by Brian Gilbert
Characters: TOM (Willem Dafoe)
           VIV (Miranda Richardson)

NOTES: Based on the life of T. S. Eliot, *Tom And Viv* is about
the tempestuous relationship between him and his first wife, Vivienne. When they meet they are deeply in love—she is wild and
impassioned—but once they are married, TOM discovered what
Vivienne's family already knows: that Vivienne is, though brilliant, emotionally unbalanced. She suffers as well from severe
menstrual disorders. The trouble starts on their honeymoon, but
they remain together for fifteen years, often sleeping in separate
rooms, while Vivienne's state causes pain and scandal to TOM
and to her family. After not being let into her husband's office
building, VIV pours melted chocolate through the mail slot. She
pulls a knife (a rubber knife, we later find out) on two women
in their social circle. She is prone to violent and outrageous behavior, mania and acute depression. Finally TOM, after accepting a tenure at Harvard that will require him to leave for
America, decides to have her committed. He has the doctors and
VIV's family waiting outside in the hall. VIV has locked herself
in the drawing room. The scene takes place in London, 1932.
TOM is an American, but he has been living as an Englishman
and desperately wants to be one.

124. INTERIOR. DRAWING ROOM—NIGHT

TOM comes in. VIV is in a dressing gown. TOM is suddenly very moved at the sight of her. His manner is extremely gentle.

VIV: I opened the curtains and unlocked the door—the minute I heard you.

Sound of laughter and music from outside—as of people leaving a pub. VIV goes to the window—watches and listens—her back to TOM.

TOM: (*a beat*) Vivienne . . . ?

VIV: . . . . It's all going on out there . . .

TOM: (*a beat*) . . . We need to be very calm.

VIV turns to him. Her demeanor is rational-seeming and pleasant.

VIV: Oh, there's no need for that. If you want to go out. Do. I want you to.

TOM: Thank you, but . . .

VIV: No, it's good for you. You can't stay trapped in here with me. I do know what goes on in your mind.

Sound of music and laughter from outside.

VIV: (*mock Cockney*) Oo is it this time? Gert or Daisy? Yer up to sumfin an no mistake!

TOM: Let's be calm, Vivvie.

VIV: (*a beat—normal voice*) I keep getting all these horrible formal letters from your lawyer. I told them I wanted to speak to you. You are my husband after all.

TOM: We are legally separated.

VIV: Oh that's just a form of words isn't it? "Whom God has joined let no man put asunder"—You're an expert on God, aren't you?

TOM: We're going to have to talk about things Vivienne.

VIV: Well, we've never done that before have we?

TOM: You have to try to understand just what you've done. We have to face this together.

TOM walks up to her—and offers her a cigarette—a touch of gallantry. VIV smiles. TOM pours himself a drink. The atmosphere, relaxed, convivial, candid—and strangely intimate.

TOM: ... The motor car, the chocolate ...

VIV: Oh that! Those rats at Fabers just wanted you to themselves. There was no room for me. I was so angry at being locked out! ... You have to remember what a success you are. A famous modern poet, director of a leading publisher. I *would* like some recognition for it. After all, the poems come out of our lives, Tom. I'd like to share just an inch of that success.

TOM: ... But why chocolate?

VIV: Because you love it! (*beat—smiles*) Not of course in quite that form, I grant you ...

TOM: (*a beat*) ... And the car? You could really have killed us ...

VIV: How are Maurice's teeth?

TOM: Fine.

VIV: Is the car fixed?

TOM: Yes.

VIV: And you and I are still standing so ... Look, I felt a rush of blood to the head—I was sitting listening to a string of trivial chatter ...

TOM: (*confused*) You were vexed by the conversation?

VIV: You were leaving me for a year and you didn't have the courage to tell me! Maurice was asking us questions about ourselves and I heard us telling him a mass of lies. Over and over! ... You see that's ... I married you to escape all that ... But you ... (*gentle, without grievance*) ... Well, Tom, you always wanted to be the perfect Englishman ...

This hits home. TOM is seated now—the drink and the smoke enveloping him—his guard lowered:

TOM: (*slowly, from the heart*) . . . All these years Vivvie, right from the start, the secrets we had to keep . . . Trying not to catch each other's eyes because we might realize we were strangers. And always the medicine, the doctors, the experts, the things I was never told. And the way people looked at us . . . "There go Tom and Viv. What do they say to each other? Whatever do they say?"

They look at each other now—sadly—tenderly. Silence. Then a brutal intrusion:

JANES: (*OS*) I have Dr. Miller and Dr. Cyriax in attendance, sir.

TOM: (*angry*) Stay out!

VIV: What's going on?

TOM: (*struggling—superhuman control*) There are two of your doctors outside Vivvie. They want to come in and look at you. And make a decision.

VIV: At this time of night?

TOM: They have your best interests at heart.

VIV: What decision?

TOM: They need to come in and ask you some questions.

They hear the people on the other side of the door. TOM is suddenly scared. VIV picks it up—but is strangely yielding, passive:

VIV: You won't let them take me away from you? . . . After all, there've been good moments in the past. We've had our splendid times, haven't we, Tom?

TOM: Yes.

VIV smiles at him. She takes out a compact from her handbag and makes up her face carefully. Then she puts on her slippers. She looks up at TOM.

VIV: Ready.

TOM goes to the door.

Truly, Madly, Deeply
(Samuel Goldwyn Co., 1991)

Screenplay by Anthony Mingella
Directed by Anthony Mingella
Characters: NINA (Juliet Stevenson)
*   JAMIE (Alan Rickman)*

NOTES: NINA and JAMIE were married and passionately in
love when JAMIE died. JAMIE was a cellist with a deep and
dramatic personality, NINA less dramatic—she works a regular
job, but has great friends who care about her. Her life was shat-
tered when JAMIE died and although she's moved to a new
apartment, she hasn't really gone on with her life; she longs for
him so fervently that he returns, as a ghost. He cannot leave the
house, however; she can only be with him there. He is cold all
the time, so he turns up the heat and wears his coat all day. And
he is lonely when she works, so he has some of his friends from
the "other side" to keep him company; they take over the bedroom watching videos, which NINA must rent for them. In the
meantime, NINA has met a man and seen him a few times—she
is coming into her own, finding her own uniqueness. Now NINA
returns home from helping to deliver her friend's baby and finds
JAMIE redecorating. This film takes place in London.

INTERIOR. NINA'S LIVING ROOM—DAY
*NINA enters just in time to see the carpet roll by her feet,
pushed by JAMIE and company.*

JAMIE: Hi! (*to his crew*) Good work.

Kneeling to inspect the revealed floorboards.

JAMIE: We just need to scrub this up a bit. It's oak. Is it oak?

ISAAC: It's definitely a hard wood.

JAMIE: —or ash?

NINA: (*absolutely exasperated*) Jamie, what are you doing?

JAMIE: Aren't these boards amazing? Who would have thought under that disgusting carpet . . . you need to burn it by the way . . . it's full of mildew and silverfish, but these boards! So, it was a girl.

NINA: I liked that carpet.

JAMIE: Don't be perverse.

NINA: Well, I did like it and you can't just go around pulling, treating my flat as—

JAMIE: Nina, the carpet was threadbare, and it's full of mold and mildew and . . . and these boards, even you must acknowledge that, these are in a different—!

NINA: I feel like I'm being burgled! Every time I come home I feel like I'm being burgled!

JAMIE: What?

He frowns at the others.

NINA: (*flailing*) Oh God. The flat—chairs are moved! The the the . . . pictures are different, they're not where, and, it's my flat! It's my flat! I mean—!

JAMIE: Do you want to have a row in public? It's actually quite embarrassing for everybody . . . for me . . . and uh . . . (*he turns and shrugs to his mates*)

NINA: Well no, I don't, no I don't want to be in public in my own home. That's right! That's absolutely right! So, in fact, could your friends go, please, could everybody just go, do you think? Is that possible? That I could have some time in my—now! Now! Please. Is that, is that asking too much?

JAMIE: (*to his cronies*) Sorry.

The ghosts leave, rather sulkily. NINA and JAMIE alone.

JAMIE: (*furious*) Satisfied?

Then he sneezes, dramatically, repeatedly.

NINA: (*acidly*) It's only dust.

JAMIE: Nina, that was really humiliating. You ask people to give you a hand, they don't need to, they lug your furniture around half the day and then you come back and throw a tantrum. That was really really really humiliating.

He sneezes again. It settles in silence.

NINA: (*desperate, floundering*) Was it like this before?

JAMIE: (*as he blows his nose*) What?

NINA: Before, were we like this?

JAMIE: What? Like what? Look, you're tired, your friend just had a baby, you were up half the night, it's traumatic, it's an emotional experience, let's not turn that into—

NINA: Tell me about the first night we spent together.

JAMIE: Why? Seriously? You want me to?

NINA: What did we do?

JAMIE: We talked.

NINA: What else?

JAMIE: Well, talking was the major component! Uh, uh, we, you played the piano—and I played and we both played a duet—something I can't remember . . . and you danced for about three hours until I fell asleep, but you were fantastic!—and then we had some corn flakes amd when we kissed—which was about eleven o'clock the following day—we were trembling so much we couldn't take off our clothes.

They remember. They're both sitting now on the bare boards. Quiet. Closer.

NINA: You see, I held that baby—so (*she makes a tangible gesture*) It's life, it's a life I want. And, and, and all my taste . . . my things, after you died. I found stuff in my trunk I'd put there because you disapproved or laughed at them— books and photographs and I couldn't, I didn't know how to mend a fuse or find a plumber or bleed a radiator but— and now I do. It is a ridiculous flat, but I'll get there, it'll be beautiful, it could be, I think it could be. I, I, I—I so much longed for you, I longed for you.

JAMIE: How's your Spanish?

NINA: What?

JAMIE: There's a poem I want you to translate. I read it, there's a bit I wanted to tell you, I wanted you to hear—

NINA: Okay.

JAMIE recites an extract from the poem, "The Dead Woman" by Pablo Neruda.

JAMIE: Uh—*Perdoname.*

NINA: (*translating*) Forgive me . . .

JAMIE: *Si tu no vives,*

NINA: I know this poem. If you are not living . . .

JAMIE: *Si tu, querida, amor mio, Si tu te has muerto*

NINA: If you, beloved, my love, If you have died

JAMIE: *Todas las hojas caeran en mi pecho*

NINA: All the leaves will fall on my breast

JAMIE: *Llovera sobre mi alma noche y dia*

NINA: It will rain on my soul, all night, all day

JAMIE: *Mis pies querran marchar hacia donde tu duermes*

NINA: My feet will want to march to where you are sleeping. Your accent's terrible.

JAMIE: *Pero seguire vivo*

NINA gets up and goes to JAMIE.

NINA: My feet will want to march to where you are sleeping but I shall go on living.

JAMIE: Do you want me to go?

She clings to him.

NINA: No, never, never, never, never, never.

Two For The Road
(20th Century Fox, 1967)

Screenplay by Frederic Raphael
Directed by Stanley Donen
Characters: JOANNA (Audrey Hepburn)
MARK (Albert Finney)

NOTES: JOANNA and MARK have been married for many
years. They have had their ups and downs, including an affair
JOANNA had, but they are still together. They reflect on their
life together as they drive to a party given by old friends.

155. EXTERIOR. PINEWOODS—NIGHT

*The Mercedes coming slowly down the drive which now
leads through the wood to the new villa. We can hear the
music from the party.*

MARK: I hate these occasions.

JOANNA: I hate these occasions. You love these occasions.

MARK: I love you.

JOANNA: I love you.

MARK: Hmmm.

JOANNA: How long is this going to go on?

MARK: I don't know. How long is this going to go on?

JOANNA: (*brightly*) For ever! (*appalled*) For ever? How
long is what going to go on?

MARK stops the car.

MARK: You used to think I wasn't ever serious. Now you're never serious.

JOANNA: (*seriously*) How long is what going to go on?

MARK: The pretense that we're happy.

JOANNA: You've never pretended we were happy! So who's pretending?

MARK: You are. That you want to stay with me. That we're happily married.

JOANNA: Those are two entirely different things!

MARK: You don't have to tell me.

JOANNA: You really want it all to be a failure, don't you?

MARK: I haven't got anyone else to go to.

JOANNA: You've got women all over the place who'd be glad to renew their subscriptions.

MARK: But I wouldn't be glad.

He restarts the car.

JOANNA: If you had someone you wanted to go to, you'd be on your way, you don't have to tell me.

MARK: Then why are you still here?

JOANNA: Because I'm not you.

MARK: How long are you going to go on resenting the past?

JOANNA: Who's talking? Just who is talking?

He stops the car.

MARK: I'm talking. What would you do if we got a divorce?

JOANNA: Cry.

MARK: Like for how long?

JOANNA: You want dates? I don't know. Why should we get a divorce?

MARK: Or if I died. If I didn't exist.

JOANNA: Look, if I hadn't had chickenpox, I'd've had chickenpox. I don't know.

MARK: (*touches her forehead*) You scratched.

JOANNA: I scratched.

MARK: I love you, Joanna Wallace.

JOANNA: Well then! Well then!

He restarts the car.

MARK: What would you do if I didn't exist?

JOANNA: The trouble with your examination is I have to answer every question.

MARK: It's a tough school.

JOANNA: I'd probably have married David.

MARK looks at her with bleak anguish and stops the car.

JOANNA: But you do exist. You knew the answer, why did you ask the question?

MARK: Because I knew the answer.

JOANNA: There'll never be anyone else like you in my life.

MARK: You promise?

JOANNA: I hope.

MARK: (*starts the car*) I thought we were going to be serious.

JOANNA: Serious isn't solemn. I am serious.

The car starts to move forward down through the woods.

JOANNA: It's you who can't accept it.

MARK stops the car again.

JOANNA: Why do you always stop the car as soon as I say anything?

MARK: What can't I accept?

JOANNA: That we're a fixture. That we're married. You go on about me leaving you when I'm always still here. Are you sure you don't want me to leave you?

MARK: Positive.

JOANNA: Michelle's at the party, you know.

MARK: Positive.

JOANNA: Suddenly you're a vegetarian?

MARK: You are my meat.

JOANNA: And so you are mine. (*MARK starts the car again.*) Why do you think I'm here?

MARK: I don't know. That's the whole—

JOANNA: That's the whole thing, you never stop to think.

MARK stops the car again.

MARK: I've stopped. To think.

JOANNA: Stop thinking.

She puts her arms round him and kisses him. She whispers to him. He looks at her.

MARK: Now?

She nods.

MARK: Here?

She nods again, vigorously.

JOANNA: I love happy endings!

He smiles at her and kisses her passionately, all in one.

MARK: You're just plain immoral.

JOANNA: How can it be immoral if you're married?

MARK: We're going to have to get a divorce.

Waiting To Exhale

(20th Century Fox, 1995)

Screenplay by Terry McMillan and Ron Bass
Directed by Forest Whitaker
Characters: BERNADINE (Angela Bassett)
JAMES (Mykelti Williamson)

NOTES: BERNADINE's marriage of eleven years has broken up. She had devoted herself to her husband's success and to her children, and they had made it. They were living a very comfortable life in the suburbs. Then her husband announced he was leaving her for a white woman. She was devastated, so hurt and furious that she set fire to his clothes and car on the front lawn. Now she is going through divorce proceedings; she has just attended a meeting with her husband and their two lawyers. It was bitter and painful. She stops into the bar at the nearby Biltmore and orders a drink. JAMES is a black man, married to a white woman who is dying of cancer. He is staying in the hotel on a business trip. Note: This scene is partially transcribed from the video.

71. INTERIOR. BILTMORE HOTEL—DAY

BERNADINE is sitting at the bar, alone, stirring the whipped cream of her strawberry daiquiri. She is the only black person in this dark, ornate room. A pianist plays classical music. She's not sure why she's here.

JAMES: *(OS, baritone)* Excuse me. Is anybody sitting here?

She swivels around to see a tall, beautiful black man in a tailored black suit, standing behind her. She is immediately embarrassed because it's undeniable that she's alone ...

BERNADINE: No. No one's sitting there.

And she basically ignores him.

JAMES: Ah, cognac please. (*he looks around; can't get her to look at him*) My name's James Wheeler. How do you do?

No answer. The bartender brings his drink and he takes a sip.

JAMES: ... so do you have a name?

BERNADINE: (*she turns to him*) Bernadine. (*she turns away again*)

JAMES: My, this is a pretty place. But I have to admit, I haven't seen anything as splendid as you since I've been here.

She gives him an "I can't believe you're trying this" look.

JAMES: (*laughs*) OK, hold on now—hold on. You don't have to give me that look. Look—I haven't seen sun for four days. I mean, it's been one meeting after the other after the other, and now I am finished. So, I decided to come downstairs, have myself a drink, and in the morning, I look forward to returning home to my lovely wife, Saluda. (*he drinks, and sighs, loosens his tie*) So—why are you sitting here all alone? (*she gives an incredulous laugh*) OK, wait, wait, now, you don't have to answer that; you don't know me, you know? I mean, you don't know me from a can of paint—here I am, all in your kool-aid and don't know the flavor.

BERNADINE: (*she cuts him short*) I'm getting a divorce, James.

JAMES: Ah—well, I'm sorry to hear that.

BERNADINE: Yeah, well, it happened so—hey, you know, it just occurred to me that, uh, I've lost something that once meant everything, and it hurts. And right now, I'm just, I'm really pissed about it. But you know what really gets me? I didn't have a plan B. My marriage was supposed to last. So I guess that's why I'm here, hmm? (*she drinks*)

JAMES is genuinely moved by her candor.

He knows what happened. Typical. She doesn't have to explain.

JAMES: But I can tell you one thing, though.

BERNADINE: Yeah, what's that?

JAMES: Well, you are one brave woman. You're bad.

BERNADINE: No ...

JAMES: Oh, yes, oh yes, I hope you recognize that.

BERNADINE: No, I don't really feel like that, James.

JAMES: Well, you're sitting all alone—(*looks around*)—ain't a black person in sight, and you sitting here looking like everything's all right. You know, you—your make-up is flawless—

BERNADINE: Oh, come on now—

JAMES: I mean, you've taken his best shot, and you're still here. Splendid.

BERNADINE: (*coy*) You just know me so well.

JAMES: No, no, no, I don't know you. But I do know a fighter when I see one. (*their eyes lock*) And I can tell that with one look in your eyes.

BERNADINE: What are you, a uh, a psychiatrist or something?

JAMES: (*laughs*) No, no, I am a civil rights attorney. My practice is in Washington, D.C. I'm going through something similar. My wife is dying. Of breast cancer.

BERNADINE: I'm sorry. I'm sorry to hear that.

JAMES: It's—Bernadine, have you ever watched someone die? I tell you, I mean, watching her suffer, just kills bit of me every day. And the worst part is that I can't help but remember all the plans we made. You know, like, we were supposed to retire in St. Thomas, you know, out there by the beach—she loves the water—take the coconut oil, rub it all over . . .

They both laugh.

JAMES: She is definitely a (*shakes his head*). I tell you, I just wish, I just wish I could have a piece of her that I could keep safely at home. Just something, something more than a bunch of memories. (*pauses*) Anyway, you look like you're out.

BERNADINE: Mm—hmm.

JAMES: How 'bout a, ah—a refill?

BERNADINE: (*looks at him, thinks*) Yeah, okay.

JAMES: Okay. (*to bartender*) Ah, she'll take another, ah, whatever it is she's got.

BERNADINE: Scotch and soda.

JAMES: Whoo, I'm scared of you.

BERNADINE laughs.

When Harry Met Sally
(Columbia, 1989)

Screenplay by Nora Ephron
Directed by Rob Reiner
Characters: SALLY (Meg Ryan)
             HARRY (Billy Crystal)

NOTES: Five years ago, HARRY and SALLY shared a car from the University of Chicago to New York City together. They didn't know each other that well; HARRY was dating SALLY's friend Amanda. They didn't exactly hit it off; HARRY completely annoyed SALLY, and when he propositioned her, she refused. He insisted that men and women can never be friends because there is always sexual tension between them. They went their separate ways, but now, five years later, HARRY recognizes SALLY's boyfriend Joe as he's dropping SALLY off, and later, on the plane, he strikes up a conversation.

INTERIOR. AIRPLANE—DAY

The plane is in flight, en route from New York to Washington. SALLY is in a middle seat in a crowded all-coach plane. She has the New York Times *on her lap, but she's staring into the middle distance, a little smile on her face. There's a man on the aisle next to her. In the row in back of her, in the aisle seat, is HARRY. His head pops up. SALLY starts to read the newspaper. The man on the aisle looks up at HARRY, who's still looming over him, trying to place*

SALLY. HARRY pops down. The stewardess comes down the aisle with the drink cart.

STEWARDESS: And what would you like to drink?

SALLY: Do you have any Bloody Mary mix?

STEWARDESS: Yes. (*she starts to pour*)

SALLY: No, wait. Here's what I want. Regular tomato juice, filled about three quarters, and add a splash of Bloody Mary mix, just a splash, and . . .

HARRY's head starts to rise again.

SALLY: (*cont'd*) . . . a little piece of lime, but on the side.

HARRY: The University of Chicago, right?

SALLY turns, sees HARRY, then turns back around.

SALLY: Yes.

HARRY: Did you look this good at the University of Chicago?

SALLY: No.

HARRY: (*he's being mischievous here*) Did we ever—?

SALLY: (*laughing, she can't believe him*) No. No! (*to man on the aisle*) We drove from Chicago to New York together after graduation.

The man on the aisle has been listening and watching all this.

MAN ON THE AISLE: (*to HARRY*) Would you two like to sit together?

SALLY: No.

HARRY: Great! Thank you.

HARRY and the MAN on the aisle change seats and HARRY sits down next to SALLY.

HARRY: (*cont'd*) You were a friend of . . . um . . . (*he can't remember her name*)

SALLY: Amanda's. I can't believe you can't remember her name.

HARRY: What do you mean? I can remember. Amanda. Right? Amanda Rice.

SALLY: Reese.

HARRY: Reese, right. That's what I said. Whatever happened to her?

SALLY: I have no idea.

HARRY: You have no idea? You were really good friends with her. We didn't make it because you were such good friends.

SALLY: You went with her.

HARRY: And it was worth it? This sacrifice for a friend you haven't even kept in touch with?

SALLY: Harry, you might not believe this, but I never considered not sleeping with you a sacrifice.

HARRY: Fair enough, fair enough. (*after a beat*) You were going to be a gymnast.

SALLY: A journalist.

HARRY: Right, that's what I said. And?

SALLY: I'm a journalist. I work at the *News*.

HARRY: Great. And you're with Joe.

SALLY nods.

HARRY: (*cont'd*) Well, that's great. Great. You're together— what—three weeks?

SALLY: A month. How did you know that?

HARRY: You take someone to the airport, it's clearly the beginning of a relationship. That's why I've never taken anyone to the airport at the beginning of a relationship.

SALLY: Why?

HARRY: Because eventually things move on and you don't take someone to the airport, and I never wanted anyone to say to me, ''How come you never take me to the airport anymore?''

SALLY: It's amazing. You look like a normal person, but actually you're the Angel of Death.

HARRY: Are you going to marry him?

SALLY: We've only known each other a month, and besides, neither one of us is looking to get married right now.

HARRY: I'm getting married.

SALLY: You are?

HARRY: (*matter-of-factly*) Um-hmm.

SALLY: *You* are?

HARRY: Yeah.

SALLY: Who is she?

HARRY: Helen Hillson. She's a lawyer. She's keeping her name.

SALLY: (*shakes her head*) You're getting married. (*she laughs*)

HARRY: Yeah. What's so funny about it?

SALLY: It's just so optimistic of you, Harry.

HARRY: Well, you'd be amazed what falling madly in love can do for you.

SALLY: Well, it's wonderful. It's nice to see you embracing life in this manner.

HARRY: Yeah, plus, you know, you just get to a certain point where you get tired of the whole thing.

SALLY: What whole thing?

HARRY: The whole life-of-a-single-guy thing. You meet someone, you have the safe lunch, you decide you like each other enough to move on to dinner, you go dancing, you do the white man's overbite, you go back to her place, you have sex, and the minute you're finished, you know what goes through your mind? (*SALLY shakes her head no*) How long do I have to lie here and hold her before I can get up and go home? Is thirty seconds enough?

SALLY: That's what you're thinking? Is that true?

HARRY: Sure. All men think that. How long do you like to be held afterwards? All night, right? See, that's the problem. Somewhere between thirty seconds and all night is your problem.

SALLY: I don't have a problem.

HARRY: Yeah you do.

EXTERIOR. NATIONAL AIRPORT—DAY

As the plane lands.

INTERIOR. NATIONAL AIRPORT—DAY

HARRY and SALLY are on a moving sidewalk, HARRY several steps behind SALLY. He makes his way past the other passengers to stand by her.

HARRY: Staying over?

SALLY: Yes.

HARRY: Would you like to have dinner?

SALLY looks at him suspiciously.

HARRY: (*cont'd*) Just friends.

SALLY: I thought you didn't believe men and women could be friends.

HARRY: When did I say that?

SALLY: On the ride to New York.

HARRY: No, no, no, no. I never said that. (*reconsiders*) Yes, that's right. They can't be friends . . . (*figuring this out*) . . . unless both of them are involved with other people. Then they can. This is an amendment to the earlier rule. If the two people are in relationships, the pressure of possible involvement is lifted. (*thinking this over*) That doesn't work either. Because what happens then, the person you're involved with doesn't understand why you need to be friends with the person you're just friends with, like it means something is missing from the relationship and you have to go outside to get it. Then when you say, "No, no, no, it's not true, nothing is missing from the relationship," the person you're involved with then accuses you of being secretly attracted to the person you're just friends with, which you probably are—I mean, come on, who the hell are we kidding, let's face it—which brings us back to the earlier rule before the amendment, that men and women can't be friends. So where does that leave us?

SALLY: Harry—

HARRY: What?

SALLY: Goodbye.

HARRY: Okay.

They look at each other. Though they have said goodbye, they are now in that awkward place of still going in the same direction next to each other on the moving sidewalk. after a beat:

HARRY: (*cont'd*) I'll just stop walking, I'll let you go ahead.

When Harry Met Sally (2)

(Columbia, 1989)

Screenplay by Nora Ephron
Directed by Rob Reiner
Characters: SALLY (Meg Ryan)
            HARRY (Billy Crystal)

NOTES: Six years after HARRY and SALLY had their conversation on the plane (*see previous scene*) they ran into each other
again at a bookstore. HARRY had been through a divorce, and
SALLY had been through a recent breakup. They became
friends—finally—and their friendship grew close over the course
of a year, as they both tried the dating scene. Then one night,
as HARRY was comforting SALLY (who had just found out her
ex-boyfriend was getting married) one thing led to another, and
they made love. Afterward, HARRY got cold feet and ran. Three
weeks later, they both are attending their friends' wedding, a
couple they introduced to each other.

INTERIOR. PUCK BUILDING—WEDDING RECEPTION
—AFTERNOON
A band is playing. HARRY approaches SALLY.
HARRY: Hi.
SALLY: Hello.
HARRY: Nice ceremony.
SALLY: Beautiful.

SALLY is clearly uncomfortable. She's going to behave like someone who simply is not going to get involved or even pretend interest in the conversation.

HARRY: Boy, the holidays are rough. Every year I just try to get from the day before Thanksgiving to the day after New Year's.

SALLY nods.

SALLY: A lot of suicides.

HARRY nods. SALLY nods. A waiter comes up with a tray of hors d'oeuvres.

WAITER: Would you like a pea pod with shrimp?

SALLY: (*with all the warmth she hasn't been showing HARRY*) Thank you.

She takes one. Waiter turns the tray to HARRY.

HARRY: No thanks.

The waiter leaves.

HARRY: How've you been?

SALLY: Fine.

A pause.

HARRY: Are you seeing anybody?

SALLY looks at him.

SALLY: Harry—

HARRY: What?

SALLY: (*cutting him off*) I don't want to talk about this.

HARRY: Why not?

SALLY: I don't want to talk about it.

SALLY turns and walks away. HARRY follows.

HARRY: Why can't we get past this? I mean, are we gonna carry this thing around forever?

SALLY: Forever? It just happened.

HARRY: It happened three weeks ago.

SALLY looks at him disbelievingly.

HARRY: (*cont'd*) You know how a year to a person is like seven years to a dog?

SALLY: Yes.

HARRY throws up his hands as if it's self-explanatory.

SALLY: (*cont'd*) Is one of us supposed to be a dog in this scenario?

HARRY: Yes.

SALLY: Who is the dog?

HARRY: You are.

SALLY: I am? I am the dog?

HARRY: Um-hmm.

SALLY: I am the dog?

People are starting to notice the intensity of the conversation. SALLY is really furious now. She starts toward the large doors in the background, thinking they can get some privacy there. Once in front of the doors, she stands angrily with her hands on her hips, away from the guests.

SALLY: (*cont'd*) I don't see that, Harry. If anybody is the dog, you are the dog. You want to act like what happened didn't mean anything.

HARRY: I'm not saying it didn't mean anything. I'm saying why does it have to mean *everything?*

SALLY: Because it does, and you should know that better than anyone because the minute that it happened, you walked right out the door.

HARRY: I didn't walk out—

SALLY: No, sprinted is more like it.

HARRY: We both agreed it was a mistake—

SALLY: The worst mistake I ever made.

INTERIOR. KITCHEN—DAY

They go through the doors SALLY was heading for and now they're in the kitchen. Waiters are banging by with trays,

dumping glasses into the sink, opening champagne, etc.
HARRY and SALLY shouting now over the din.

HARRY: What do you want from me?

SALLY: I don't want anything from you.

HARRY: Fine, fine, but let's just get one thing straight. I didn't go over there that night to make love to you. That's not why I went there. But you looked at me with those big, weepy eyes. "Don't go home tonight, Harry. Hold me a little longer, Harry." What was I supposed to do?

SALLY: What are you saying? You took pity on me?

HARRY: No, I . . .

SALLY: Fuck you!

SALLY slaps HARRY across the face. Then bursts out of the kitchen with a stunned HARRY right behind her.

White Palace
(Universal, 1990)

Screenplay by Ted Tally, based on the novel by Glenn Savan
Directed by Luis Mandoki
Characters: NORA (Susan Sarandon)
MAX (James Spader)

NOTES: MAX and NORA have met once before. Earlier in the evening, NORA was at work at White Palace, a hamburger joint, when MAX and his friends came in on their way to a bachelor party. They were wearing tuxes, and NORA called MAX Fred Astaire. MAX was rude to her, especially when he returned to say he had been shorted a few burgers. MAX has had a bad time at the party and he ends up at the same bar where NORA is having a drink. NORA and MAX are from opposite sides of St. Louis, physically, culturally, financially. He is an ad executive in his twenties, successful, Jewish; she is a waitress in her forties, poor, Christian.

INTERIOR. "COUSIN HUGO'S" BAR AND GRILL— NIGHT
We're in a dark, smoky, very crowded honky-tonk. MAX cautiously surveys the joint from the doorway. He's never been here before. Finally he decides to make his way to the bar, where he takes a stool. An angry looking bearded bartender with a Grateful Dead tee-shirt appears.

MAX: Chivas and a splash.

With a lingering glance at the tuxedo, the bartender fixes MAX his drink, slides it over. MAX sips it, then turns to swivel a glance around the room. The clientele is heavily blue collar. At the far end of the bar, a woman sits staring at him, bold as a child. Slinky maroon dress, thin shoulders, thick hair piled high, a burning cigarette. She looks somehow familiar. MAX hesitates, then raises his glass in a half-salute. Back on the woman, expressionless, as she slowly stubs out her cigarette, picks her purse up off the bar, and slides off her stool. She walks past MAX wordlessly, almost brushing against him, and disappears into the crowd, in the direction of a "Restrooms" sign, as his eyes follow her. MAX turns back towards the bar, frowns; did he offend her? Then he shrugs: what the hell. He drains his drink, then tries to signal the bartender for another. But Grateful Dead is locked in conversation with a waitress, and MAX's polite little signals get him nowhere. Suddenly a hand reaches into the shot, taps his shoulder insistently.

WOMAN'S VOICE: (*OS*) Well, hello there!

MAX turns, surprised. It's the woman in maroon again. By now we have recognized her as the White Palace waitress with whom MAX quarrelled. But he still can't quite place her.

WOMAN: My lord—what a tiny little world!

MAX: (*stares at her with a cautious smile*) Is it?

She shifts her weight, a bit girlishly.

WOMAN: Honey, don't you know who I am?

MAX: You're going to have to refresh my memory.

WOMAN: (*laughs*) Well, I'll give you a hint, Fred. I ain't Ginger Rogers.

And MAX finally recognizes her. He stares at her for a moment, more closely . . . NORA CROMWELL is a woman of striking and mercurial contrasts. She's 41, but looks younger. An arresting face, yet one that is not convention-

ally pretty. An innate reserve—something about her almost always feels held back—and yet she radiates a very powerful, even raw sensuality. A woman, above all, who's seen some hard times, but who just now is playfully, almost recklessly, high.

NORA: You gonna invite me to sit down? Or you still p.o.'d at me?

MAX: (*hesitates*) Have a seat.

She sits on the next stool over, drops her purse on the bar. She smiles, fishes for a cigarette, lights it.

NORA: Well now, Fred! Isn't this just the strangest thing, runnin' into you again?

MAX: It's strange, all right.

NORA: I guess I owe you some kinda apology, don't I? But see, I had me one helluva rotten day, and you come in at the wrong time. I'm what you might call short-tempered . . . Lord, listen at me blabber! That's just my drinks talkin'. (*beat, pointedly*) Vodka tonics.

MAX hesitates again. She is so direct, so totally unlike him—and yet . . . and yet there is this heat about her. He turns to the bartender.

MAX: One vodka tonic, and one Chivas, okay?

She raises an eyebrow, pleased by this thawing.

MAX: I guess maybe I owe you an apology, too. I was pretty rude, myself.

NORA: (*smiles*) So! How'd you end up in this dump? Doesn't 'xactly seem like a Fred Astaire kinda place.

MAX: I don't know. Pure serendipity.

NORA: (*slight pause*) Come back in English?

MAX: It means a lucky accident.

NORA: (*slyly, teasing*) Well, you ain't got lucky yet, Fred. That remains to be seen.

MAX colors a bit. The bartender sets their drinks down, moves away. She starts on hers fast, hungrily.

MAX: What, ah—what's your name?

NORA: Why would you wanna know?

MAX: (*shrugs*) So I don't have to call you Mildred.

NORA: (*grins*) What if my name is Mildred?

MAX: Is it?

NORA: No.

MAX: Then what is it?

She takes a deep drag on her cigarette, lets the smoke roll out of her mouth. She's seen quite a few '40's movies.

NORA: Nora.

MAX: Nora what?

NORA: Just Nora. (*stubs out her cigarette*) What's yours?

MAX: Mildred.

NORA: (*laughs, slapping his arm slightly*) Come on!

MAX: Max. Max Baron.

NORA: I like that . . . short and classy. So how come the monkey suit, Max Baron?

MAX: I was at a bachelor party . . . friend of mine's getting married.

NORA: Yeah . . . ? Are *you* married? (*He hesitates, shakes his head.*) Engaged? (*no response*) You're wearin' a ring.

MAX turns away, facing out into the room. Slight pause.

MAX: My wife died, a couple years ago.

NORA: (*surprised*) But honey, you're so young! How old're you?

MAX: Twenty-seven. (*pause*) It was a car accident. She was alone . . . She was twenty-five.

NORA: (*genuinely touched*) Well, my lord, that's just—I'm sorry. Shit . . . (*pause*) Lemme get the next round.

MAX: No, it's okay. My treat tonight.

He signals the bartender. There is a silence, while she searches for a way of changing the subject.

NORA: So . . . What d'you do? No, wait. Don't tell me. You're an actor.

MAX: (*surprised*) Why do you say that?

NORA: You look a little like Tony Curtis. You know that picture, *Some Like It Hot*? With Marilyn Monroe . . . ? Well, I don't mean when he had the dress on. (*MAX can't help smiling*) You know what I mean. Anybody ever tell you you look like Tony Curtis?

MAX: No. Not really. But my wife used to—(catches himself, stops) People used to tease me and say I look sort of like a Ken doll. You know—Ken and Barbie? (*he grins shyly*) 'Cept, of course, that I have a navel.

NORA: Honey, I bet you got all the rest of it, too.

She hoots with laughter. He shifts uneasily, glancing at the bartender, who is just setting down their new round. The bartender gives MAX a faint smile, then moves away. MAX rises.

MAX: Look, it's been great meeting you, Nora—Whatever-Your-Last-Name is. But I've really gotta—

NORA: Oh, you can't leave yet. We just got these! (*sees his hesitation*) C'mon, *stay*. Stay just a little while . . . C'mon— we'll sit right over there, get more comfy. What d'you say? (*pause*) Honey, I won't bite you!

Before he can object again, she takes his arm firmly, leads him over towards an empty table nearby. She sways a bit as she walks. By now MAX is pretty wasted, too. Angle on the table with its oilcloth, ketchup bottle, cheap plastic ashtray. MAX puts down their drinks, and they both sit.

NORA: So! What do you do, Max?

MAX: I work for an ad agency. Spindler Advertising? I write copy there. And before that I taught high school English.

NORA: You mean, like, TV commercials? (*He nods. She's impressed*) Well, what d'you know! Hey, you ever wrote any I might've seen?

MAX: (*modestly*) Well . . . there's one out now for Baumann's Hams. Bunch of starving kids in an orphanage? That one's mine.

NORA: (*face falling a bit*) Oh.

MAX: What . . . ?

NORA: Well, its just—that one's so sad.

MAX: It's supposed to be funny. It's very funny.

NORA: What's so funny about goin' hungry?

She sees that he's a bit peevish over this, and quickly tries to lighten the mood.

NORA: Hey, Max, you know what? This is great! This is almost like meetin' somebody famous! Just wait'll I tell the girls at Shit City. (*off his puzzled look*) Oh—that's what we call White Palace.

MAX: Ah! (*pause*) So, so—you haven't told me anything about yourself, yet.

NORA: (*shrugs*) What's there to tell?

MAX: Well . . . are you married?

NORA: Shoot, you think I'd be sittin' here with you if I was?

MAX: I have no idea.

NORA: Then you don't know me very well.

MAX: I don't know you at all. (*beat*) So I guess—you're *not* married?

She lights another cigarette, blows smoke.

NORA: (*coyly*) Maybe I'm just not sayin'.

MAX: (*becoming irritated*) Let me get this straight. You might be married, or you might not, and you have a last name, but you won't tell me what it is. (*She looks back at him evenly*) D'you have any children? Or do you have them and not have them at the same time?

NORA: How come you're askin' me all these pushy questions?

MAX: How come you're not answering any of them? What is this, classified information?

NORA: (*slight pause*) What kind of soap did your wife like to use, Max?

MAX: (*taken off guard*) What?

NORA: That's not such a hard question, is it? Every woman has a particular kind of soap she likes to use. What was your wife's—Ivory? Camay . . . ? Or something fancier.

MAX stares at her for a moment, then down at the table.

NORA: Oh, you remember, all right. Don't you? You just don't wanna talk about it. So I guess there's no tellin' what some folks consider too personal . . . (*he colors at this, a bit surprised*) You wanna know who I am? My last name's Cromwell. I was married for fourteen years. Jack and me had us one little boy, Charlie. He died . . . leukemia. After that, Jack run off. And good fuckin' riddance. (*pause*) Satisfied, Max? Now you can go back out to West County and tell 'em all you met a real live hoosier.

She stubs out her cigarette—quick, angry little jabs. MAX stares at her with new respect. But he is also stirred by an almost unfamiliar feeling: he has, in spite of himself, become aroused.

MAX: Hey, I'm sorry . . .

NORA: Aw, forget it. Me and my big mouth. (*she drains her glass*) Hell, I get any more drunk and I'm liable to fall all over you! (*after a pause; her voice softens*) How would you like that, Max Baron? If I fell all over you?

MAX: (*pause, tensely*) Nora, it's—this's got nothing to do with you . . . Okay? But I've just—lost interest in women since my wife died.

NORA: (*suddenly suspicious*) You haven't gone queer, have you?

MAX smiles, shakes his head.

NORA: Well, don't you like me at all?

MAX: It's not you, Nora! I'm just—not very keen on sex right now.

Her hand goes up to her right ear, begins to twist the tiny earring there—a characteristic gesture of hers in moments of stress. She is embarrassed.

NORA: I think you mean to say you're not very "keen" on me.

MAX: Nora, no! That's not true.

NORA: Well, hell. I guess I was just outta line, thinkin' I could interest a slick young advertisin' man. I guess I was just way outta line!

She struggles, with as much dignity as she can muster, to rise, but is overcome by dizziness. He moves quickly to steady her, ease her back into her seat.

NORA: Whoa . . . ! Jesus.

MAX: Take a deep breath . . . Are you okay?

NORA: Hey. Gotta ask you somethin', Max Baron. You think I'm too drunk to drive?

MAX: You're too drunk to stand up.

NORA: Well, you think maybe you could give me a lift home? Or's that askin' too much? (*sees that he's hesitating*) Just a few blocks, c'mon. Couldn't you do that for me— be a real nice gen'leman, 'n' drive me home?

MAX: Nora—I really don't—

NORA: You wouldn't want me t' go an' have a car wreck, would you?

An innocent grin. MAX stares back at her angrily, trapped.

White Palace (2)
(Universal, 1990)

Screenplay by Ted Tally, based on the novel by Glenn Savan
Directed by Luis Mandoki
Characters: NORA (Susan Sarandon)
*   MAX (James Spader)*

NOTES: MAX and NORA met under strange circumstances (*see notes for previous scene*), perhaps the only way their worlds might have collided. They have been seeing each other for a little while now and there are strong feelings there, which scare both of them, for different reasons. Now NORA's electricity has been cut off, and she's sitting in the dark, fuming, not about the electricity, but about the fact that MAX went to his friend's wedding without her; in fact, without telling her. MAX now shows up at her house after the wedding.

EXTERIOR. NORA'S FRONT DOOR—NIGHT

MAX stands by NORA's door, hesitating. He looks left and right; the house is mysteriously dark and silent. Dogs are barking in the distance. MAX has changed to jeans, a knit shirt; he carries a bag of Chinese takeout. Finally he pushes open the unlocked door, looks in.

MAX: (*calls out*) Nora . . . ?

No response. He goes inside. He makes his way cautiously into the kitchen, bumping into the table in the gloom. He curses under his breath.

MAX: Nora . . . ?

He sets his bag down on the counter, reaches for a light switch. It clicks uselessly up and down.

MAX: (*puzzled, and a bit alarmed*) Nora, where *are* you . . . ?

Another silence, then her distant voice, very subdued.

NORA: (*OS*) Out here.

EXTERIOR. NORA'S BACKYARD—NIGHT

MAX comes to the kitchen's screen door, peers outside. The red glow of a cigarette arcs up through the darkness, then glares brighter as NORA drags on it. She is lying on a lawn chair, facing away from him. In her other hand is a glass, with clinking ice. There's a vodka bottle by her foot.

NORA: Dark enough for you in there?

MAX: What happened?

NORA: 'Lectricity's out.

MAX: How come?

NORA: 'Cause I didn't pay the bill, that's how come. Three months overdue.

MAX: Oh, Jesus, Nora . . .

NORA: Poor people are a real hoot, ain't they?

MAX reacts to this, staring at her across the little strip of lawn. There is an unfamiliar tone in her voice—hostile and self-pitying. He takes a folded lawn chair from against the house, crosses over to her.

MAX: Nora, why didn't you say something? I would've given you a—a loan or something.

She turns to look at him for the first time.

NORA: (*fiercely*) I don't need your charity or anybody else's. I'm doin' just fine, thank you.

MAX: (*opening his chair*) Oh yeah, this is "doin' fine." "Doin' great" is when they kick you out of your house.

NORA: (*abruptly*) Have a nice time at the wedding, Max?

He stares at her, surprised and ashamed.

NORA: Yeah, that's right. Think hard. I saw the invite at your apartment.

A long silence. He sets his chair down beside her, sits, trying to collect himself and think of a response.

NORA: Why'd you lie to me? Are you goin' out with somebody else . . . ? Some college girl, huh Max? Somebody young and pretty that likes "Spaghetti Carbonation"?

MAX: (*angrily*) There's no other woman, Nora! I almost wish there were, sometimes. Jesus . . . ! (*a pause, then with great intensity*) Everything was so—so clear before I met you. I mean, my life was lousy, but at least it was clear! Everything was in its place . . . And now nothing is! Some of my oldest friends were at that wedding today, and they looked like strangers to me . . . I sit at my desk, at work, and I can't even think straight . . . ! I don't know what's happening to me, Nora. All I know is, no woman *ever* made me feel the way you do. Not even my wife.

NORA: (*frightened*) Don't say that. How can you say that?

MAX: It's true! Nora—I love you!

They stare at one another. MAX is just as shocked as NORA at his own blurted admission. He struggles for more words, can't find any. She turns away.

NORA: Oh, Jesus, Max . . . You can't say that. You can't say that to me if you don't really mean it. Words like that could kill a person.

MAX: But I did say it! I do mean it.

NORA: Are you drunk? Are you crazy?

MAX: I don't know what I am, anymore! Nora, look at me . . . !

He takes her face into his hands and kisses her passionately. She pushes him away, near tears.

MAX: I love you! And I know you love me, too! The hell with everything else!

NORA: Max, if you love me, then why did you lie to me about this wedding? *Huh*?

MAX: (*uneasily*) Nora, look—it's just—(*hesitates*) Have you ever been to a Jewish wedding . . . ? Okay, well, lemme tell you, compared to those *yentas*, Perry Mason is still in law school! "When's the big day, dear?" "Isn't it about time you two thought about a family, dear?" "And when are you converting, dear?"

NORA: (*pause*) Well hell, every wedding's like that. Jewish or not.

MAX: (*improvising*) I just thought—it's not fair to put you through that, right now. So, so I decided maybe it was better if I didn't even mention the wedding. I know now that was wrong, Nora . . . I'm sorry. Can you forgive me?

MAX has managed to make this sound quite plausible. She looks at him for a long moment, searchingly. She dries her eyes.

NORA: One thing I can't abide is bein' lied to. Hell, I'd rather have a man beat up on me than lie to me. Bruises will heal . . . I trusted you, Max.

MAX: Nora, I said I was sorry . . . I said that I love you. I wish you'd say you forgive me.

NORA: I'll forgive you once, Max . . .

She flips away her cigarette, a curving spark in the darkness. Then she stares at him—wary, tough, irreducibly proud.

NORA: But I'll be damned if I forgive you twice.

The Wings Of The Dove
(Miramax, 1997)

Screenplay by Hossein Amini
Directed by Iain Softley
Characters: MILLIE (Alison Eliott)
                MERTON (Linus Roache)

NOTES: This film is set in Edwardian London and Venice. Kate is a beautiful and brilliant young woman, but she is a "poor relation" and lives with her wealthy aunt in London, on whom she is completely dependent. She knows her life depends on making a "good marriage," but she is immersed in a love affair with MERTON. She wants to marry him, but she can't bear the idea of poverty stripping them of their passion. When a young American heiress, MILLIE, enters her social circle and the women become fast friends, Kate learns that MILLIE is dying. She also notices MILLIE's attraction to MERTON. Kate hides her love for MERTON and arranges that they accompany MILLIE to her villa in Venice. Kate wants MILLIE to fall in love with MERTON and leave her money to him. MERTON half-heartedly agrees, and gets sucked into the deception. Kate soon finds an excuse to leave Venice, and MERTON and MILLIE are left there. MILLIE does indeed fall in love with MERTON, and MERTON, while his passion is always for Kate, develops feelings of admiration and respect for MILLIE. Now MILLIE is dying, and MERTON comes to see her; her companion Susan tells him that MILLIE's been informed of Kate and MERTON's love by a jealous man.

INTERIOR. SALON—PALAZZO LEPORELLI—DAY

MERTON doesn't notice her at first ... MILLIE is lost in the whiteness and vastness of the room. She sits on the sofa, wearing the same white dress she wore the night of the carnival. She looks pale and tired, but more beautiful than she's ever looked before ... MERTON walks toward her in silence ... She smiles at him softly ...

MILLIE: I was hoping you'd find a way to see me.

MERTON: All you have to do is ask.

MILLIE: I couldn't do that. I had to be a little difficult.

MERTON notices the bloodstained handkercheif on the table ...

MERTON: You look well.

MILLIE: Apparently not.

She smiles at him gently ...

MILLIE: You've heard I'm ill?

MERTON: Yes.

MILLIE's face shines with sweat ... She dabs it with her hand ...

MILLIE: I went out yesterday morning. I feel better in the mornings. This is such a big city, but I really thought I might see you.

MERTON: I did the same.

MILLIE: Where did you go?

MERTON: San Marco, the Rialto, everywhere ...

MILLIE: The Guidecca?

MERTON: I went to all the places we went together.

MILLIE: Maybe we just kept missing each other. Me turning the corner, just as you went the other way.

MERTON: I thought of that. I stayed in the same place and waited for hours.

MILLIE: And we still didn't see each other ...

She smiles ironically . . . They stare at each other in the silence . . .

MILLIE: When are you going back?

MERTON: Going back where?

MILLIE: To London.

MERTON: I'm not going anywhere.

MILLIE: But what will you do here?

MERTON: The same things we did before.

MILLIE: Do I look like I can climb a church scaffold?

MERTON: You can do anything you want.

MILLIE: Don't encourage me . . .

MERTON: Millie. I saw you get better. With my own eyes . . .

MILLIE: That was before . . .

She smiles at him sadly . . .

MILLIE: I kicked for a while. Now I've tired myself out . . .

The rain patters in the silence . . .

MILLIE: And whatever I have inside me hasn't gone away . . .

She looks deep into his eyes . . .

MILLIE: I have to face the truth. For the first time . . .

She seems to be staring right into his soul . . . MERTON hears the rain drumming all around him . . . And the whisper of her voice . . .

MILLIE: It isn't so bad . . .

MERTON loses himself in her eyes . . .

MERTON: It isn't true, Millie. What he told you isn't true . . .

She says nothing for a moment . . . And then looks away . . .

MILLIE: He brought me these from London . . .

MILLIE points to a box of biscuits in a decorated tin . . .

MILLIE: Look at the print on the box. I think it's Ophelia drowning. Or someone dying anyway. He only realized at the last moment . . .

MERTON: Millie . . .

MILLIE: You should have seen him. He was so embarrassed. He kept trying to turn the tin on its side without me noticing . . .

MERTON: Millie, please . . .

MILLIE: Mark never does anything quite right. He came to hurt me and he bought a box of biscuits . . .

MERTON: What he told you isn't true.

MILLIE looks into his eyes again . . .

MILLIE: I said that to him myself. That it wasn't true. And then I sent him away in the rain.

MERTON: But you believed him?

MILLIE smiles softly . . .

MERTON: Millie, what can I do to persuade you . . .

MILLIE: Merton, please . . . Don't.

Her eyes plead with him not to lie anymore . . .

MILLIE: We're past that. You and I.

MERTON stares in silence . . . She smiles at him . . . Kindly . . . Forgiving him . . . MERTON can't speak . . . tears begin to fill his eyes . . . They look at each other for what seems an eternity . . .

MERTON: You look so beautiful . . .

MILLIE: Really?

MERTON: Really.

MILLIE: Considering I'm . . .

MERTON: Considering nothing.

There's a passionate conviction in his voice . . . Even though his voice is cracked . . . And his eyes are wet and bloodshot . . . she gets up to see him out . . .

MILLIE: Goodbye.

MERTON stares at her . . . There's so much he wants to say . . . There's nothing to say . . .

The Wings Of
The Dove (2)
(Miramax, 1997)

Screenplay by Hossein Amini
Directed by Iain Softly
Characters: KATE (Helena Bonham Carter)
MERTON (Linus Roache)

NOTES: After Millie's death (*see notes for the previous scene*), MERTON returns to London, but doesn't inform KATE of his return. He is grieving Millie's death even as a letter arrived from her lawyers informing him of his inheritance. KATE finally comes to his apartment to see him. The ordeal of the events that have taken place have strained their sureness of each other.

INTERIOR. MERTON'S ROOMS—LONDON—DAY

A burst of flame as the fire catches . . . MERTON pushes the embers around with a stick . . . He hears footsteps on the stairs outside . . . He keeps prodding the fire . . . There's a knock on the door . . .

KATE: (*offscreen*) Merton?

MERTON keeps poking at the fire . . . The knocking continues . . . Eventually MERTON gets up and opens it . . . KATE smiles at him softly . . .

KATE: You couldn't hear me?

MERTON: I was next door.

He invites her in . . . KATE takes her rain-soaked jacket off and throws it over the sofa . . .

KATE: When did you get back?

MERTON: A fortnight. A fortnight Friday.

KATE looks confused . . . And hurt . . .

MERTON: I was keeping with our wonderful system. I couldn't rush to you could I?

There's a touch of bitterness in his voice . . .

KATE: She was my friend too, Merton.

MERTON: Of course she was. Our great friend. The three of us . . .

KATE: Stop it.

MERTON: Why did you tell Lord Mark?

KATE: Tell him what?

MERTON: About us.

They stare at each other in silence . . .

MERTON: You knew he'd go to her . . .

KATE doesn't say anything . . .

MERTON: What about all your plans?

KATE: I was scared of losing you.

Her voice is soft and sincere . . . It's almost as if she needs him to forgive her . . . MERTON keeps staring at her coldly . . . Her words don't change anything . . .

KATE: You are in love with her, aren't you?

MERTON: With a dead girl.

MERTON smiles bitterly . . . KATE approaches and touches him tentatively . . . She slips her hand through his shirt and touches his chest . . . MERTON takes her hand away . . . He holds it and kisses it softly . . . And then reaches into his pocket . . .

MERTON: This is for you . . .

MERTON holds out a letter for her . . . KATE takes it . . .

MERTON: Open it . . .

KATE: It's addressed to you.

MERTON: It's from Millie's lawyers.

KATE: It's for you.

She gives him back the letter . . .

MERTON: You're not interested to know what it says?

KATE: I know what it says. It's her last will and testament. She's left you everything.

MERTON: This is your prize . . .

KATE looks at him sadly . . .

MERTON: Don't you want it?

KATE: It's yours.

MERTON walks over to the fire and throws the letter into the flames . . . KATE looks surprised but makes no attempt to retrieve it . . . She walks into the bedroom . . . MERTON follows her . . .

INTERIOR. BEDROOM—MERTON'S ROOM—DAY

KATE walks through and starts to take her clothes off . . . She folds her clothes neatly on a chair. She doesn't look at him . . . MERTON watches her . . . KATE sits on his bed, completely naked now . . . She stares up at him . . .

KATE: Why did you give me the letter?

MERTON: I wanted to see what you'd do?

KATE: You'll still get her money. Burning a letter doesn't change that.

MERTON: No.

KATE turns on her front . . . MERTON starts towards her . . . He sits down and starts to rub her back . . .

KATE: That feels nice.

He lets his fingers trickle down her back . . .

MERTON: I'm going to write another letter. To her lawyers.

KATE turns around slowly. She looks up at him . . . He lets his hands drift over her breasts . . .

KATE: You want me to persuade you to keep the money? Is that what you want?

MERTON shrugs . . . KATE sits up and holds him close to her for a moment . . . She starts to kiss his neck. Her fingers stroke his face . . . He doesn't respond . . . She starts to unbutton his shirt . . . She rolls him gently on his back and starts to take his clothes off . . . MERTON stares up at the ceiling . . .

MERTON: I love you, Kate.

His voice is almost a whisper . . . KATE takes off his socks . . .

KATE: I love you too.

She moves on top of his naked body and looks down at him . . . MERTON smiles gently and raises his arms to her shoulders . . . He touches them lightly . . . KATE looks into his eyes . . .

KATE: What are you thinking about?

MERTON: Millie.

KATE: You are still in love with her.

MERTON: I was never in love with her.

KATE: Whilst she was alive, no.

KATE smiles gently and moves him inside her . . . She winces slightly from the pain . . . She lies down softly on his chest and starts to move . . . They both look close to tears . . .

MERTON: I'm sorry, Kate.

KATE: It doesn't matter.

MERTON: I think she wanted us to be together.

KATE: We will be.

KATE wipes his tears away with tender fingers . . . She sways a little faster now . . . They turn around together . . . They move in slow perfect time . . . Neither looks at the other . . . KATE groans softly as he finishes inside her . . . She moves quickly to his breast. She doesn't want him to see her crying . . . MERTON breathes hard. He holds her for a moment in his arms . . . His fingers gently explore her face . . . He feels her tears . . . For a moment neither speaks . . .

MERTON: I'm going to write that letter.

KATE: Do whatever you want.

MERTON: I want to marry you, Kate.

There's a long silence . . .

MERTON: Without her money.

KATE: Is that your condition?

MERTON: Yes.

KATE: Am I allowed one too?

MERTON: Of course you are.

KATE buries her face deeper in his chest. She kisses it softly. Her eyes are wet . . .

KATE: Give me your word of honor . . . You word of honor that you're not in love with her memory?

MERTON stares out . . . He doesn't reply . . . They stay there a moment longer in each other's arms . . . KATE rolls away from him and gets out of bed . . . She takes her clothes and walks into the next door room . . . MERTON doesn't follow her . . . He lies in bed and listens to her put her clothes on . . . He hears her walk out of the door and close it behind her . . . He hears her footsteps on the stairs . . . He makes no attempt to follow her . . . He lies back and stares at the ceiling . . . There are tears in his eyes . . . He rolls over on his front . . .

Working Girl
(20th Century Fox, 1988)

Screenplay by Kevin Wade
Directed by Mike Nichols
Characters: TESS (Melanie Griffith)
KATHERINE (Sigourney Weaver)

NOTES: TESS is a working girl from Staten Island; her friends
and her boyfriend are also from Staten Island. Her ambitions
run higher, however, and she feels limited by and out of place
in her old milieu. She works in Manhattan, at a powerful media
company, and has just been promoted from the typing pool to a
position as secretary to KATHERINE. KATHERINE is the head
of Mergers and Acquisitions; she is well-bred and successful,
everything that TESS thinks she wants to be. On the first day of
work, KATHERINE shows TESS the "ropes" and TESS battles
with her fear of inadequacy.

25. INTERIOR. OFFICE—MERGERS AND ACQUISI-
TIONS—MONDAY MORNING

*Angle on a desktop, bare save for a telephone and a type-
writer. Quickly, ceremonially, it is covered with a stack of
newspapers and magazines (everything from Forbes to
WWD), a Walkman, a make-up kit, four packets of No-Doz,
a copy of "The Search for Excellence", a framed photograph of Dugan, a plain yogurt, some tape cassettes, and
her birthday bunny vase.*

Another angle—TESS sitting behind her new desk, looking around anxiously. It is quieter here, private offices lining the perimeter of the floor, secretaries in adjoining anterooms, lesser execs and clerks and interns in clustered cubicles in the center.

Another angle—KATHERINE PARKER striding up, leather briefcase in hand. She is tall and beautiful and impeccably dressed, with a confident air and a throaty, patrician-sounding voice. She is, in short, everything TESS longs to be.

KATHERINE: I'm Katherine Parker, you must be Tess.

She extends her hand for a shake. TESS takes it, gets shook.

KATHERINE: (*cont'd*) Nice bunny.

TESS: I don't usually have a bunny on my desk. It was my birthday, a couple of days ago.

KATHERINE: (*brightly*) Well, no kidding. Mine's next Tuesday. How old?

TESS: Thirty.

KATHERINE: I'm going to be thirty next Tuesday. We're practically twins!

TESS sags a little.

TESS: Except that I'm a little older.

KATHERINE: Just barely . . .

TESS: It's just . . . I've never worked for someone younger than me. Or a woman.

KATHERINE: First time for everything. (*a beat*) Tess, that's not going to be a problem, is it?

TESS: No, no. No no no no no . . .

KATHERINE: *Good.* Then why don't you pour us a couple of coffees and come inside. I'm light, no sugar.

KATHERINE breezes into her office.

INTERIOR. KATHERINE'S OFFICE—SAME

KATHERINE and TESS and coffee and an office with a

view. KATHERINE pacing, TESS unsure of where to stand. A little dance.

KATHERINE: A few ground rules. The way I look at it, you're my link with the outside world. People's impression of me starts with you. You're tough when it's warranted, accommodating when you can be. You're accurate, you're punctual, and you never make a promise you can't keep. Let's put our feet up, Tess. Go ahead, put 'em up.

KATHERINE abruptly sits and TESS does like it's musical chairs and KATHERINE swings her feet up on the desk. TESS follows suit, tentative. Each notices the other's awkwardness.

KATHERINE: (*laughs*) This just doesn't work in skirts, does it.

TESS: No.

BOTH put their feet back on the floor.

KATHERINE: You know how I take my coffee, I lunch at one, you might want to keep a pack of Larks in your desk for my weak moments. I'm never on another line, I'm in a meeting. I consider us a team, and as such, we have a uniform. Dress shabbily, they notice the dress, dress impeccably and they notice the woman. Coco Chanel.

TESS: How do I look?

KATHERINE: You look wonderful. You might re-think the jewelry.

TESS: Got you.

KATHERINE: I want your input. I welcome your ideas. And I like to see hard work get rewarded. It's a two-way street on my team. Am I making myself clear?

TESS: Yes, Katherine . . .

KATHERINE: (*blithely*) And call me Katherine.

TESS: O.K.

KATHERINE: Let's get to work then, shall we? This department's profile last year was damn pitiful. Our team's got its work cut out for it.

KATHERINE stands up and reaches across the desk and vigorously shakes TESS's hand, and TESS returns it just as vigorously, pleased, snowed, and fired-up.

Index of Scenes by Gender

*Due to a cross-gender character, this scene is included in two categories.

Scenes for a Man and a Woman

Index of Scenes
by Category

Many of these scenes ride the line between comedy and drama. Please use this index only as a general reference.

Comedy

Drama

Index of Original Actors